NEW ZEALAND'S
TOP
100
HISTORY-MAKERS

NEW ZEALAND'S
TOP
100
HISTORY-MAKERS

JOSEPH ROMANOS

TRIO
BOOKS

Photograph credits

The photographs in this book have come from the following sources:

Alexander Turnbull Library 11, 12, 14, 15, 19, 21, 23, 24, 25, 27, 29, 30, 31, 33, 35, 38, 39, 51, 55, 57, 63, 65, 67, 69, 75, 79, 83, 89, 91, 95, 103, 115, 117, 119, 123, 129, 135, 137, 141, 147, 149, 151, 155, 157, 165, 167, 169, 175, 179, 183, 185, 199, 201

The Dominion Post 41, 47, 53, 61, 71, 81, 85, 97, 99, 101, 107, 111, 121, 125, 131, 133, 145, 159, 173, 187, 193, 195, 197, 207, 209, 211, 213, 215, 217

Evening Post Collection, Alexander Turnbull Library 18, 73, 87, 105, 127, 161, 181, 191, 203, 205

Canterbury Museum 49, 59 (Davidson), 109

Archives New Zealand 17, 36

Wellington College Archives 45, 77

Visionary Film and TV 93, 163

The Otago Settlers Museum 59 (Brydone)

The Timaru Herald 113

C W F Hamilton Ltd 139

The Gallagher Group 143

Home of Compassion, Wellington 153

Nelson College for Girls 171

New Zealand Sports Hall of Fame 177

Don Neely Collection 189

Stock Image Group 219

Cover photographs

Peter Jackson – *The Dominion Post*

Peter Snell – Joseph Romanos Collection

Helen Clark – *Evening Post* Collection, Alexander Turnbull Library

Ernest Rutherford – Alexander Turnbull Library

Janet Frame – Barry Harcourt, *The Southland Times*

Apirana Ngata – Alexander Turnbull Library

Edmund Hillary – Archives New Zealand

National Library of New Zealand Cataloguing-in-Publication Data

Romanos, Joseph.
New Zealand's top 100 history-makers / by Joseph Romanos.
A spin-off from the television programme of the same name.
ISBN 0-9582455-6-8
1. New Zealand-Biography. 2. New Zealand-History-Biography.
I. New Zealand's top 100 history-makers (Television programme)
II. Title.
920.093-dc 22

Text © Joseph Romanos 2005
First published 2005
The author has asserted his moral rights in the work.
This book is copyright. Except for the purpose of fair reviewing, no part of this publication (whether it be in an eBook, digital, electronic or traditionally printed format or otherwise) may be reproduced or transmitted in any form or by any means, electronic, digital or mechanical, including CD, DVD, eBook, PDF format, photocopying, recording, or any information storage or retrieval system, including by any means via the Internet or World Wide Web, or by any means yet undisclosed, without permission in writing from the publisher.

Published by Trio Books Limited
PO Box 17-021
Wellington
New Zealand
Email: enquiry@triobooks.co.nz
www.triobooks.co.nz

Printed by Printlink, Petone, Wellington

Contents

Contents		5
Acknowledgements		8
Introduction		9
1. Ernest Rutherford	*Lord of the atom*	10
2. Kate Sheppard	*Nothing less than equal*	13
3. Edmund Hillary	*The man who took New Zealand to the top of the world*	16
4. George Grey	*The Governor who shaped New Zealand*	19
5. Michael Joseph Savage	*The Prime Minister who set up the welfare state*	22
6. Apirana Ngata	*Maori leader in a Pakeha world*	25
7. Hone Heke	*Formidable warrior, man of intellect*	28
8. Truby King	*Plunket Society visionary*	31
9. William Hobson	*Treaty of Waitangi author*	34
10. Jean Batten	*The Garbo of the skies*	37
11. Brian Barratt-Boyes	*Heart surgery pioneer who preferred to work at home*	40
12. Peter Snell	*Like a Sherman tank in full flight*	42
13. William Pickering	*The rocket man*	44
14. Peter Jackson	*Giant of the big screen*	46
15. Janet Frame	*The author whose writing literally saved her*	48
16. Te Rauparaha	*The Napoleon of the Southern Hemisphere*	50
17. Colin Meads	*The famous five*	52
18. Whina Cooper	*Tireless campaigner for Maori rights*	54
19. Katherine Mansfield	*The shooting star who has continued to shine*	56
20. Thomas Brydone and William Davidson	*The men whose big chill ideas launched the meat export industry*	58
21. Richard Pearse	*A world first for a flying Kiwi?*	60
22. Te Whiti	*The Gandhi of the South Pacific*	62
23. Richard John Seddon	*The political giant*	64
24. Peter Buck	*Master of many trades*	66
25. Julius Vogel	*The expansionist whose policies shaped a fledgling country*	68
26. Maurice Wilkins	*The scientist who helped unravel the mystery of DNA*	70
27. Helen Clark	*Labour's First Lady*	72

28.	Mabel Howard	*The woman who shocked Parliament*	74
29.	Bernard Freyberg	*The soldier who became Governor-General*	76
30.	Harold Gillies	*The father of plastic surgery*	78
31.	Kiri Te Kanawa	*The diva who sang for royalty*	80
32.	Keith Park	*Fearless in mind and duty*	82
33.	Alan McDiarmid	*The boy chemist who won a Nobel Prize*	84
34.	Peter Blake	*The Hillary of the seas*	86
35.	Clarence Beeby	*The visionary behind New Zealand's education system*	88
36.	Jack Lovelock	*An enigma who was our first great runner*	90
37.	John Bedbrook	*The biotech pioneer*	92
38.	James K Baxter	*The gifted poet who challenged society*	94
39.	Fred Hollows	*The wild colonial boy of eye surgery*	96
40.	Murray Halberg	*Champion sportsman, generous human being*	98
41.	Neil Finn	*The dream's not over*	100
42.	Edward Gibbon Wakefield	*Self-serving, but a man who got things done*	102
43.	David Lange	*Right man, right time*	104
44.	Rob Muldoon	*The feisty Nat who changed the face of politics*	106
45.	Thomas Edmonds	*The businessman who rose to the top*	108
46.	Colin McCahon	*The modernist who enhanced cultural nationalism*	110
47.	Colin Murdoch	*The lateral thinker who saved millions of lives*	112
48.	Archie McIndoe	*The maestro who worked miracles with the Guinea Pig Club*	114
49.	Samuel Marsden	*The driving force behind Christianity in New Zealand*	116
50.	Peter Fraser	*The great war-time leader*	118
51.	John Clarke	*The comic genius who showed New Zealand how to laugh at itself*	120
52.	Ettie Rout	*The free spirit who was born too soon*	122
53.	Arthur Lydiard	*The coach who revolutionised athletics training*	124
54.	Kupe	*The voyager who discovered Aotearoa*	126
55.	Te Puea Herangi	*The greatest Maori woman of her time*	128
56.	John Walker	*The third of New Zealand's great middle-distance champions*	130
57.	Tim Finn	*The creator of Split Enz*	132
58.	John A Lee	*From Labour Party pin-up boy to exile*	134
59.	James Wattie	*The man who gave us baked beans and frozen veges*	136
60.	William Hamilton	*Jet-boat inventor*	138
61.	Norman Kirk	*Big Norm, champion of ordinary New Zealanders*	140
62.	Bill Gallagher	*His electric fence took farming into a new era*	142
63.	Michael King	*The writer who explained New Zealand to New Zealanders*	144
64.	Frances Hodgkins	*The Dunedin painter who became world-renowned*	146

65.	George Nepia	*The prince of All Black fullbacks*	148
66.	James Fletcher	*The engaging immigrant who built an empire*	150
67.	Suzanne Aubert	*New Zealand's Mother Teresa*	152
68.	Charles Heaphy	*The adventurer with many strings to his bow*	154
69.	Alfred Reed	*Pioneering publisher and inspirational wanderer*	156
70.	Frank Sargeson	*The writer who captured New Zealand working-class vernacular*	158
71.	Roger Douglas	*The man who shaped New Zealand's modern economy*	160
72.	Matt During	*The neuroscientist who is making a difference*	162
73.	Te Kooti	*Tribal leader and prophet*	164
74.	Hongi Hika	*The Nga Puhi leader who encouraged European settlement*	166
75.	David Low	*The free-spirited cartoonist who would not be cowered*	168
76.	Kate Edger	*Pioneer of women's education*	170
77.	Marie Clay	*The Michael Jordan of reading*	172
78.	Rewi Alley	*New Zealand's gift to China*	174
79.	Tom Ellison	*Rugby legend and astute Maori leader*	176
80.	Rua Kenana	*The Maori prophet who established his own community*	178
81.	Tahupotiki Wiremu Ratana	*The faith-healer who spawned religious and political movements*	180
82.	Maud Basham (Aunt Daisy)	*The diminutive giant of radio broadcasting*	182
83.	Charles Upham	*The ultimate soldier*	184
84.	Ralph Hotere	*The "black" artist*	186
85.	Richard Hadlee	*New Zealand cricket's one-man destruction unit*	188
86.	Billy T James	*The irreverent entertainer who was loved by a nation*	190
87.	Keith Sinclair	*The historian's historian*	192
88.	Charles Goldie	*The man who turned portrait painting into an art form*	194
89.	John Minto	*The activist with an acute social conscience*	196
90.	Rudall Hayward	*Early master of the silver screen*	198
91.	Witi Ihimaera	*Maori storyteller, New Zealand novelist*	200
92.	John Rangihau	*Bridging the Maori-Pakeha divide*	202
93.	Dave Dobbyn	*The beloved entertainer*	204
94.	Russell Coutts	*The yachtie who made the America's Cup his cup*	206
95.	Jonah Lomu	*The softly-spoken giant who took the rugby world by storm*	208
96.	Peter Mahon	*The judge whose Erebus crash report made him a household name*	210
97.	Georgina Beyer	*From drag queen to Member of Parliament*	212
98.	A J Hackett	*The man who took bungy-jumping to the world*	214
99.	Denny Hulme	*The quiet achiever who snared the greatest prize in motor sport*	216
100.	Russell Crowe	*Rough diamond, brilliant actor*	218
Index			220

Acknowledgements

This book would never have been written if there had not been a television series of the same name. Visionary Film and TV conceived the concept, walked the long road to having their idea turned into a seven-part television series, and then offered me every imaginable assistance when I suggested I might write a book from the series. Though they were exceedingly busy putting together their series, the Visionary people were ever helpful, sending information, contact details, photos... whatever I asked for. So to Richard Driver, the executive producer of the series, and to Hayley Cunningham, Samantha Blackley, Doni Karatau, Claire Thompson, Sarah Murphy, Ian Hart, Mitchell Hawkes and John Bates, my grateful thanks.

Thanks go to Prime Television, which eagerly grabbed the chance to screen the series, and to New Zealand On Air, for helping fund it. Without their enthusiasm, there would have been no television series, and therefore no book. Andrew Shaw at Prime, and the good folk at New Zealand On Air were most encouraging when I suggested to them I might write a book out of the series.

There would be no list, of course, without my fellow panellists, Stacey Daniels, Raybon Kan, Robyn Langwell, Douglas Lloyd-Jenkins, Melanie Nolan, Tainui Stephens and Kerrie Woodham. They put in hours of research in compiling their lists and I found our group discussion most informative and entertaining. Our panel included one of the funniest people I have met, and another whose campaign manager I want to be, should he ever decide to run for Parliament.

I was confronted by a tight deadline writing this book, so did not have time to hunt down the photographs. Don Neely, a good friend, was the photo researcher, and what a marvellous job he did. Some of the photos he uncovered are exceptional and have seldom seen the light of day.

Others helped with specific photos. Dave Wood (*Timaru Herald*), Fred Tulett and Barry Harcourt (*Southland Times*), Ron Palenski (New Zealand Sports Hall of Fame), Winton Cleal and Susanna Joe (*The Dominion Post*), Joan McCracken and Heather Mathie (Alexander Turnbull Library), Paddianne Neely (Wellington College archives), Libby McCreadie (Nelson College for Girls archives), Teresa Steele of the Gallagher Group, Tony Kean of C W F Hamilton and Co, and the Home of Compassion, in Wellington.

For my research I sought the assistance of a variety of people. Marie Clay, John Bedbrook, Matt During and John Minto, who are profiled in the book, helped me with details of their careers.

Tom Larkin, Sarah Williams, Rod Hamel and Gregor Fountain, very wise people with such wide general knowledge, read all or part of my manuscript and offered vast amounts of support and advice. I shudder to think what this book would have been like without them. Chris Bourke assisted with the musical entries; Paddianne Neely provided information on William Pickering, Mark Harris on Bill Gallagher.

I have met several of the 100 profiled, though not always through my journalism endeavours. I recall having a game of snooker with John Clarke in the St George poolrooms, Wellington, in the 1970s. I ran into Michael King while we were both doing research in the Chatham Islands in 1988. I interviewed Rob Muldoon at Eden Park and spoke with David Lange at a motor racing jubilee dinner. I've met many of the sports figures in this list through the course of my reporting career.

Many I knew little about before I began writing this book. *The Dictionary of New Zealand Biography* was a magnificent resource, full of detail and interesting snippets about so many of our achievers. Wikipedia, the Internet encyclopaedia, is another wonderful resource. The Prime Ministers of New Zealand website was extremely helpful. After that, it was a matter of scanning the Internet for other relevant websites, visiting the library to read specific books and asking questions. It was time-consuming, but extremely enjoyable.

There are several other people who need particular acknowledgement. Phil Murray and Gael Woods were dedicated proof-readers. It took a while to sort out our style – is Moon capped, what about scholar in Rhodes scholar and fellow in Menton fellow, should the names of boats be italicised, were we using metric or imperial measurements? It soon fitted into place.

And to Lisa Wright of Printlink. What a gem. Quick, efficient, accurate and ever-cheerful.

Introduction

I was surprised and delighted to be asked to be a panellist for the *New Zealand's Top 100 History-Makers* series. The work involved for the eight panellists – scanning the original list of 250 nominations, adding our own, then voting on the final list of 403 – proved time-consuming, but enjoyable.

It was something of a voyage of discovery for me. I was comfortable talking about notable sports figures, because I have been a sports journalist for the past 30 years. But our great inventors, politicians, scientists, historical figures, painters, musicians, historians and so on? That required much research and consulting of people more knowledgeable in those areas.

The whole exercise was tremendously stimulating, yet I felt I was really only scratching the surface. So I resolved to take the panel's final 100 and write a book, profiling each of our choices. The stories on each of the 100 aren't especially long, but hopefully they provide enough information to give a picture of that person's life and to allow readers to understand why they were voted into the top 100.

It was an eclectic panel that the Visionary Film and TV people put together, containing journalists drawn from different fields, and historians. I don't agree with our final 100 – none of the panel does, actually. But that's democracy for you. We voted and our combined vote produced this final list. Another panel might produce a different list, but I would wager that nearly all the people in this top 100 would figure prominently on any such list.

Our panel was:

Stacey Daniels. Television and radio personality.

Raybon Kan. Comedian, newspaper columnist, radio host.

Robyn Langwell. *North and South* magazine editor.

Douglas Lloyd-Jenkins. Historian, academic, and design, art and architecture writer.

Melanie Nolan. Associate Professor of History at Victoria University and author.

Joseph Romanos. Sports journalist and author.

Tainui Stephens. Television producer.

Kerrie Woodham. Broadcaster and print media columnist.

On a personal note, I was disappointed at some of the omissions from the final 100. Susan Devoy, Keith Holyoake, Maui Pomare, Rosina Buckman, Barry Crump, Arthur Porritt, Helen Connon and Bob Charles, among others, seemed to have undeniable claims to me. On the other hand, I could not fathom how Kupe, whom I regarded as a mythical being, made it. And on the basis of some of those named, I wondered if Abel Tasman and Captain Cook should have been there, too. But I bow to the panel's combined wisdom. No-one made the top 100 merely because of the vote of just one panellist.

As I set out to write profiles on the chosen 100, I discovered that even the ones I knew little about, or was sceptical of, had far stronger claims than I'd understood. Hongi Hika and Te Rauparaha were far more than simply successful Maori warriors, Hone Heke's legacy goes way beyond cutting down the British flagpole. Charles Heaphy was a multi-talented individual, not merely a person who painted pretty scenes. I learnt about John Bedbrook, Matt During, Thomas Brydone and William Davidson, Colin Murdoch, Maurice Wilkins, Rudall Hayward and many others.

This project has given me an immense admiration for New Zealanders. What a lot of pioneering, innovative, brave people the country has produced. New Zealand is just a tiny country in the scheme of things, but has made a significant impact in all sorts of ways, from sport to science, international affairs to entertainment.

This then is our 100, the combined vote of eight New Zealanders. Disagree with the 100 by all means, but read their stories and acknowledge them for their greatness.

Joseph Romanos
November 2005

Ernest Rutherford

Lord of the atom

BORN: SPRING GROVE, NELSON, AUGUST 30, 1871. DIED: CAMBRIDGE, ENGLAND, OCTOBER 19, 1937.

No New Zealander has done work of greater significance to the future of the world than Ernest Rutherford. Those seeking a quick one-phrase summary describe Rutherford as "the man who split the atom". While that's true, it hardly does justice to his incredible work as a pioneering scientist. He was the father of nuclear physics and ushered in the atomic age. Einstein called him "the second Newton".

Rutherford was a Nelson boy, though he spent much of his youth at Havelock in Marlborough. He was one of 12 children of James, a farmer from Scotland, and Martha, a local schoolteacher. He attended Nelson College on a Marlborough Education Board scholarship from 1887-89 and was a dream student – head prefect, dux, a member of the First XV.

He moved on to the University of New Zealand in Christchurch on a New Zealand Junior Scholarship. Again, he revealed his academic gifts, earning a BA in 1892, an MA the following year (double first-class honours in mathematics, mathematical physics and physical science), then a BSc in geology and chemistry.

Rutherford's study was always notable for its practical purposes. In 1893 he produced his first original research, into high-frequency magnetisation of iron, and developed a timing device that could switch circuits in less than one-hundred-thousandth of a second.

In 1895, after a brief spell teaching at Christchurch Boys' High School, Rutherford was granted an Exhibition of 1851 Scholarship, which enabled him to go anywhere in the world to carry out research of importance to New Zealand industry. He chose Cavendish Laboratory at Cambridge University, England, studying under the esteemed Professor Joseph Thomson. It didn't take Rutherford long to make a mark at Cambridge. In 1896 he set a record for the distance over which "wireless" waves could be detected. Two years later he discovered that rays from uranium radiation were of two main types, which he named alpha and beta.

By 1898 Rutherford had an international reputation as a scientist and he was lured to McGill University in Montreal, Canada, to take the Macdonald Chair of Physics, where he remained until 1907. He outlined the principles of what we now call smoke detectors in 1899 and shortly afterwards discovered a radioactive gas that was later named radon.

Despite the acclaim he gained in Britain and North America, Rutherford maintained strong links with New Zealand. He remained in close contact with his family and returned home four times. In 1900 he married his long-time fiancée, May Newton, in Christchurch. Rutherford, a prolific and practical scientist who developed a reputation for rigorous experimentation, attributed much of his success to his upbringing, saying: "In New Zealand we don't have money, so we have to think." He was appointed a DSc at the University of New Zealand in 1901, so becoming Dr Rutherford, and in 1904 was awarded the prestigious Rumford Medal. Among the areas he studied at this time were radioactivity and research into Earth's ageing process.

From 1907-19 he was Langworthy Professor of Physics at Manchester University. Rutherford won the Nobel Prize for Chemistry in 1908 for his "investigations into the disintegration of the elements, and the chemistry of radioactive substances". Over the next two decades, he mentored or worked with many other outstanding scientists, including Niels Bohr, Hans Geiger, James Chadwick, Patrick Blackett, Robert Oppenheimer, John Cockroft and Ernest Walton. Some won Nobel Prizes as a result of research that he instituted. Charles Ellis, who wrote two books with Rutherford, said that "the majority of the experiments at the Cavendish were really started by Rutherford's direct or indirect suggestion".

Rutherford was a generous-spirited person, noted for his "benevolent guidance, leadership and intellectual authority", as one student put it. When work was going well in Rutherford's laboratory he would stride about singing a hearty rendition of *Onward Christian Soldiers*. He was tall, radiated good humour and had lively blue eyes.

In 1910 his investigations into the scattering of alpha rays and the nature of the inner structure of the atom that caused such scattering led to his concept of the "nucleus". This is often described as his greatest contribution to physics.

During World War I he did pioneering work on acoustic methods of detecting submarines and determining the direction of the sound they emitted. He travelled to the United States in 1917 to present his findings to officials there. Besides his work for the war effort, he continued his research into atomic science and

in 1917 he changed nitrogen into oxygen – he split the atom – which he had been working towards for many years. Significantly, Rutherford said at the time that he hoped mankind would not discover how to extract the energy from the nucleus until man was living in peace with his neighbour. His sense of danger turned out to be prophetic.

Rutherford became director of Cavendish Laboratory at Cambridge in 1919, a position he held until his death 18 years later. He continued to do ground-breaking work – in 1920 he proved the existence of the neutron.

Having been knighted in 1914, he received the Order of Merit (restricted to 24 living persons) in 1925, and was elevated to the peerage in 1931, when he became Ernest, Lord Rutherford of Nelson. He was elected a fellow of the Royal Society in 1903 and was its president from 1925-30. He received honorary doctorates from 21 universities around the world. Craters on the Moon and Mars have been named after Rutherford.

On his trips back to New Zealand, Rutherford was invariably greeted as a hero. There were civic receptions for him and he packed out halls when he delivered lectures. He strongly supported education and research, and urged that New Zealand scientists focus on research of benefit to farmers. His backing helped establish New Zealand's Department of Scientific and Industrial Research in 1926.

Rutherford's portrait was placed on the New Zealand $100 note in 1992. Four countries – Sweden, New Zealand, the Soviet Union and Canada – have issued stamps depicting him. In 1969 element 104 was named rutherfordium. In 1991 the Rutherford Origin was built on the site of his birth. It is a permanent outdoor display of information about his life and work.

Kate Sheppard

Nothing less than equal

BORN: LIVERPOOL, ENGLAND, MARCH 10, 1847. DIED: CHRISTCHURCH, JULY 13, 1934.

When Kate Sheppard died in 1934, the *Christchurch Times* noted: "A great woman has gone, whose name will remain an inspiration to the daughters of New Zealand while our history endures." By 2005, New Zealand had women as Prime Minister, Governor-General, Chief Justice, and Parliamentary Speaker. Sheppard had indeed proved an inspiration to the women who followed her.

Sheppard had a mild personality. She was quiet, determined and utterly capable, but never strident or demanding. Perhaps that was one of the secrets of her remarkable achievements.

Though named Catherine Malcolm, she always preferred to be called Katherine or, even better, Kate. She was born in Liverpool, but was raised primarily in Scotland, with spells in London and Dublin. She was a particularly bright student, with notable ability in the sciences and law. She had a strong religious education and throughout her life never deviated from her Christian principles. After her father died, her mother brought Kate, aged 21, her two brothers and a sister to Christchurch, where another sister, Marie Beath, was living. In 1871 Kate married Walter Sheppard, a storekeeper. They were to have one son, Douglas.

Sheppard was an active member of the Trinity Congregational Church, spending much of her time in temperance work, taking Bible classes and fund-raising. She was already showing the organisational skills that were to make her a world figure within a few years. She was a natural leader who was tolerant and charming, but ever persuasive. In 1885 Sheppard became a founding member of the New Zealand Women's Christian Temperance Union. Many New Zealand women blamed alcohol for the disorder of society and welcomed a women's organisation that sought to ban it. To carry out its work more effectively, and get social and legislative reforms accepted, the union realised it would be helped considerably if women could vote.

From 1887 Sheppard pursued this goal. She wrote and distributed pamphlets, sparked debate in the press and attended church and political meetings. She was a fine speaker, with a clear sense of logic and no rancour, and was disarmingly feminine. One of her major successes was in persuading Sir John Hall, a leading MP, to support the women's cause. With Sheppard in the vanguard, the union presented three petitions to Parliament from 1891-93, seeking to give women the right to vote. Until then, only males over 21 could vote. Women were excluded, along with juveniles, lunatics and criminals. The women's path was a tough one – suffrage bills in Parliament were defeated in 1888, 1891 and 1892.

The heat was turned up when Sheppard began contributing a women's page in the *Prohibitionist*, the national temperance magazine. She kept women up to date with the suffrage movement, not just in New Zealand, but in other countries. In a pamphlet she put together called *Ten Reasons Why the Women of New Zealand Should Vote*, she wrote: "Because it has not yet been proved that the intelligence of women is equal only to that of children, or that their intelligence is on a par with that of lunatics or criminals."

Her 1893 petition contained 32,000 signatures, a huge number for that time. Finally, on September 19, 1893, the Electoral Act was passed by a vote of 20–18. Sheppard received a telegram from the Premier, Richard Seddon, who had been staunchly opposed to women's suffrage, conceding victory to the women. The Governor, Lord Glasgow, acknowledged Sheppard's work by presenting to her the pen with which the bill granting women suffrage had been signed.

It was a world event – New Zealand was the first country (though not the first territory) to grant universal adult suffrage to men and women equally, and Sheppard's equivalents in the United States, Britain and Europe drew much inspiration from her success. British women did not get the vote until 1928 and American women were not granted it nationally until 1920. In the 10 weeks before the 1893 election, Sheppard and her assistants set about enrolling women. They were so successful that 65 per cent of women voted in the election. (Women, however, still had a long way to go to achieve political equality. They did not gain the right to stand for Parliament until 1919, and the first female MP, Elizabeth McCombs, was not elected until 1933.)

Sheppard was a trend-setter in other ways as well. At a time when many felt that women should avoid vigorous physical activity because they were too fragile, Sheppard become one of the first female cyclists in Christchurch. She favoured women playing sport and was a member of the women's Atalanta Cycle Club. She was very disparaging of women who sat around trying to look delicate.

Though she did not seek such praise, Sheppard was fêted as a celebrity when she travelled to London in 1894. Two years later she was elected president at the inaugural National Council of Women of New Zealand meeting. In 1895 the Women's Christian Temperance Union began publishing its own newspaper, *The White Ribbon*. Under Sheppard's editorship the newspaper covered a range of issues, including health, education, proper attire, equal wages for women, education against alcohol, and women's political and legal rights.

Sheppard was always clear that she regarded the family as the foundation of the state and asked: "If the mother is dwarfed, repressed, how can the children grow to their full mental and moral stature?" Besides her temperance union and National Council of Women responsibilities, Sheppard was also a long-serving convener of the Canterbury Women's Institute economics department.

Her health broke down in 1903 and she and her husband decided to retire to England. On the journey across, she met Carrie Chapman Catt and other leading North American feminists. In London, she was in constant demand as a public speaker and wrote numerous letters to national newspapers, pushing the women's cause in the suffrage debate. She was to be a keynote speaker at the International Council of Women meeting in Berlin in 1904, but was too ill to attend. Her paper was read to the conference.

With her health continuing to decline, she decided to return to New Zealand. She lived sedately, though she continued to influence the women's movement with her writings. In 1909, at the Toronto meeting of the International Council of Women, Sheppard was elected vice-president, even though she was unable to attend.

She was made a life member of the National Council of Women in 1923. Two years later, having been widowed for 10 years, she married 72-year-old Christchurch printer William Lovell-Smith, an old friend and a long-time

supporter of women's rights. An independent thinker with a keen sense of social responsibility right to the end, Sheppard died in 1934.

Sheppard's image is found on the New Zealand $10 note. The Kate Sheppard National Memorial, a large bronze sculpture marking the centenary of the women's suffrage vote, was unveiled at Oxford Terrace, on the banks of the Avon River in Christchurch, in 1993.

Edmund Hillary

The man who took New Zealand to the top of the world

BORN: AUCKLAND, JULY 20, 1919.

Edmund Hillary never fancied himself as a photographer. But on one day in his life – and what a day – his photographic skills were crucial. "Tenzing Norgay and I had reached the top of Mt Everest," Hillary recalled. "I had to take photos on all sides, as proof we'd made it. I had one of those cameras that you wind on manually, or you double-expose the film, and I got quite paranoid about it. When the film was developed in London, there'd be one image, then a couple of blanks, then another image, then another couple of blanks. I'd taken a photo, then wound on the film. Then before taking the next photo, I'd wound on the film again, for insurance. Thankfully the photos came out all right."

Taking photos was just one task Hillary performed that famous day – May 29, 1953 – when he and Norgay became the first people to reach the top of the world's highest mountain, the 8824m (29,028ft) Mt Everest.

The day began for them at about 4am. "Norgay and I had left the main party the previous day and set out for the final push to the top," Hillary said. "We made a barely adequate snow cave and settled down for the night. It was a terrible night, and neither of us slept more than a few minutes. I was relieved when it got light enough for us to get started."

Others had climbed to within 2000 feet of the summit, only to be defeated, usually by the weather. "Two thousand feet at that height is an enormous distance," Hillary says. "It refers to vertical height, but you may have to climb a long way before making any vertical progress." On and on they climbed, hacking their way up the mountain, Hillary two or three steps ahead. Hillary recounted the moment he reached the top in his autobiography *Nothing Venture, Nothing Win*: "I realised that the ridge ahead, instead of monotonously rising, now dropped sharply away. A few more whacks of the ice axe in the firm snow and we stood on top." It was not really a sharp point, said Hillary. "It's a summit you can stand on reasonably comfortably. Six or eight people could stand on it together. A nice summit."

Once they knew they'd reached the top, Hillary proffered a handshake. "Tenzing wasn't having any of that, and hugged me vigorously. Having been brought up along Anglo-Saxon lines, it was almost embarrassing. It was a very satisfying moment, but we weren't hooped up too much. After all, there was the knowledge that we had to get back down."

The view was beautiful, he said. "It was a reasonably clear day, and when I took off my oxygen mask, this great swoop of air came over the summit, filled with little bits of ice, and there were prickles all over my face." Norgay posed on top of the mountain, waving an axe containing the flags of the United Nations, Britain, Nepal and India, while Hillary got busy with his camera. Norgay placed some food in a hole, a gesture to the gods Buddhists believed had their home on the summit, and Hillary placed a crucifix in the same hole.

After about 20 minutes, the pair prepared for the return journey. "That's often more dangerous than the climb. You're tired, maybe low on oxygen, trying to hurry." They descended steadily and there came the moment, 1000 metres below the summit, when Hillary and Tenzing reached their companions in the party mounted by Englishman Colonel John Hunt. It was the other New Zealander in the party, George Lowe, who greeted Hillary. "How did it go, Ed?" he asked anxiously.

"Well, George, we knocked the bastard off," replied Hillary.

"It was a comment made between two friends after a day that could never be repeated. But when we got to London, and George was asked by the BBC World Service what my first words had been, he recounted it. The comment seemed to reverberate around the world. My mother was appalled that I had used such language, and reproached me suitably."

By then, Hillary was a world celebrity, and has remained so ever since. "I thought we'd done something that would be of interest in the mountaineering world. I never had any concept of the impact the climb would have, or how it would affect my life. It occurred just days before the Queen's coronation, and by really stretching themselves, newspapers were able to report news of the climb before the coronation. The two events were linked by the headline writers, which greatly increased the publicity."

When he climbed Mt Everest, Hillary was a tall, lean, Auckland 33-year-old who had established himself as a fine mountaineer: strong, resourceful, ambitious and technically efficient. He was delighted to be invited by

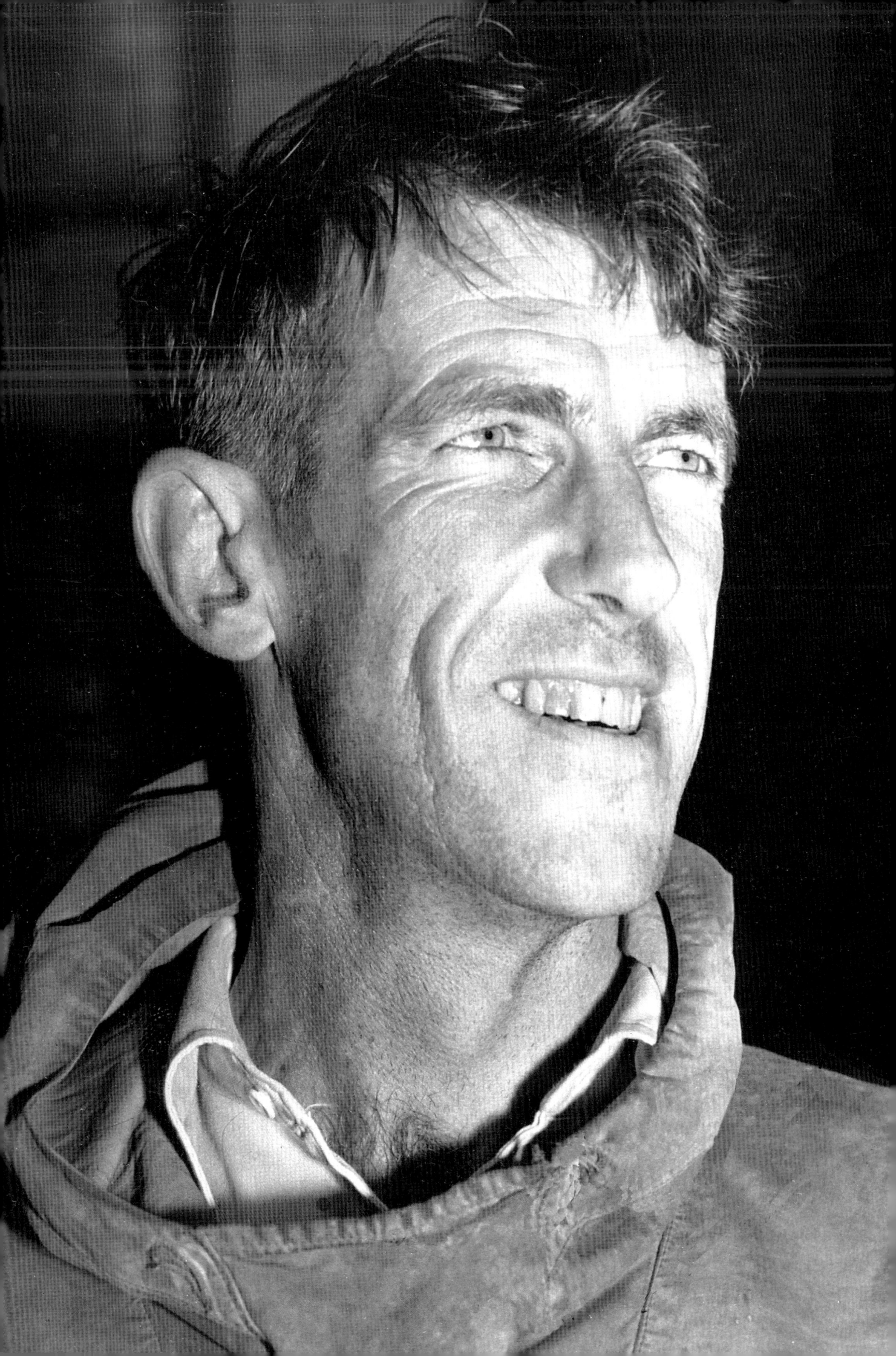

Hunt to be part of the Everest expedition, and even happier when he learnt that Lowe was also to be a member of the party.

Once the assault on Everest began, it became clear that Hillary was one of the most qualified technically and physically for the final push. "Of the party of 13 [excluding sherpas], three or four of us could have reached the top. George Lowe could certainly have, but I don't think the English wanted two New Zealanders grabbing all the kudos! Tenzing had stood out as a strong and reliable sherpa. He didn't speak much English, but certainly more than I spoke of Nepalese, and while we were not able to discuss the meaning of life, we were able to communicate sufficiently." After their climb, the two men were linked forever. Norgay became a national celebrity and he and Hillary remained friends until Norgay's death in 1986.

Hillary was knighted immediately. On their slow trek back to Kathmandu, the climbers were met by ever more mail runners, laden with congratulatory cables, telegrams and even letters. One of these was addressed to "Sir Edmund Hillary, KBE".

"I thought it was a joke," said Hillary. "I didn't take it seriously, but George Lowe realised it wasn't a joke and thought it was very funny. Well, I didn't laugh at all. It wasn't something that I'd have chosen personally. Even though I realised it was a great honour, I was just a beekeeper and I didn't really feel quite right to have an honour like that."

Hillary has more than justified his knighthood. His has been a life full of accomplishments. He has travelled by jet boat up the Ganges, climbed Mount Herschel in Antarctica, and been on a three-year four-wheel-drive expedition to the South Pole. He served in New Delhi for four-and-a-half-years as New Zealand High Commissioner in India. In Nepal, where he returned frequently to front efforts to build schools and hospitals, he is revered.

Home in Auckland, he receives dozens of letters a week from all around the world. He is a national celebrity, whose face is on our $5 note. Through it all, he has never got carried away with himself. He signs himself "Ed Hillary", and that's how he sees himself, even if he is the most famous New Zealander of all.

George Grey

The Governor who shaped New Zealand

BORN: LISBON, PORTUGAL, APRIL 14, 1812. DIED: LONDON, SEPTEMBER 20, 1898.

George Grey was one of the most influential figures in early New Zealand history, an emissary of Britain who, as Governor, forged close links with Maori and later became the Premier. He was also a significant personality in South Australian and South African politics. Although he was autocratic and egotistic, Grey had vision and a good deal of pragmatism. Those traits stood him in good stead through more than half a century of politics in three countries.

His father, George, died during the attack by the Duke of Wellington on Napoleon at Badajoz, Spain, in 1812. A week later, George was born in Portugal. He was educated at Guildford and, from 1826, at the Royal Military College at Sandhurst.

Grey served with the 83rd Foot Regiment in Glasgow, then, from 1830-36, in Ireland. The appalling poverty in Ireland affected him greatly and he became an advocate of emigration. He developed his political liberalism in Ireland. After rising to the rank of captain he was sent to Australia in 1837. He undertook two arduous exploratory trips to Western Australia, and served for a time as Resident Magistrate at King George Sound, before becoming Governor of South Australia in 1841.

He took charge of a state that was virtually bankrupt and in which there was constant and fierce fighting between the Aborigines and the settlers. Grey all but balanced the books and showed more understanding of the Aborigines' situation than those who had preceded him.

His empathy with the Aborigines encouraged the Colonial Office to send him to New Zealand, where the situation was threatening to spin out of control. He arrived in New Zealand on November 11, 1845, and found that not only was there little money, but that there were pockets of fighting between Maori and Pakeha all over the country.

New Zealand had not had especially strong leadership from Governors Hobson and FitzRoy and much work needed to be done. Grey steered a middle line, appeasing Maori where necessary and adopting sterner measures elsewhere. He stayed clear of the aggressive Hone Heke in the far north, but arrested and imprisoned without trial Te Rauparaha in Wellington.

Generally he managed Maori affairs well from 1845-53, observing some of the provisions in the Treaty of Waitangi that recognised Maori land rights. He tried, with only limited success, to "Europeanise" Maori in terms of schooling, law, hospitals and agriculture. He developed a

good understanding of the Maori people. He learnt the language, and later published books on various aspects of Maori culture. Grey became the Governor-in-Chief of New Zealand on January 1, 1848, and was knighted later that year.

He was practical and effective and not above bending the truth to suit his own ends. He deferred the introduction of self-government for five years, claiming it would have been a minority government, with Maori outnumbering Pakeha, and instead remained in charge as Governor. In 1852 he wrote to the Secretary of Colonies: "Both races already form one harmonious community... insensibly forming one people." Such a comment looked absurd a few years later when the New Zealand Wars re-ignited. However, Grey was largely instrumental in writing the 1852 constitution that set up provincial and two central representative assemblies in Wellington.

He made an extensive trip through the Pacific Islands in 1853 and the following year became Governor of Cape Colony and High Commissioner of South Africa. He had a mixed time in South Africa, declining to take orders from London and eventually being recalled to England in disfavour.

In 1861 he returned to New Zealand as Governor. This time he had to share power with an elected government and had to deal with a new force, Kingitanga (the King Movement). This pan-tribal group, based in the Waikato, resisted the sale of land and established the position of a king to rule Maori within the rohe (territory). Grey assembled a vast number of troops, ordered the building of Great South Road as a military supply line and invaded the Waikato. Although Kingitanga survived the invasion, the movement was weakened through confiscation. Grey had removed a major threat to British sovereignty over New Zealand.

His term as Governor was terminated in 1868. Whereas he was once hailed among Maori as "Good Governor Grey", that reverential attitude did not persist in the wake of several examples of Grey's lack of scruples and the severity with which Maori were treated after the 1860s wars.

There was another brief stay in England, where he made an abortive attempt to win a parliamentary seat as a Liberal, then he returned to New Zealand to settle. He lived in a grand house on Kawau Island in the Hauraki Gulf.

In 1875 Grey re-emerged into public life. He won a seat in Parliament, representing Auckland City West, and became Superintendent of Auckland province. The following year he won the Thames seat. In Parliament, Grey unsuccessfully opposed Julius Vogel's moves to abolish provincial governments.

In 1877 he became Premier, pushing a "one man-one vote" line at a time when wealthy land-owners held an inordinate amount of voting sway. It was a difficult time to run the country though, because the Depression had hit hard and there was widespread unemployment. Not only that, but Grey had made some important political enemies. He had often clashed with Vogel, who had had two terms as Premier, and then fell out with a rising political figure, Robert Stout. After two undistinguished years he resigned as Premier, though he remained in Parliament, as an increasingly embittered backbencher. In 1891 Grey was one of three New Zealand representatives at the Australian Federal Convention. It was a triumphant return to Australia for Grey, who was received with warm feeling. He strongly opposed suggestions that New Zealand should federate with Australia, hardly surprising when he had drafted New Zealand's constitution as a separate crown colony.

Back in New Zealand, he represented Newton in Parliament, then in 1893 Auckland Central. But his health became increasingly fragile and he returned to England for good in 1894. His death, in 1898, came only a fortnight after that of his wife, Eliza. They had married in 1839, split acrimoniously in 1860, and then, improbably, reconciled 36 years later.

Grey was an inveterate collector of many things, notably rare books. He donated most to libraries in Cape Town and Auckland. He was also a keen botanist and linguist, who studied and wrote books about the Aborigine and Maori languages.

The Grey River on the West Coast of the South Island, Greymouth, Greytown, Grey Lynn, the Grey Glacier in the Southern Alps, Grey Pass, which crosses the Grey Glacier, and Mt Grey in central Canterbury are just some of the places named after him.

Michael Joseph Savage

The Prime Minister who set up the welfare state

BORN: TATONG, VICTORIA, MARCH 23, 1872. DIED: WELLINGTON, MARCH 27, 1940.

Michael Joseph Savage was the most popular of all New Zealand Prime Ministers. His friendly, caring personality and the sweeping changes he introduced when leading the first Labour Government made him an icon. Like those of today's rock stars and sports heroes, Savage's photo hung in the homes of thousands of New Zealanders.

He was born in Victoria and after limited schooling was working in a wines and spirits shop by the time he was 14. Savage's brother, Joe, died in 1891 and as a mark of respect he adopted Joseph as his middle name. Thereafter he was known by his full name of Michael Joseph Savage, though this was sometimes shortened affectionately to Mickey.

Through most of his 20s he was a labourer in New South Wales. When he returned to Victoria he took odd jobs – fireman, gold-miner, train-driver, bakery manager. He enjoyed all sport, particularly weightlifting and boxing, and was a keen dancer. He gradually became more involved in union politics and was active in the Political Labor Council of Victoria before moving to New Zealand in 1907.

After a spell cutting flax in Manawatu, he based himself in Auckland, boarding with the family of Alf and Elizabeth French (Savage never married and stayed with the family until his death). He quickly became immersed in Auckland political and union activity. He was president of the Auckland Trades Council by 1910 and ran for Parliament in 1911, finishing second in Auckland Central when representing the Socialist Party. A young Scotsman named Peter Fraser, who was also an active unionist in Auckland, was his campaign manager.

Savage was involved in the Auckland labourers' strike of 1912, the Waihi miners' strike the same year and the big Auckland waterfront dispute in 1913. He stood for Parliament in 1914, this time as a Social Democratic Party candidate, but was beaten again.

After trying for some years to draw together various strands of the union movement, Savage decided to start again. He helped establish the New Zealand Federation of Labour (The Red Feds, as they were known), becoming Auckland branch chairman, and was an important figure in the formation of the New Zealand Labour Party in 1916. During World War I, Savage argued for the conscription of wealth, not men.

Representing Labour, he was finally elected to Parliament in 1919, standing for Auckland West. He was also voted on to the Auckland City Council in 1919 (he remained until 1923) and the Auckland Hospital and Charitable Aid Board. He stayed on the board for three years and had another stint from 1927-35.

Savage quickly became one of the Labour Party's most important figures. He was the party vice-president from 1918 and secretary from 1919. In 1922 he became deputy-leader to Harry Holland, who was far more radical. Through the 1920s Savage did much to spread the Labour message into the rural community and helped formulate Labour's policies on pension schemes, superannuation and finance. When Holland died in 1933, Savage beat Fraser in the race for the leadership and under him Labour swept to power in 1935, winning 55 of the 80 seats. He also formed an alliance with the Ratana Movement.

Savage, much affected by what he had seen during the Depression years, proved to be a decisive leader. He immediately gave the unemployed a bonus and set up a state housing construction programme. He nationalised commercial broadcasting, introduced minimum prices for dairy products and made unionism compulsory. These policies were made more acceptable to an anxious public by Savage's sincerity and reassuring air.

Though he was a genial figure, he was firm in his convictions. When he visited England in 1937 to attend the coronation of King George VI, he criticised Britain's policy of appeasement towards Germany, Italy and Japan, drawing criticism from the British, Canadians and Australians and the National Party in New Zealand. Undaunted, he continued to make his point, despite suggestions he was damaging the British Empire with his comments.

In 1938 Savage was diagnosed with cancer but delayed treatment to campaign before the election. And what a campaign it was. Savage, always a good orator, drew crowds of up to 30,000 at his rallies and they were emotional, memorable occasions. He proposed the Social Security Bill, which would introduce free healthcare, give a pension at 60 and superannuation at 65. This bill would be enacted on April 1, 1939 and thus became the central issue of the campaign. Labour won with an even bigger majority. To introduce the bill, Savage dealt ruthlessly with opposition from Treasury, the New Zealand branch of the British Medical Association and the National Party.

That election victory cost Savage dearly, though. By the time he finally sought treatment, his cancer had spread and for much of the last year of his life he was gravely ill.

When war was declared, Savage gave a series of "fireside chats", speaking to his countrymen through the medium of radio and attempting to recruit volunteers. Though increasingly ill, he rallied long enough to call for the rebellious John A Lee's expulsion from the Labour Party. Lee had made a barely-disguised attack on Savage in an article for *Tomorrow* newspaper called "Psychopathology in Politics" and Savage was determined to be rid of him. Fraser read Savage's speech to the 1940 Labour Party annual conference and quoted Savage as saying that Lee had made his life a "living hell" for the past two years. Savage said of Lee: "During my illness he has tried to destroy me as a political figure." Lee was expelled by a 546–344 vote. Within two days, Savage had died.

Savage's body was transported by train to Auckland and as it stopped along the way, hundreds of thousands of New Zealanders paid tribute to him. He was buried at Bastion Point. Above the grave is the impressive Savage Memorial. Savage began his life a Catholic and returned to the church during his final years.

Savage was not alone in devising Labour's far-reaching policies of the 1930s. Fraser, Walter Nash and Lee, among others, played a hand, but he was one of the chief architects of the welfare state. In addition, Savage delivered the message in a most convincing manner. He was sincere and New Zealanders trusted him. In any list of New Zealand Prime Ministers, he must be near the top.

Apirana Ngata

Maori leader in a Pakeha world

BORN: TE ARAROA, EAST CAPE, JULY 3, 1874. DIED: WAIOMATATINI, JULY 14, 1950.

With better luck and timing, Apirana Ngata might have become New Zealand's first Maori Prime Minister. During a distinguished career that bridged law, politics and Maori affairs, he was one of the country's most important figures for more than half a century. His influence was not confined to just a single Maori tribe or political party.

Ngata's upbringing combined the Maori and Pakeha worlds. His father, Paratene, was a Native Land Court assessor and a tribal lore expert. His grand-uncle, Ropata Wahawaha, had led Ngati Porou troops against the Crown during the 1860s land wars. These two men shaped the young Apirana's views on loyalty to the Crown. However, his mother, Katerina, the daughter of a Scot, was important because through her influence Apirana received a solid grounding in Pakeha learning and traditions.

Ngata spent eight years at Te Aute College, and gave early signs of his leadership talent. In 1891-92 he travelled around the Ngati Porou villages with Reweti Kohere, talking on health reform. On leaving Te Aute, Ngata studied at Canterbury College, courtesy of a Te Makarini Scholarship. He earned a BA in political science in 1893, and later completed an MA. He completed his LLB in Auckland in 1897, becoming the first Maori to complete a New Zealand university degree.

But Ngata did not pursue a law career. He married Arihia Tamati in 1895 and they moved to the East Coast, where he built a large home at Waiomatatini. Eleven of the couple's children survived to adulthood. Ngata set off

on what became his life's work: reforming and improving the social and economic conditions for Maori. He spoke at hui, wrote numerous newspaper articles and impressed with his clarity of thought, tenacity and courtesy.

Ngata was convinced that the only hope for Maori survival and development in an environment controlled by Pakeha lay along two lines of endeavour – mastery of Western skills and the determined retention of Maori culture. He exemplified both approaches, as did several other Te Aute college pupils, who, with Ngata, formed the Young Maori Party. They included Maui Pomare and Peter Buck.

As early as 1900, Ngata was working with James Carroll, the Minister of Native Affairs, on two significant pieces of legislation, the Maori Lands Administration Act and the Maori Councils Act.

Ngata began his 38-year stint as an MP in 1905. Representing the Liberals, he won Eastern Maori handsomely over long-time incumbent Wi Pere. Ngata was a magnificent parliamentarian. He spoke commandingly and researched meticulously, and rose through the ranks quickly. By 1909 he was on the Executive Council, representing the "native race", and was then elevated to Cabinet and placed in charge of Maori councils. The Liberals lost power in 1912, but Ngata remained a leading member of the House. Though he was not in Government again until 1928, he always wielded considerable power.

In 1912 Ngata founded the Waiapu Farmers' Co-operative Company, which was owned by Ngati Porou farmers. His legal knowledge and business acumen helped the co-operative thrive, and Ngata encouraged other tribes to replicate the concept.

At 40, Ngata was too old to serve in World War I, but busied himself recruiting and pushing to have a Maori battalion formed. He never shied away from causes that might prove unpopular. For years he sought justice on behalf of Maori who had lost land during the land wars decades earlier. He was rewarded in 1927, when a royal commission of inquiry investigated the confiscation of that land in a similar fashion to the Waitangi Tribunal decades later.

Another area where Ngata's role was far-reaching was in promoting Maori social and cultural activities. He encouraged Maori sport, promoted the performing arts through inter-tribal competitions in haka and poi, and supported Maori carving and tukutuku work. He helped to establish the Maori School of Arts in Rotorua in 1927. He was also heavily involved in the Anglican Church and in 1928, swimming against the rising tide of the Ratana movement, persuaded the general synod to create a Maori archdiocese.

Despite these various interests, his major preoccupation was the land reform movement. He had success first with Ngati Porou and then guided other tribes into following suit, pushing his famous "Ahuwhenua" policy, which, in effect, involved working the land hard to produce maximum output.

When the renamed United Party won power in 1928, Ngata became Native Minister. He was ranked third in Cabinet and on occasion filled in as Deputy Prime Minister. As Native Minister, his pace of decision-making became frenetic, as he pushed ahead with his land development schemes. He was a folk hero to Maori, though many Pakeha were suspicious of him.

All went well – even if Ngata proved more of a visionary than a details person – until one of his aides on the East Coast was exposed as a fraudster. This dented Ngata's reputation. Prime Minister George Forbes launched a commission of inquiry into Ngata's handling of his department. The inquiry's report was critical of Ngata's eschewing of bureaucratic regulations, and there were suggestions he had favoured Ngati Porou. Though personally cleared of corruption, Ngata resigned from Cabinet.

He finally lost his parliamentary seat in 1943, to Ratana-Labour candidate Tiaki Omana. He was the last non-Ratana Maori MP of the time. By then he was the Father of the House, the title bestowed on the longest-serving MP.

Ngata remained involved in all manner of Maori affairs. He helped organise the Treaty of Waitangi centenary celebrations in 1940, recruited Maori and pushed again for a Maori battalion in World War II, and assisted with Auckland University College adult education courses. Among other projects were a revision of the Maori Bible, and an increasing interest in anthropology, sparked by his friendship with Peter Buck.

He married three times. Arihia died in 1929. He married Te Riringi Tuhou in 1932 and when she died in 1948, he married Hene Te Kira.

Until his death aged 76, he remained active, working on the Rangiatea Church restoration and a planned 600-year anniversary celebration of the coming of the Great Fleet. He maintained an interest in Te Aute College, filling a variety of roles, including serving on the college's centennial committee.

His famous advice to a young girl, "E tipu e rea..." encapsulates his philosophy. Translated, it was: "Grow and branch forth in the days of your world, your hand grasping the material things of the West so that your body may prosper. Your heart to the treasures of your ancestors, adornments for your head. Your spirits with the Lord, who made all things."

When he died, people from all over New Zealand honoured him at his tangi. He is featured on the New Zealand $50 note. In 1927 Ngata became the third Maori to be knighted, after James Carroll and Maui Pomare.

Hone Heke

Formidable warrior, man of intellect

BORN: PAKARAKA, BAY OF ISLANDS, c1808. DIED: KAIKOHE, AUGUST 6, 1850.

Hone Heke's name is recalled today because he was said to be the first Maori chief to sign the Treaty of Waitangi, on February 6, 1840, and because he later three times cut down the flagpole flying the British flag to protest against the way Maori people were being treated by the Crown. This was the act that sparked the Northern War. Only rarely is appropriate weight accorded his intelligence, common-sense, sense of chivalry and vision.

Heke Pokai was born just south of Kerikeri. He was a member of the Nga Puhi tribe, and a nephew of the great warrior Hongi Hika. He also had connections to Rahiri that significantly increased his mana. His advance to adulthood needed a large measure of good fortune – his family became caught up in the tribal warfare of the time and he had some narrow escapes during his early years.

He was a clever and inquisitive youngster who was much influenced by the teachings of missionary Henry Williams, who became somewhat of a father figure to him, especially while he was attending the mission school at Kerikeri. Heke and his first wife, Ono, the daughter of Nga Puhi leader Te Pahi, converted to Christianity in 1835. He took Hone (John) as his first name and developed a deep knowledge of the scriptures. Using his excellent oratorical skills, he became a lay preacher. Hone and Ono's two children, who both died young, were baptised.

Ono died soon after her baptism and in 1837 Heke married the strong-minded Hariata Rongo, Hongi Hika's daughter. This further increased Heke's stature.

Heke, who spent his time mainly at Paihia and Kaikohe, established his reputation as a warrior during the first battle of Kororareka (Russell) in 1830, when he took part in Titore's expedition to Tauranga in 1833, and when he fought with Titore against Pomare II in 1837. Tall and sturdily built, Heke impressed with his bravery, leadership skills and quick thinking during these musket wars.

By the time Lieutenant Governor William Hobson arrived at the Bay of Islands in 1840 to negotiate an agreement with Maori chiefs to extend British sovereignty to New Zealand, Heke was one of the north's most influential Maori chiefs. Hobson presented what is now known as the Treaty of Waitangi, which was read in English and Maori, on February 5. It was greeted sceptically by the Maori, but after a day and night of pondering and discussion, Heke became the first of 45 northern chiefs to sign. He believed that the treaty would protect Maori rights, recognise their trusteeship of the lands and give them the privileges of British subjects. He did not foresee or accept the extensive powers that British settlers claimed had been conferred on them by the treaty.

It did not take long for Heke and his allies to become disenchanted. The capital was shifted south to Auckland just months later, which hurt the northern Maori economically. Customs duties were introduced as a means of raising revenue for the Government, and that forced up prices, while revenue from whaling ship levies was now directed to the Government. Heke was angry that British law had been placed above any authority wielded by the Maori chiefs and that the treaty had left Maori worse off economically.

Rather than engage in open warfare, he focused on the British flag as the symbol of the way British sovereignty was reducing chiefly authority. At daybreak on July 8, 1844, his second-in-command, Te Haratua, cut down the flagstaff at Kororareka. On three more occasions over the next year, Heke himself cut down the flag, despite increasing military protection around it. The final act of cutting down the flagpole sparked the Northern War. The British viewed his actions as open rebellion and offered a £100 reward for his capture. Heke and his ally, Kawiti, were pursued not just by the British, but by kupapa Maori, led by Tamati Waka Nene, who believed that Heke would scare away the Pakeha settlers and that Nga Puhi economic prosperity would be lost.

Over the next few years, a series of key battles took place. The British marched north to attack Heke and Kawiti at their pa at Puketutu, but, after sustaining 50 casualties, withdrew. Waka Nene seized Heke's pa at Te Ahuahu and when Heke tried to retake it, he was defeated and seriously wounded. Kawiti built a pa and made a stand at Ohaeawai. The British bombarded it for a week and then, expecting Kawiti's men to be shattered, attacked the pa. However the Maori, secure in their trenches, cut them down with crossfire. The British suffered 114 casualties.

George Grey, who had replaced Robert FitzRoy as Governor, sent 1700 men through dense bush to attack Ruapekapeka. After bombarding the pa for two weeks, they took it, but it was a hollow victory. The Maori had

Hone Heke — Eruera Maihi Patuone

abandoned the pa, which was not near population centres, did not contain food and was not the home of Heke or Kawiti.

Heke lived at Kaikohe while he recuperated from the injury he suffered at Te Ahuahu, and, always a keen letter-writer, waged a campaign by written word. He wrote many letters to FitzRoy and then Grey voicing his distress at how Maori had been treated since the signing of the treaty. He wrote to Grey: "God made this country for us. It cannot be sliced. If it were a whale it might be sliced... It is not for any stranger or foreign nation to meddle with this sacred country."

Eventually Heke, Kawiti and Waka Nene decided to seek peace with the British. Grey agreed, though for some time he and Heke remained implacably opposed to each other. They eventually came to have grudging mutual respect and were reconciled at a meeting in 1848.

During his final years, Heke suffered from tuberculosis and became extremely frail, though he continued to command respect as the unofficial king of northern Maori. He married again, though still legally married to Hariata. The third marriage did not last and he returned to Hariata at Kaikohe. Once her initial anger died down, Hariata took him back and nursed him until his death.

While at Kaikohe, Heke petitioned his treaty partner, Queen Victoria, to right the injustices his people had suffered. He stressed the need to let his people determine their own destiny. In what was to become a familiar royal response, the Queen declined to reply. Heke was given a Christian burial service. There was great secrecy about where his body was buried, though it is believed to be in the burial ground called Kaungarapa at Pakaraka.

Truby King

Plunket Society visionary

BORN: NEW PLYMOUTH, APRIL 1, 1858. DIED: WELLINGTON, FEBRUARY 10, 1938.

Frederic Truby King was a medical visionary who has had a far-reaching impact on infant health and child-rearing methods in New Zealand, Australia and England.

His father, Thomas, was a wealthy and prominent Taranaki banker/politician. From an early age, Truby showed himself to be an unusually gifted scholar. He was mainly home-schooled and later credited his tutor, Henry Richmond, for much of his success. After setting out to be a banker, with stops along the way in New Plymouth, Auckland, Wellington and Masterton, King decided to pursue a career in medicine. He sailed to Britain in 1880 and studied at the University of Edinburgh, where he was

awarded the Ettles Scholarship as the most distinguished student of his year. He then completed a BSc in public health and took up residencies at the Edinburgh and Glasgow royal infirmaries.

While in Scotland, he met and married Bella Millar, who was also an outstanding scholar. She was to become critical to his work for 40 years.

Back in New Zealand, King was the medical superintendent at Wellington District Hospital, until, in 1889, he was appointed to run the Seacliff Lunatic Asylum, north of Dunedin. He was also a lecturer in mental diseases and an examiner in public health and medical jurisprudence at the University of Otago.

King did excellent work at Seacliff, and in some of his dealings with his patients proved ahead of his time. He attempted to set up a community where the patients maintained their self-respect, in contrast to the very harsh way some other institutions were run. He was an innovative and effective thinker, and not just on medical issues. He wrote papers on plant and animal husbandry and remodelled the institution's sewerage system.

In the early years of the 20th century, King turned his attention to children's health. On May 14, 1907, he addressed a meeting at the Dunedin town hall on the promotion of the health of women and children, and from this the Society for the Promotion of the Health of Women and Children was born. This became the Plunket Society, named after Lady Victoria Plunket, the Governor's wife, and a strong supporter of his beliefs.

The society aimed to "inculcate a lofty view of the responsibilities of maternity" and promoted breast-feeding, trained nurses in maternal and infant welfare, and educated parents in domestic hygiene. King persuaded many wealthy women to devote their energies to promoting the cause of child welfare. Committees were formed throughout the country, local clinics were opened and nurses trained in infant welfare visited mothers in their homes, advising them on feeding and sleeping times, nutrition and so on. King also took ailing infants into his holiday home at Karitane, and thus began the first of the Karitane hospitals.

Like many visionaries, King was an inspiring speaker. He used graphs and charts, and quoted figures that showed how much the health of infants and children had improved under his regime. Things had undeniably improved, but many claimed this was happening anyway, with increased hygiene and more advanced medical practices.

King became a noted figure nationally. He had strong views, especially on making raising children easier for mothers. He said breast-feeding should be four-hourly, but not at nights. He favoured toilet training from two weeks. He was a staunch advocate of the effects of fresh air on babies. He frowned on cuddling and felt masturbation led to moral decline. His creed was: "Help the mothers and save the babies."

In 1912 he was seconded to the Department of Public Health for six months, and travelled the country promoting infant welfare. He took the cause abroad in 1913 when he was appointed as the Government's delegate to an international infant welfare conference in London. In 1917 the founders of the Babies of the Empire Society invited him back to England to advise on training at its Mothercraft Training Centre. In 1913 he wrote a best-selling book, *Feeding and Care of Baby*.

King was never the healthiest of people himself. He suffered from tuberculosis throughout his life and eventually went blind in one eye. He had a difficult personality, and was inclined to be autocratic, intolerant and crusty.

He left Seacliff in 1921 to take up the post of director of child welfare and was knighted in 1925. After his death in 1938 he was accorded a state funeral, the first private citizen to be so honoured.

His status was endorsed in 1957 when he became the first New Zealander to have his image on a New Zealand postage stamp.

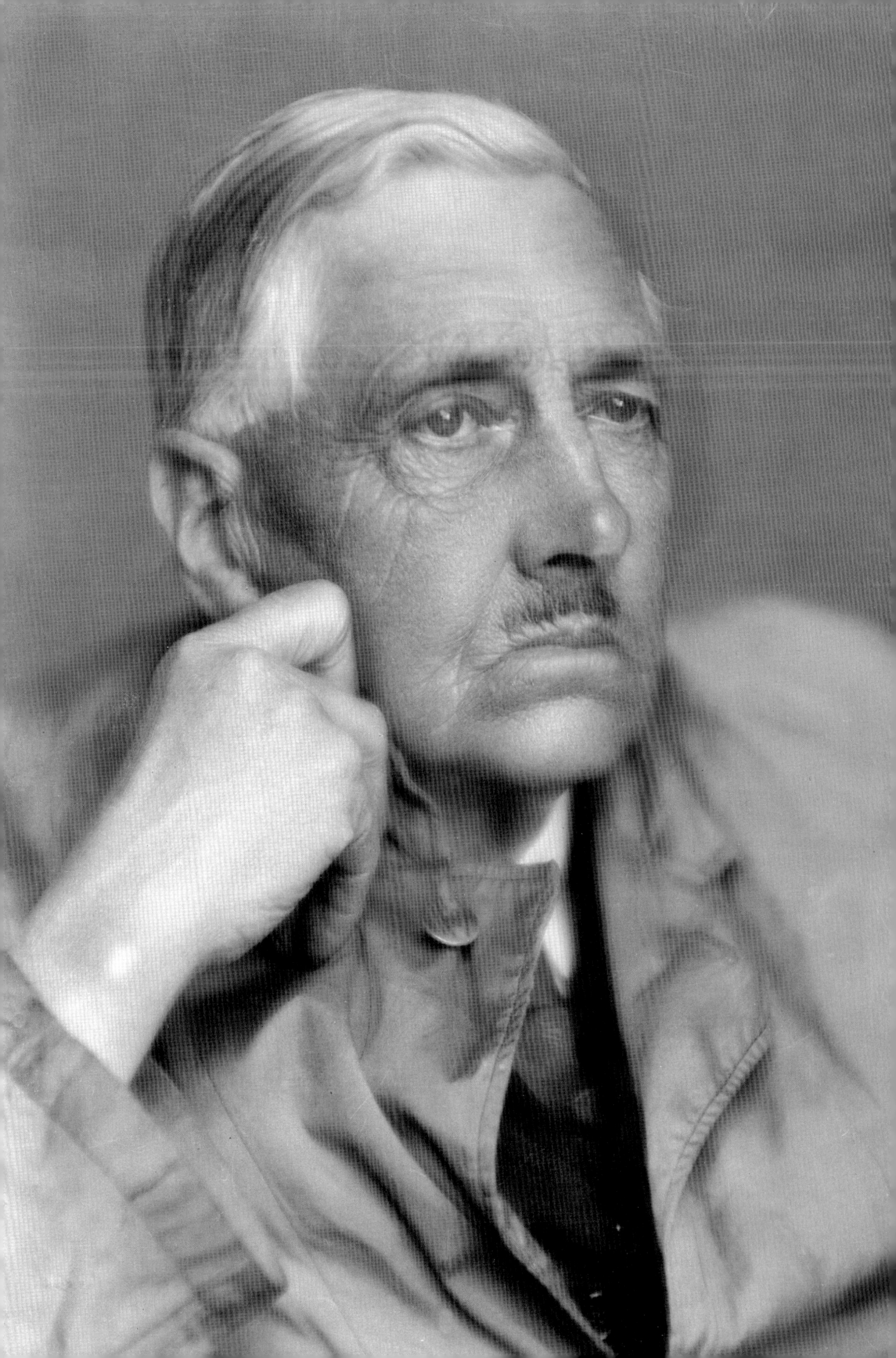

William Hobson

Treaty of Waitangi author

BORN: WATERFORD, IRELAND, SEPTEMBER 26, 1792. DIED: AUCKLAND, SEPTEMBER 10, 1842.

There is debate over how good a Governor of New Zealand William Hobson was and evidence to suggest that, but for his sudden death, his reputation might have been sullied by a recall to London. Regardless, his place in New Zealand history is secure because he was one of the principals at the historic signing of the Treaty of Waitangi on February 6, 1840.

Before Hobson had heard of New Zealand, he had proved himself a fine British naval commander. He was born in Ireland and retained strong links with the country, but when he was just nine he signed on in London as a second-class volunteer in the Royal Navy. It was the beginning of several decades of life at sea.

He served in the North Sea, West Indies, Mediterranean and North America and took part in the Napoleonic wars. He became a lieutenant in 1813 and a commander in 1824 and endured some hair-raising experiences, which included being captured by pirates several times in the Caribbean. While in the West Indies, Hobson suffered from yellow fever, the lingering effects of which were to bedevil him for the rest of his life.

He met Eliza Elliott, the daughter of a Scottish West Indies merchant, while in the Bahamas and married her in 1827. They were to have five children.

Under the patronage of Lord Auckland, Hobson was appointed commander of the frigate Rattlesnake in 1835 and sailed for the East Indies. The following year the Rattlesnake was dispatched to Australia, where it helped with the founding of Williamstown (later Melbourne) and surveyed Port Phillip.

In 1837 the British Resident in New Zealand, James Busby, sent word that inter-tribal musket wars were running out of control and Hobson sailed to New Zealand to lend support. He wasted no time, meeting Busby, missionaries, Maori leaders and prominent settlers. He attempted to reconcile the warring chiefs, then a couple of months later sailed for England.

While in England, Hobson submitted a crucial report, in which, among other suggestions, he pushed for an agreement with the Maori to regularise land purchases. He was appointed Lieutenant Governor of New Zealand on July 30, 1839, and set sail with the instructions that he was to obtain land from Maori "by fair and equal contracts", reselling to settlers at a profit to fund future operations.

Hobson arrived in the Bay of Islands on January 29, 1840 and immediately invited Maori leaders to a meeting at Waitangi. Then he and Busby very imaginatively – this had not been the original idea back in England – drafted a treaty, translated by Henry Williams, a missionary. Through the English version of the treaty, the Maori chiefs would cede sovereignty to Britain, in return for guarantees respecting their lands and possessions and their rights as British subjects. The Maori translation was much less explicit about Maori chiefs ceding sovereignty. Instead they were only to give up "kawanatanga", or governorship. The meeting was held on February 5, beginning at noon. Williams was the interpreter and Hobson was joined on the platform by Busby and several missionaries. The treaty was read out in English and Maori. Gradually the Maori leaders warmed in their support of the treaty, especially after long evening discussions at Te Tii marae and its approval by the influential Tamati Waka Nene, Hone Heke and Patuone.

The following day, Hobson received the signatures of more than 40 chiefs. He intended to arrange similar signings throughout the country and travelled to Waitemata Harbour in search of more signatures, and to survey a location for a new capital. Hobson also sent the Deputy Surveyor-General, William Symonds, to other parts of the country to obtain signatures.

However, on March 1, 1840, Hobson suffered a stroke that affected his right side and his speech. He recovered somewhat, but did not enjoy good health in the remaining 30 months of his life.

Not surprisingly, he was beset by problems constantly as the new country was settled. For example, New Zealand Company settlers arrived at Port Nicholson (later Wellington) and laid claim to the area. Hobson rushed to draft a proclamation asserting British sovereignty over the whole of New Zealand, despite the fact that the treaty-signing had achieved far from blanket coverage.

The Port Nicholson settlers' leader, William Wakefield, travelled to the Bay of Islands and pledged allegiance to the Crown. He wanted the new capital to be Wellington. However, Hobson continued to be plagued by problems from the principals around Wellington. Eventually they sent a petition to Queen Victoria calling for Hobson's dismissal. He had more trouble when the

New Zealand Company attempted to pursue dubious claims for land at Wanganui and Taranaki.

An equally sticky predicament arose when the French frigate L'Aube arrived in New Zealand and headed for Banks Peninsula, where the Nanto-Bordelaise Company planned to found a settlement. Hobson rushed two magistrates to Akaroa to hold court sessions as a signal that the land was subject to British rule.

In September 1840 the British flag was raised on the shores of Waitemata Harbour and the first immigrants to settle in the area arrived from Australia the following month. Hobson named the area Auckland, in honour of his patron. Within a few months, Auckland had become the capital.

On the strength of the treaty that Hobson negotiated, the Queen signed a royal charter for New Zealand to become a Crown Colony separate from New South Wales in November, 1840. Hobson was sworn in as Governor and Commander in Chief on May 3, 1841. Hobson was a civil, courteous man and had a measure of success, especially considering he was chronically underfunded and had such a limited number of troops at his call.

He seemed to have some empathy with the Maori, and appointed George Clarke as Protector of Aborigines, which was a distant predecessor of today's Maori Affairs department. A man of Christian beliefs, Hobson showed a desire to protect Maori while establishing British rule.

However, journalists in Wellington and Auckland hammered Hobson, especially over his land policy, which involved establishing whether land had been fairly purchased from Maori prior to 1840, and his government's expenditure. Never one to respond well to criticism, Hobson replied by shutting down the *New Zealand Herald and Auckland Gazette*. Lack of funds was a constant concern, the more so because it took the best part of a year for Hobson to contact the Colonial Office in London, then receive its reply. After a while, to try to overcome his crippling lack of money, he issued unauthorised bills on the British Treasury.

Hobson suffered another stoke and died in 1842, at the age of 49. He was accorded a military funeral and was buried in what is now known as the Grafton cemetery.

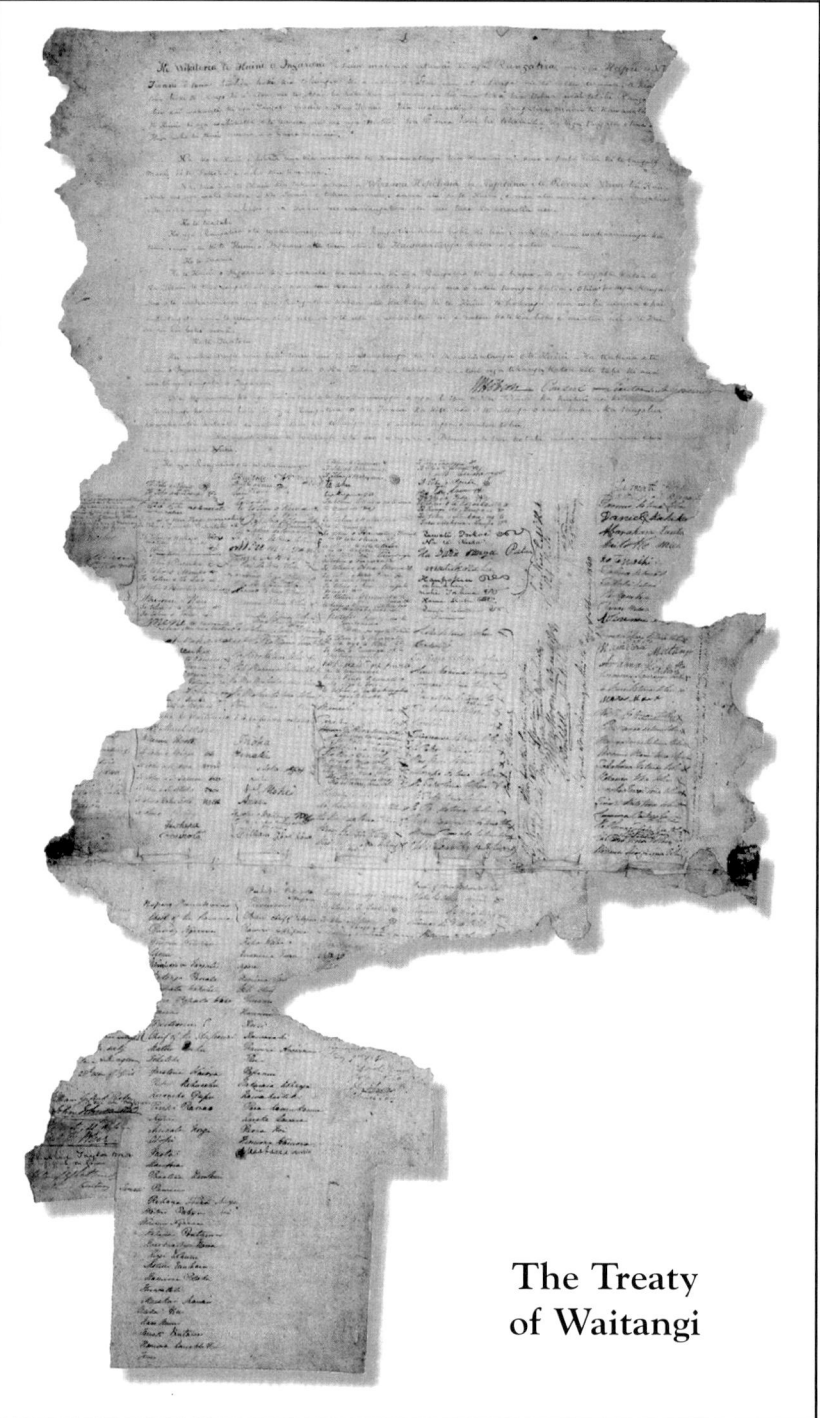

The Treaty of Waitangi

Jean Batten

The Garbo of the skies

BORN: ROTORUA, SEPTEMBER 15, 1909. DIED: MAJORCA, SPAIN, NOVEMBER 22, 1982.

Jean Batten was the most famous New Zealander of the 1930s. The pioneering aviatrix mixed adventure with glamour and became a source of immense pride for New Zealanders. She endured sandstorms over deserts, gale-force winds over Rome and monsoons over India. She became so hot in her tiny cockpit that the rubber soles of her shoes melted, and so cold that she could not bend her fingers. Though she was a celebrity who received massive publicity, she often recoiled from the spotlight. Newspapers tagged her "the Kiwi Garbo", after famous reclusive actress Greta Garbo.

Jane Gardner Batten was born in 1909 in Rotorua, where her father was a dentist. When she was four, her family, including two older brothers, moved to Auckland. Jean, as she was called, finished her schooling at Auckland Ladies College in Remuera. She was a fine scholar, but a rather insular personality. She had an unusually intense relationship with her mother, Ellen, especially after her parents separated in 1920.

When she was 20 Batten accompanied her mother, a strong feminist, to England, intending to become a concert pianist. It was a journey that would set her course for the rest of her life. Flying for the first time – as a passenger – from Richmond aerodrome in Sydney, she vowed she would become a pilot. That first flight was on the Southern Cross and the pilot was Charles Kingsford-Smith.

In London she wasted no time getting to Stag Lane aerodrome, the London Aeroplane Club headquarters. She earned her commercial pilot's licence in 1930, having borrowed £500 from Fred Truman, a New Zealand pilot serving with the Royal Air Force. Truman wanted to marry Batten, but she was not interested. After gaining her advanced pilot's licence in 1932, she exited his life, never having repaid him. She turned to Victor Dorée, the son of an English linen merchant, who was also infatuated with her. He borrowed £400 and bought Batten a de Havilland Gipsy Moth.

In April 1933 her first attempted flight to Australia ended near Karachi, where she made a forced landing that wrecked her plane. She hitched a camel ride to the nearest town. Back in London, Batten asked Dorée to buy her another plane. When he refused, she ended the relationship. She approached Castrol oil company head Charles Wakefield, who was impressed by her grit and glamour. He bought her a second-hand Gipsy Moth for £240.

Batten, now engaged to London stockbroker Edward Walter, made her second attempt to fly to Australia in April 1934. After battling head-winds for hours, she ran out of fuel over Rome, crash-landed skilfully in the dark and suffered minor injuries.

She was nothing if not determined and on May 8, 1934, she set off again for Australia. It took her 14 days, 22½ hours, breaking British pilot Amy Johnson's record by nearly five days. There were stopovers at Rome, Athens, Cyprus, Baghdad, Basra, Karachi, Allahabad, Calcutta, Rangoon, Singapore and Darwin. In Sydney, Batten fell in love with Australian pilot Beverley Shepherd (later to die in an air crash). She broke her engagement to Walter, who was so angry that he billed her for the plane wings he had lent her. She flew back to England, becoming the first female pilot to fly from England to Australia and back.

Batten, brave and a wonderful navigator, was on the lookout for more challenges, and in 1935 became the first female pilot to cross the Atlantic solo, flying from England to Brazil. She won the Royal Aero Club's Britannia Trophy and, for three successive years, the Harmon International Trophy for the most outstanding flight by a woman. She was also awarded a CBE.

Her greatest achievement was in 1936, when she flew from England to New Zealand in 11 days, 45 minutes. She had to land in a space of 200 metres at Mangere, where she was met by 35,000 excited well-wishers. She emerged from her plane wearing her white kidskin helmet, trailing a red, white and blue scarf and flashing a brilliant smile. Batten later wrote: "I realised my greatest ambition when I landed at Auckland. My mother always said I reminded her of Kipling's dreamer whose dream came true." In October 1937 she flew to England from Australia in five days, 18 hours, another solo record.

Batten wrote *My Life* in 1938. It was reissued in 1979 as *Alone in the Sky*. Of her well-groomed appearance, she wrote: "I always managed to tidy myself up. I dabbed my forehead with cologne, and put on lipstick. I've always been a fastidious girl."

She continued to fly around Europe, giving lectures. She was in Sweden two days before World War II began and, courtesy of the Germans, was permitted to fly back

to England. During the war she drove ambulances around London, and worked on the assembly line in a munitions factory in Poole. In 1943, she joined the National Savings Committee lecture tour, raising money for the war effort. She also fell in love again, to an RAF bomber pilot named Richard. They planned to marry, but he was killed flying over Europe.

After the war, Batten, always with her mother, lived at various times in Jamaica, England, and Spain. Following her mother's death in 1966, she became very depressed and did not leave Tenerife for several years.

Then, in 1969, she bounced back to public life. With hair dyed black and wearing a miniskirt, Batten flew to London and re-immersed herself, amid much publicity, in the aviation world. In 1970, she flew to New Zealand, booking into an Auckland motel under an assumed name. Discovered by the media, she was fêted and photographed. She visited New Zealand again in 1977 and opened the aviation pavilion at the Museum of Transport and Technology in Auckland.

Batten returned briefly to London in 1982, then vanished. For five years friends could not find her. Finally it was learned that she'd died in Majorca. She had rented a flat there and had been found dead by a maid. Local authorities, unaware of her fame, had mistakenly identified her by her middle name of Gardner and had buried her in a pauper's grave, a strange end for someone who had been so famous.

Brian Barratt-Boyes

Heart surgery pioneer who preferred to work at home

BORN: WELLINGTON, JANUARY 13, 1924.

Brian Barratt-Boyes was one of the world's heart surgery pioneers, and he did it in New Zealand, helping earn Auckland's Green Lane Hospital an international reputation.

Barratt-Boyes attended Wellington College, then studied at Otago University Medical School, graduating (MB, ChM) in 1946. He worked at the Mayo Clinic at Rochester, Minnesota, from 1953-55. This was an important time for several reasons, not the least of which was that, while there, Barratt-Boyes met John Kirklin, with whom he developed a life-long friendship and working relationship. From Mayo, Barratt-Boyes attended the University of Bristol in England on a New Zealand Nuffield Travelling Fellowship.

In 1956 he was lured back to Auckland by thoracic surgeon Douglas Robb and was soon doing groundbreaking work on the development of the cardiopulmonary bypass. The first such operation took place at Green Lane Hospital in 1958. Barratt-Boyes built an innovative team that seemed to thrive despite Auckland's remoteness from the hotspots of the medical world. One of the engineers in his team, Sid Yarrow, built an early external pacemaker for intra-operative use. The first aortic valve replacement took place in 1962, though Barratt-Boyes spent years afterwards perfecting the valve.

There were huge advancements made in heart treatment throughout the world in the 1960s. Christian Barnard gained fame when he conducted the world's first heart transplant in South Africa in 1967, and that same year Argentinian Rene Favaloro performed the first coronary bypass. Barratt-Boyes belonged in the company of those pioneers, as Barnard acknowledged.

Writing an introduction for Barratt-Boyes' biography, *From the Heart*, Barnard mentioned the Aucklander's "single-mindedness, clear-sighted striving towards a goal and vision". He wrote: "He refused to suffer bureaucratic limitations on his work and plans. I can identify strongly with his epic fights with bureaucracy for a better deal for his unit and an improved health service for his country. Fame he had, fortune he spurned, turning down lucrative overseas offers and preferring instead to stay with the team he had built up and the country of his birth."

Through the 1960s Barratt-Boyes advanced the treatment of babies with complex congenital defects and developed coronary artery surgery, whereby a vein from a leg is used to bypass a blocked artery to the heart.

From 1957-65 Barratt-Boyes was the senior thoracic surgeon at Greenlane Hospital. For the following 25 years he was the surgeon in charge of the Cardio Thoracics Surgical Unit at the hospital. He hosted numerous international workshops at Greenlane, one of the most significant being the 1987 Asian Pacific conference.

Barratt-Boyes' international reputation can be seen in countless ways. He lectured all over the world. He received honorary fellowships from a vast number of medical organisations in New Zealand, Australia, the United States, Britain and Asia. He was president of the Australia and New Zealand Cardiac Society through the 1980s and later became president of the Asian-Pacific Society of Cardiology and a member of the executive board of the International Society and Federation of Cardiology. Barratt-Boyes was knighted in 1971, and in 1987 received the prestigious Rene Leriche Prize and Medal from the International Society of Surgery. In 1995 he had the rare privilege of having a stamp issued in his honour.

Ironically, Barratt-Boyes had two major heart operations. In 1974 he received a double bypass and in 1983 a triple bypass.

He has sometimes been described as aloof and arrogant, but has never been one to shy away from political controversy. He has criticised successive governments for their health policies and before the 1975 election was especially critical of the Labour Government's handling of health care, pushing for health authorities to be free of political interference. He has also taken issue on occasion with the Auckland City Council and the Auckland Area Health Board.

In 1986 Barratt-Boyes and Kirklin wrote the definitive *Cardiac Surgery*, a 1550-page masterpiece that has been reissued several times.

After his retirement from Greenlane Hospital – there is now a room at National Women's named after him – Barratt-Boyes continued his research into heart tissue valve replacements through an American-funded private research company, Systematics, and lectured around the world. Growing grapes on his 80-hectare Waimea property north of Auckland filled some of his spare time.

Barratt-Boyes has been married twice. He had five sons in his first marriage and in 1986 married Sara Monester.

Peter Snell

Like a Sherman tank in full flight

BORN: OPUNAKE, DECEMBER 17, 1938.

It would be difficult to make a case for anyone other than Peter Snell as our greatest sportsman or woman. Three Olympic gold medals, two Empire Games golds, and a clutch of world records is mighty impressive. He was Sportsman of the Year twice. He was named Athlete of the Decade by the authoritative *Track and Field News* and in 2000 was voted New Zealand Athlete of the Century at the Halberg Awards.

Snell was so outstanding that his name has become a figure of speech. As "Titanic" signals a disaster, so in New Zealand "Snell-like" signifies excellence. Along with Murray Halberg and other leading runners in coach Arthur Lydiard's stable, Snell ushered in the golden era of New Zealand athletics. Massive crowds flocked to see him, not just in the main centres, but in Wanganui, Invercargill, Tokoroa and Masterton. He was a cult figure. Meetings featuring him drew crowds of 25,000, even 30,000. Today 3000 is considered good for a big athletics meet in New Zealand.

He nominates two races that stand out in his glittering career:

"The first was the 1960 Olympic 800 metres final at Rome," he says. "Arthur and Murray told me I was in with a chance. But I was just 21, and when I burst through to win the final from Roger Moens I was stunned. I recall looking up at the giant results board above the track and seeing 'P G Snell NZL' at the top of the list. That was one of the great thrills of my life."

Another came on January 27, 1962 when he lined up for the mile at Cook's Gardens, Wanganui. A crowd bigger than the population of Wanganui gathered, the forbidding thunder clouds held off and Snell pounded around the grass track, fighting off a challenge from Englishman Bruce Tulloh. His time was 3min 54.4s and he not only bettered four minutes for the first time, but broke Herb Elliott's world record. "That race changed my career," he says. "After that I was regarded primarily as a miler. Even though I set world records for 800 metres and 880 yards in Christchurch the following week, any overseas invitations I received were for the mile."

By 1964 Snell – who fitted in quantity surveying study during his career – was looking for a great performance at the Tokyo Olympics to cap his career. He got it, winning gold medals in the 800m and 1500m in emphatic fashion.

Snell nipped back to Auckland and broke two world records – the 1000m and the mile. There was one more overseas trip, in 1965, but his motivation was waning and he retired at the age of just 26. "We weren't paid to run in those days, and I felt I'd achieved all I could in my sport. I'd run out of goals," he said.

Snell was such a powerful figure – "like a Sherman tank in full flight," *Time* magazine said – that it seemed he was coasting, even when he was running away from the world's best runners.

After his retirement Snell was the Rothmans Foundation's director of coaching. But he found his name and reputation cloying and longed to achieve more off the track. He had never been an outstanding student, but a year at Loughborough College in England in 1971 convinced him that he had the ability to achieve academic distinction. So he packed up his family and moved to the United States. He studied at the University of California from 1974-77 and earned a BSc degree.

That might have ended his study, but for the Superstars craze of the time. He won the New Zealand section and represented his country at the world event. His prize-money paid for his graduate studies at Washington State University. After gaining a PhD at Washington he moved to Dallas to do a post-doctoral fellowship. He met his second wife, Miki, in Dallas. Snell has continued to do research and Dr Snell, as he is now, is in huge demand these days to present papers and make speeches on exercise physiology.

He has maintained his contact with New Zealand, primarily through the Peter Snell Institute of Sport in Auckland. In 1990 Snell ran the final lap at the Auckland Commonwealth Games opening ceremony. In 2002 he was made a Distinguished Companion of the New Zealand Order of Merit, the equivalent of a knighthood under the previous system.

William Pickering

The rocket man

BORN: WELLINGTON, DECEMBER 24, 1910. DIED: LA CANADA FLINTRIDGE, CALIFORNIA, MARCH 15, 2004.

From small beginnings in a tiny school at Havelock, Marlborough, William Pickering climbed so high that he was a key figure in the space race of the 1950s and 1960s. He played a pivotal role in the United States getting astronauts into space, in sending spaceships to explore several planets and, finally, in getting man on the Moon.

There were propitious omens early in Pickering's life. He went to Havelock Primary School, which Ernest Rutherford, one of the world's greatest scientists, had attended 30 years earlier. From there Pickering, whose father was a pharmacist, boarded at Wellington College, an important time in his life because he was introduced to astronomy by his maths teacher, Charles "Pop" Gifford, who founded the school's observatory. Gifford and Pickering spent hours in the observatory with their telescopes trained on the skies. After a year at Canterbury University College, in 1929 Pickering was persuaded by an uncle who spent much of his time in the United States to apply to study at the California Institute of Technology.

He earned his bachelors and masters degrees in electrical engineering at the institute and completed a PhD in physics in 1936. By 1946 he was a professor of electrical engineering. He had considered a return to New Zealand but a trip home in 1932, when he was hoping to land a job as an engineer, had produced no enticing job offers, so he had returned to the United States, and that's where he made his life, joining the California institute's faculty in 1936.

Pickering worked for the Pasadena-based Jet Propulsion Laboratory from 1944. He became involved initially through his studies into telemetry – the science of radio control. By 1954 he had become the laboratory's director, remaining in charge after it was placed under the umbrella of NASA and until his retirement in 1976. Pickering excelled in his dealings with people, bringing his powers of diplomacy to bear when working with scientists, politicians and military leaders during the pressure-cooker environment of the Cold War.

His work initially centred on developing missile systems for the United States Army, and he became project manager for Corporal, the first operational missile the laboratory launched.

The laboratory's work assumed even more national importance in the late 1950s, after the Soviet Union surprised the Americans by launching Sputnik on October 4, 1957. There was pressure on the Americans for a quick response. Within four months Pickering's team provided the satellite, telecommunications and upper rocket stages that launched Explorer I into orbit from Cape Canaveral on January 31, 1958. Explorer I, which eventually orbited Earth for 10 years, was the forerunner to a series of successful Earth and deep-space satellites.

Pickering, known as "the rocket man", described his work as "a mix between engineering and science, between the world and the research laboratory". Over the next two decades his laboratory set the agenda for space exploration. Explorer III discovered the radiation field around Earth that is now known as the Van Allen Belt. In 1962 Mariner 2 successfully completed a fly-by of Venus. Three years later Mariner 4 made a 228-day journey and covered more than 525 million kilometres to obtain close-up images of Mars. There were Ranger photographic missions to the Moon in 1964-65 and Surveyor lunar landings in 1966-67. Until these missions, most believed the Moon's surface was covered in a thick layer of dust. Ranger disproved this and paved the way for Neil Armstrong's first steps on the Moon in 1969.

Before he departed the Jet Propulsion Laboratory, Pickering's team was responsible for exploratory missions to Mercury, Jupiter, Saturn, Uranus and Neptune.

After retiring from the laboratory, Pickering took up a two-year teaching post in Saudi Arabia, then returned to the United States and founded Lignetics Inc, which made wood pallets from wood waste.

Pickering appeared twice on the cover of *Time* magazine in the 1960s. Among his many awards was the National Medal of Science, presented by President Gerald Ford in 1975. Though he became an American citizen in 1941, he was knighted in 1976 and in 2003 he became a member of the Order of New Zealand. Pickering and his wife, Inez Chapman, had two children.

When Pickering died, at the age of 93, Jet Propulsion Laboratory director Charles Elachi said: "Dr Pickering was one of the titans of our nation's space programme. It was his leadership that took America into space and opened up the Moon and planets to the world."

Peter Jackson

Giant of the big screen

BORN: PUKERUA BAY, OCTOBER 31, 1961.

It was appropriate that Peter Jackson, New Zealand's most acclaimed film producer, writer and director, should in 2005 turn his considerable talents to a remake of the 1933 classic *King Kong*. Seeing the original *King Kong* as a nine-year-old inspired Jackson to become a movie-maker. "It was on TV on a Friday night in New Zealand and the very next day I started making little stop motion films with a Super 8 movie camera my parents had used for home movies," said Jackson.

From such small beginnings... *Premiere* magazine ranked Jackson the most powerful man in Hollywood on its 2005 Power list. As a director, he ranks alongside such illustrious figures as Steven Spielberg and Oliver Stone.

Jackson was an only child, who liked taking photos so much that his parents bought him a movie camera. His early attempts at movie-making, while amateurish, revealed his flair for effects and his imagination.

In 1987 he produced *Bad Taste*, which had been four years in the making. It was a typical Jackson movie of the time – low-budget, lots of special effects, and with Jackson filling a variety of roles, from actor to producer. He even played Derek, the hero. He made the latex models for the movie in his mother's kitchen oven. The film, characterised by its wacky humour, became a hit. It was well-received at the Cannes film festival, was sold to a dozen countries, and is now a cult-classic. So 25-year-old Jackson, who had worked in *The Evening Post* photo production section and for a local photographer, became a full-time director of horror movies.

His first big commercial success came in 1992 with *Braindead*, but it was *Heavenly Creatures*, the story of how two young girls with an unhealthy bond plotted to kill one of their mothers, Honorah Parker, that gained him a world reputation, because of the remarkable filming techniques used to reveal the states of mind of the girls.

In 1995 he revealed his sense of humour when he produced the hoax movie *Forgotten Silver*, which was narrated by Sam Neill. The film caused an uproar in New Zealand when viewers briefly believed there had indeed been an old film found and restored. The following year came *The Frighteners*, starring Michael J Fox. Like most of Jackson's work, it was filmed around his home town of Wellington. Even as Jackson's star has risen, he has preferred to let Hollywood come to him rather than basing himself in California.

His most audacious undertaking was the *Lord of the Rings* trilogy. He shot the three movies simultaneously and released them over a period of two years. First there was *The Fellowship of the Ring*, then *The Two Towers* and finally *The Return of the King*. The first two movies picked up only minor Academy Awards, but the 2004 ceremony was an Oscar bonanza for Jackson and his team. Jackson became the first director in 10 years to win Academy Awards for producing, directing and writing in one movie. *The Return of the King* was voted Best Picture and the movie won 11 Academy Awards.

It was a coup for Jackson and spoke volumes for his vision, organisation, innovative use of computer technology, meticulous attention to detail and persuasive personality. He is incredibly popular. Even on set, when seeking yet another retake, he will win over actors with his "One more for luck" line.

Jackson has quickly become a New Zealand icon. His countrymen love his success on the world stage, the fact that he has poured so much money into Wellington, and Miramar in particular, and that his production companies, including Stone Street Studios, Weta Workshop, Three Foot Six and WingNut Films, are based there. Most importantly, he never appears to get carried away with himself, remaining the typical down-to-earth New Zealander. He has been known to wear shorts on the bitterest Wellington winter days and often goes bare-footed.

For years he was a bespectacled, unkempt, rather woolly figure. Eye surgery means he no longer wears glasses, and he lost 32kg while filming *King Kong* in 2004-05. He has also tidied himself up, but still appeals as the same unpretentious Peter Jackson.

Jackson married Fran Walsh in 1987. They have two children. She co-writes his scripts with him and they were made Members of the Order of New Zealand in 2002. Jackson, a devotee of The Beatles, collects World War I model aeroplanes and in 1998 he bought the National Film Unit. He has announced that after *King Kong*, he will turn his attention to converting to the screen *Halo*, Microsoft's sci-fi video game, and Alice Sebold's novel, *The Lovely Bones*.

Janet Frame

The author whose writing literally saved her

BORN: DUNEDIN, AUGUST 28, 1924. DIED: DUNEDIN, JANUARY 29, 2004.

New Zealand has produced several exceptional novelists, but none more gifted than Janet Frame. She was 27 when her first work, a collection of short stories called *The Lagoon and Other Stories*, was published in 1951. For the next half-century she was acclaimed as a literary genius for her work as a novelist, essayist and short-story writer. Her experiences frequently fed into her work, though she stressed that her fictional statements should not necessarily be regarded as autobiographical.

Frame was born in Dunedin in 1924. She was the third of five children of an impoverished railway engineer. She had a difficult childhood. A brother was epileptic and two sisters drowned. She was raised in Oamaru, and attended Oamaru North School and Waitaki Girls' High School. She spent two years at Teachers' Training College in Dunedin and taught for a short time before suffering a mental breakdown. She was wrongly diagnosed as schizophrenic and became a voluntary patient at Seacliff Mental Hospital. From 1947 she spent eight years in psychiatric institutions, and underwent more than 200 electric shock treatments.

Many of the stories in *The Lagoon and Other Stories* are told from the viewpoint of children or outcasts whose imaginative worlds are dismissed by socially conformist adults. She won the Hubert Church Memorial Award for this work and was saved from a lobotomy when doctors, about to operate, realised that their patient was an award-winning writer.

In 1954-55 she lived on the Takapuna property of leading writer Frank Sargeson, who became her mentor. In 1956 she received a State Literary Fund grant and spent the next seven years living in Ibiza, Andorra, and England.

The first of her 11 novels to receive international recognition was the strongly-autobiographical *Owls Do Cry*. After that she produced a succession of outstanding works, including *Faces in the Water, The Edge of the Alphabet, Scented Gardens for the Blind, The Reservoir: Stories and Sketches, Snowman, Snowman: Fables and Fantasies, The Adaptable Man, A State of Siege, The Pocket Mirror, The Rainbirds, Mona Minim and the Smell of the Sun, Intensive Care, Daughter Buffalo, Living in the Maniototo, You are Now Entering the Human Heart,* and *The Carpathians*.

Though she returned to New Zealand in 1963, she spent extended periods in the United States and several of her later novels were set in that country.

She wrote an autobiographical trilogy that comprised *To the Is-land, An Angel at My Table,* and *The Envoy from Mirror City*. It was later published in one volume as *An Angel at My Table* and adapted by director Jane Campion to a television series.

Frame received numerous literary honours, including the New Zealand Scholarship in Letters and the Robert Burns Fellowship. She was short-listed twice for the Nobel Prize for Literature. She won the Turnovsky Prize for Outstanding Achievement in the Arts, and was made an Honorary Doctor of Literature at the University of Otago. She held overseas fellowships in New York, New Hampshire, and Menton, France, and received Italian and Chilean awards. She received a CBE in 1983 and was later made a member of the Order of New Zealand.

She was chronically shy, tending towards reclusive, though friends maintained that she had a unique sense of humour. For many years she lived a rather nomadic lifestyle. She was always distinctive because of her thick, flame-red hair. In 1972 she changed her name to Clutha by deed poll to preserve her privacy, though she continued to write under her own name. She was always at pains to deflect attention from herself to her writing.

Her work was widely heralded overseas. Australian Nobel Laureate Patrick White once wrote: "Janet Frame seems to me the most considerable New Zealand novelist yet. Her innocent eye can show one the commonest object for the first time, her sensibility can convey, and has perhaps experienced, the bloodiest tortures of the mind." Harvard critic John Beston described her as "the most distinguished woman writer in English". Frame felt that her best writing was in the fable *Bird, Hawk, Bogie*.

In 2003 she was awarded one of the Prime Minister's inaugural awards for Literary Achievement in fiction, and was named among New Zealand's 10 greatest living artists. She died of leukaemia, aged 79.

Te Rauparaha

The Napoleon of the Southern Hemisphere

BORN: KAWHIA, c1768. DIED: OTAKI, NOVEMBER 27, 1849.

Te Rauparaha, the Napoleon of the Southern Hemisphere, was one of the great Maori chiefs and at the peak of his powers controlled much of central New Zealand.

Legend suggests he was born in 1768, before Captain Cook reached New Zealand. He lived long enough to meet and negotiate with Samuel Marsden, William Wakefield and George Grey, all important British figures in New Zealand in the mid-19th century.

His father, Wera Wera, was a Ngati Toa chief and his mother, Parekowhatu, was from the Ngati Ruakawa tribe. When Te Rauparaha was a boy, his father was killed during the inter-tribal fighting around Waikato. In his teens he married Marore, the first of his eight wives.

Soon Te Rauparaha was accompanying Ngati Toa into battle around Kawhia, where the tribe was established. Though short, Te Rauparaha was strong, courageous and ferocious, and established himself as one of his tribe's leaders. When Te Rauparaha married his fifth wife, Te Akau, the deceased Ngati Ruakawa chief's widow, the alliance of Ngati Toa and Ngati Ruakawa tribes strengthened his position.

In about 1810 Te Rauparaha obtained his first firearms, from the Ngati Maru tribe near Hauraki. This was decisive. From then, Te Rauparaha was a commander to be reckoned with. In 1819 he led his people south in a great migration to find a better home and with new opportunities. The constant fighting among the Waikato tribes had made Kawhia unsafe for settlement.

Te Rauparaha's men travelled through Taranaki, Wanganui, Manawatu and into Horowhenua. Armed with muskets, they over-ran the comparatively defenceless tribes they encountered. While at Otaki, Te Rauparaha spotted Kapiti Island, and decided this would be the ideal base from which to attack the South Island. So he returned to Kawhia, gathered his tribe and led them south, promising more food, the presence of Pakeha ships (with consequent supply of muskets), and a wealth of pounamu (greenstone) in the South Island.

Once at Otaki, Te Rauparaha set his sights on Kapiti Island, which, after several attempts, he conquered. By 1827 he ruled the North Island's west coast, from Wanganui to Wellington. His position was strengthened by his tribe's willingness to supply visiting European sailors with flax and potatoes in return for muskets.

In 1830 Te Rauparaha travelled to Sydney to meet Samuel Marsden, the New South Wales chaplain.

It did not take long for Te Rauparaha to wrest control of the northern part of the South Island. His advance was finally halted near Kaiapoi when Ngai Tahu Maori, who had obtained guns from whalers in Otago, resisted him.

Te Rauparaha was a signatory twice to the Treaty of Waitangi – on May 14, 1840, before Henry Williams, and a month later in the presence of Major Thomas Bunbury. He believed the treaty would guarantee his ownership of land he had conquered before 1840.

In 1839 the New Zealand Company's William Wakefield began moving British settlers to Wellington. Company officials aboard the Tory met Te Rauparaha off Kapiti Island and negotiated to buy some land. Soon they were claiming that they had bought far more than Te Rauparaha thought he had sold. One disputed area was the Wairau Plain in Marlborough. Te Rauparaha, supported by his nephew, Te Rangihaeata, another mighty chief, insisted he had never sold the land. Further disputes arose over land in Porirua and Hutt Valley.

Feelings simmered until, in 1843, they boiled over and the British surveyors' huts at Wairau were burnt. Fighting broke out, Te Rongo, wife of Te Rangihaeata, was killed and settlers who had survived were executed. Governor FitzRoy investigated the Wairau Incident and decided to take no punitive action against Te Rauparaha.

However, Te Rauparaha was viewed as a threat to British sovereignty, even though he was ageing and reluctant to attack European settlements. The new Governor, George Grey, tricked him into boarding a naval vessel and arrested him at Porirua in 1846, then held him without trial for a year – a clear breach of the treaty, which promised Maori full rights under British law. Eventually he was allowed to live in Auckland. In 1848 Te Rauparaha was permitted to rejoin his Ngati Toa tribe at Otaki, where he died soon after. His mana never recovered from the disgrace of being arrested and imprisoned. His grave is in the cemetery of Te Rangiatea Anglican church in Otaki, but his body is believed to be buried on Kapiti Island.

The All Black haka ("Ka mate! Ka mate! Ka ora! Ka ora!...") is known as Te Rauparaha's Haka.

17
Colin Meads
The famous five

BORN: CAMBRIDGE, JUNE 3, 1936.

When the New Zealand netball team was in Wales in 1982, captain Lyn Parker was seldom required for an interview. Reporters instead sought fledgling goal shoot Rhonda Meads, daughter of the legendary All Black lock Colin "Pinetree" Meads. Most questions were not about netball.

In 133 matches for New Zealand from 1957-71 (no-one has played as many matches for the All Blacks), including 55 tests, the King Country farmer became recognised throughout the world as the face of New Zealand rugby.

Meads had long, rugged duels with tough men like Willie John McBride of Ireland, Benoit Dauga of France and Frik du Preez of South Africa.

Though he began his international career as a flanker, it was as a 1.92m (6ft 4in), 102kg lock wearing the No. 5 jersey that he played most of his football. In the tight exchanges his hill country strength made him a man not to be messed with, and in the open his ball skills and athleticism were admired by team-mates and feared by tacklers. There was no more spine-tingling sight in rugby than Meads charging down the field with the ball in one hand.

His career had its dark moments. In 1966 he punched British Lion David Watkins; in 1968 Australian halfback Ken Catchpole's career was effectively ended when he was torn from a ruck by the leg by Meads, badly injuring his groin; and in 1969 Welsh hooker Jeff Young suffered a broken jaw, courtesy of Meads.

His most infamous run-in with officialdom was in 1967, when he was ordered from Murrayfield during the test against Scotland for kicking dangerously. As with the Catchpole incident, Meads felt he was blameless: "With Catchpole I was clearing him from a ruck. I wasn't to know he was pinned in there. With the ordering off, I was really only trying to kick a loose ball."

He was also often the victim. During the 1967 French test in Paris, he was brutally kicked in the head. In South Africa in 1970, his arm was broken when he was kicked by an Eastern Transvaal forward. Incredibly, he played out the match, with a huge bandage covering the wound. Later he appeared in the test series, with his arm protected by a splint.

Stories about Meads grow in the telling. Once, he was playing so ferociously in a Ranfurly Shield challenge that Hawke's Bay captain Kel Tremain asked the referee to count the Hawke's Bay players. "I think Meads has eaten one," said Tremain, or so the story goes. Future test referee Keith Lawrence deferentially addressed Meads as "Mr Meads" when controlling one King Country game.

Meads began his 19-season provincial career in 1955. He made his All Black debut at 20, playing at flanker in both tests on the 1957 tour of Australia. In the second, he scored a try while deputising on the wing. He became an indispensable part of a great forward pack, alongside his brother Stan, Wilson Whineray, Tremain, Ken Gray, Brian Lochore and Waka Nathan.

In a career of many highlights, Meads recalls fondly the try he scored in the second test against South Africa in 1960 because "we won the game". A decade later, in the first match of another South African tour, he scored such a brilliant try that team-mates believed the All Blacks would be unbeatable with him on board. With two arms, that might have been so. Meads was 35 when he led the All Blacks against the 1971 Lions. The series loss was a sad end to the test career of a man whose devotion to New Zealand rugby was unparalleled. As Fergie McCormick said: "To Colin, the All Black jersey was pure gold." Meads' motivation was simple: "I wanted to be not just an All Black, but a good All Black."

In 1973 Meads retired after a record 361 representative matches. He continued to play for his Waitete club until 1975. His status was confirmed when *Colin Meads All Black* sold a record 59,000 copies. A second Meads book three decades later sold nearly as well.

Meads coached King Country and was a North Island selector before winning promotion to the All Black selection panel in 1986. He became embroiled in controversy when he coached the rebel Cavaliers in South Africa in 1986 and was thrown off the national panel. Some said his involvement with the Cavaliers was misguided, but no-one doubted he was doing what he felt was best for New Zealand rugby.

He has become the most iconic figure in New Zealand rugby history and a sought-after speaker. In 2000 he was voted New Zealand Rugby Player of the Century.

Whina Cooper

Tireless campaigner for Maori rights

BORN: TE KARAKA, DECEMBER 9, 1895. DIED: HOKIANGA, MARCH 26, 1994.

The image of Whina Cooper, in her 80th year, marching from Northland to Parliament in 1975, walking stick in her right hand and leading a child with the other, is one of the most enduring in New Zealand history. The revered leader of the Maori people, who knew her as Te Whaea o te Motu (Mother of the Nation), led 5000 marchers and took 60,000 signatures to Parliament. That Maori land march was a significant step along the path to the acknowledgement and redressing of the wrongs of more than a century.

For the New Zealanders who witnessed the march, Cooper was inspiring. She might have been wizened and stooped, but she spoke with style and wit when explaining the march's objectives. But then, she had always been a clear, forceful and reasoned campaigner for Maori rights.

Hohepine (Josephine) Te Wake was born near Hokianga, the daughter of Heremia Te Wake, a leader of Ngati Manawa. Her mother, Kare Pauro Kawatihi, was of Te Rarawa and Taranaki descent. Whina was the first child of her father's second marriage. Her father's role as a community and Catholic Church leader in Whakarapa influenced her, and from an early age she showed unusual organisational ability and confidence as a speaker. She was educated at St Joseph's Maori Girls' College in Napier, courtesy of funding secured from Native Minister James Carroll, a family friend.

Back in Whakarapa, she became a teacher, storekeeper, postmistress and farmer. In 1917 she married (in secret) Richard Gilbert, who worked for the Native Land Court. The couple went through tough times after the death of Whina's parents and it wasn't until they received a loan from Fr Charles Kreymborg and were able to set themselves up in a store at Whakarapa that their lives turned around. With Whina the driving force, the store became a huge success.

By the late 1920s Whina, who had two children, was a leading force in her community. At her urging, the name of her town was changed to Panguru (there was already a Whakarapa in Northland). She formed and became president of the New Zealand Farmers Union's Panguru branch. With her energy and persuasiveness, she played an ever-increasing role in church and community activities, and became a prominent national Maori figure.

However, she left her husband and began a relationship with William Turakiutu Cooper, of Ngati Kahungunu. When Richard Gilbert died of cancer in 1935, she was already pregnant to Cooper. This caused her problems in the church and the Maori community and she and Cooper eventually moved to Kamo, where they had four more children and lived relatively quietly. They married in 1941, the day Cooper's divorce from his first wife was finalised.

After their marriage, they returned to Panguru. Though Cooper's popularity was somewhat diminished, she continued to be an outspoken presence in Northland, even becoming president of the Hokianga Rugby Football Union.

In 1949, the year her second husband died of a heart attack, she took part in Royal Commission meetings about surplus lands, and was elected founding president of the Maori Women's Welfare League. She stumped the country setting up local and regional branches of the league and shone in this role, partly because of her exceptional powers of oratory. The league was established to care for the young, the elderly and the sick, and was for many years the most effective voice of Maori hopes and aspirations. Cooper moved to Auckland in 1951. When Cooper resigned from the league presidency in 1957, it had 300 branches. Working through the league, Cooper had turned Auckland and national attention to the plight of Maori in housing, education, crime, health and employment.

During the 1960s she was a strong advocate on treaty issues, but said, when awarded a CBE in 1974, that she felt her days of public life had passed. She couldn't have been more wrong. She was at her best leading the march to Parliament and presenting the petition to Prime Minister Bill Rowling on October 13, 1975.

She remained a prominent figure among Maori for the last two decades of her life, presiding over the Waitangi Day celebrations and the Maori Women's Welfare League. She became Dame Whina in 1981 and returned to Hokianga two years later. She was given the privilege of speaking at the 1990 Auckland Commonwealth Games opening ceremony and, typically, used the opportunity well, saying tellingly: "Let us all remember that the treaty was signed so that we could all live as one nation in Aotearoa."

She was made a member of the Order of New Zealand in 1991. Cooper died, aged 98, in 1994. Her televised funeral was watched by more than one million viewers.

Katherine Mansfield

The shooting star who has continued to shine

BORN: WELLINGTON, OCTOBER 14, 1888. DIED: FONTAINEBLEAU, FRANCE, JANUARY 9, 1923.

Katherine Mansfield once said: "I shall not be fashionable long." But more than 80 years after her death, she is New Zealand's best-known writer and her work has been translated into 25 languages. She was one of the first New Zealanders of genuinely international significance and her writing was compared with that of Russian short story master Anton Chekhov.

Kathleen Mansfield Beauchamp was fortunate that her parents were wealthy and educated. From 1898 she attended Wellington Girls' High School, where it was noted that *Enna Blake*, a story she wrote for the school magazine, "shows promise of great merit". Mansfield's education was completed at Mary Anne Swainson's exclusive Fitzherbert Terrace School. She did not endear herself to teachers, being described as surly, untruthful and a poor student. In 1903 her family sailed to England. She discovered the works of some great contemporary writers and formed a strong friendship with Ida Baker, whom she renamed "Leslie Moore" or "LM", and with whom she would remain close throughout her life.

After four years, the Beauchamps returned to Wellington, against Kathleen's wishes. Her diaries reveal a young woman desperate to be back in London. Several of her short stories were published in Australia in 1907. By now, she wrote as "K Mansfield" or "KM" (she took the first name Katherine in 1910). Her writing successes persuaded her father to permit her to live in England, with an annual allowance of £100. She never returned to New Zealand. Mansfield was talented, energetic, neurotic and, astoundingly for the times, openly bisexual.

She became pregnant to former Wellingtonian Garnet Trowell, but married singing teacher George Bowden in March 1909, with Baker as witness. Within days she had left Bowden. Her parents were alarmed by how she was handling her life. Her mother travelled to England, separated her daughter from Baker and escorted her to a German spa, where she miscarried.

While in Germany, Mansfield wrote satirical sketches of German characters, publishing them in 1911 as *In a German Pension*. In many of her stories the female characters are vulnerable and naïve, questioning the double standard that allowed men but not women to enjoy sexual pleasures. Mansfield was already being troubled by illness. She suffered from pleurisy and the effects of a long-term venereal infection.

In 1911 she met John Middleton Murry, an Oxford student and editor. Seven years later, when she finally divorced Bowden, she and Murry married. Mansfield helped Murry edit *Rhythm* and its successor, *Blue Review*. Yet they often lived apart and it was Baker who provided the unconditional devotion.

Mansfield and Murry became friends briefly with DH and Frieda Lawrence, but the Lawrences were shocked at her brief affair with French writer Francis Carco. Among Mansfield and Murry's circle of literary friends were Dora Carrington, Lytton Strachey, T S Eliot, Aldous Huxley, Siegfried Sassoon, Leonard and Virginia Woolf, Samuel Koteliansky and Bertrand Russell.

Mansfield's brother Leslie's death in World War I focused her writing on New Zealand and her family and led to *Prelude*, one of her most famous stories.

She suffered from tuberculosis from 1918 and in her last years lived mainly in Menton, southern France, and Switzerland, seeking better health.

She wrote much about her childhood. In 1920 she produced *The Daughters of the Late Colonel*, which she described as "the only story that satisfies me to any extent". *Bliss and Other Stories* (1920) cemented her reputation. Over the next two years she produced the much-praised *Garden Party and Other Stories*. It included famous New Zealand stories, such as *At the Bay* and *The Garden Party*. One significant piece of work was *Je Ne Parle Pas Français*, which caused a stir by examining sexuality and social behaviour.

Mansfield underwent radiation therapy in Paris. While there, she wrote *The Fly*, a story of pointless struggle and destruction. She died in 1923, aged 34.

Murry spent decades publishing Mansfield's work. He turned her into a cult figure, which partly explains why her life, as well as her work, remains of such interest.

Mansfield was unarguably influential in the development of the short story as a form of literature. But she was an erratic, moody, unconventional personality and her creative years were marked by loneliness and ill-health, which are reflected in her short stories, poetry, letters, journals and reviews. She also occasionally wrote grimly realistic stories, of which *The Woman at the Store* is an outstanding example.

The Katherine Mansfield Fellowship to Menton remains a sought-after prize for New Zealand writers.

Thomas Brydone
BORN: WEST LINTON, SCOTLAND, APRIL 14, 1837. DIED: LONDON, JUNE 17, 1904.

William Davidson
BORN: MONTREAL, JUNE 15, 1846. DIED: LEUCHIE, NORTH BERWICK, JULY 17, 1924.

The men whose big chill ideas launched the meat export industry

For more than a century the frozen meat industry underpinned the New Zealand economy. New Zealand now exports meat to 200 countries. It's difficult to imagine a time when farmers routinely disposed of their sheep, pushing them over cliffs, because they had no way of exporting meat and too few residents to eat it. New Zealand's only major exports then were wool and wheat. That changed, as did New Zealand's overseas earnings, with the introduction of refrigeration on ships, which opened the world to New Zealand sheep and dairy meat produce.

Shipping refrigeration was used first by Argentina in 1875 and by Australia five years later. Two forward-thinking agriculturalists, Thomas Brydone and William Davidson, introduced it to New Zealand in 1882. It was Brydone and Davidson who were responsible for the early consolidation of European markets for New Zealand.

Brydone grew up in Scotland, establishing a reputation in England and Scotland as a capable, industrious land steward and travelling inspector. In 1867 he was appointed a superintendent of the New Zealand and Australia Land Company, a large pastoral association whose New Zealand interests were located mainly in Canterbury and Otago. Brydone rose steadily through the company's ranks, the more so when it amalgamated with the Canterbury and Otago Association in 1877.

He was a successful farmer himself, as well as an able superintendent. It was Brydone who first applied lime and other fertilisers to enrich farm land and it was his idea to establish New Zealand's first dairy farm, at Edendale, in Southland, in 1882.

Though he was born in Montreal, Davidson, like Brydone, had Scottish roots. After attending the Edinburgh Academy, he seemed headed for a commercial career, but he enjoyed outdoor life and, at the suggestion of Glasgow financier James Morton, travelled to New Zealand to help run the Canterbury and Otago Association. The timing was propitious – until Morton's intervention, Davidson was planning a move to Argentina.

Davidson arrived in Timaru in 1865 and managed a vast amount of land. He was initially in charge of 150,000 acres on the Levels Estate, and by 1868 was controlling more than 500,000 acres. He became skilled in accounting, building construction, estate management, surveying and negotiating and was soon promoted to the position of inspector. One of his significant steps was to introduce the corriedale sheep breed to New Zealand. He was involved with Brydone in the Edendale dairy farm project, using the Danish example as the basis for butter and cheese production.

Davidson lived in New Zealand for 12 years and realised that the country's future lay in being able to sell meat overseas. He discussed this with Brydone and they began exploring methods of preserving, transporting and refrigerating meat.

In 1878 Davidson gained a further promotion in the company and returned to Britain. This proved important in the progress of the refrigeration work. Brydone remained in New Zealand, building a slaughter factory at Totara, selecting stock and organising rail and road distribution networks, while Davidson dealt with insurance, distribution and sales in Britain.

Finally, on February 15, 1882, the Dunedin, loaded with frozen meat, left Port Chalmers. Brydone was there to see off the ship and Davidson returned to New Zealand for the occasion, though he was back in London by the time the ship arrived there. It must have been incredibly difficult to keep the ship's hold refrigerated and the sheep carcasses from bouncing around too much below decks. The first shipment of frozen meat was so successful – only one carcass was spoilt – that the business never looked back.

Davidson went on to forge an extremely successful business career in Britain. He made regular trips to New Zealand. He married twice. He met his first wife, Jane, in Edinburgh and married her in 1873. She died 11 years later and in 1889 he married Caroline Thierens in Timaru.

Brydone remained in New Zealand, where he became a successful farmer and helped found the New Zealand Refrigerator Company. He became ill in 1904 and travelled to London seeking specialist medical help, but died soon after. There are memorials to Brydone at Totara, south of Oamaru, and at the Edendale Dairy Factory. The one at Totara is an impressive tower atop a hill.

Thomas Brydone

William Davidson

Richard Pearse

A world first for a flying Kiwi?

BORN: TEMUKA, DECEMBER 3, 1877. DIED: CHRISTCHURCH, JULY 29, 1953.

For more than a century, debate has raged about whether South Cantabrian Richard Pearse beat the Wright brothers to the honour of being the first to fly an aeroplane. Orville and Wilbur Wright made their famous flight at Kitty Hawk, North Carolina, on December 12, 1903. It's possible – probable even – that Pearse flew the earliest version of what might today be termed a microlite in March 1903. Writing about the flight years later, Pearse suggested it occurred in 1904. However, eyewitness accounts point to 1903, or even 1902, as equally likely.

It wasn't what air travellers today would term a flight. Pearse travelled perhaps 100 metres along Main Waitohi Road, then crashed into a gorse fence on his farm. However, he did achieve a powered take-off. Frustratingly, no proof exists to pinpoint the date – records of the visit Pearse made to hospital after injuring his collarbone in the crash were destroyed by fire, and a photograph of the aircraft in the hedge, taken the following day, was lost in flooding.

Not surprisingly, proud Timaru folk – who have named their airport after Pearse – are quick to claim his place in history. Regardless of whether they are correct, Pearse was an amazing inventor who should be hailed as such.

He was born on a farm near Temuka, the fourth of nine children who grew up in a musically-minded family. Pearse was a quiet, introverted child, who excelled at one subject – engineering. He hoped to study at Canterbury College, but there was not enough money to send him there. Instead, when he was 21, he was given a 100-acre block of land at Waitohi to farm.

While never a successful farmer, Pearse used the land to good effect by building a workshop, complete with forge and lathe. He was forever inventing gadgets, ranging from a zoetrope for his sisters, to a steam engine, gramophone, motorised plough, fertiliser applicator, needle threader, power generator, recording machine, power cycle, harp, top dresser, potato planter and two types of music box. He was the embodiment of the classic Kiwi cliché, using not No 8 fencing wire, but bamboo, scrap metal and anything else he could find.

Pearse was an avid reader of *Scientific American* – he was often seen with his head buried in the magazine while trudging behind a horse-drawn plough.

He experimented with various engines and modes of transport. In 1902 he had his first patented invention, a bicycle with a vertical-drive pedal action. But his dream was powered flight, or "aerial navigation", as he termed it. With a vivid imagination and unlimited resourcefulness and patience, he gradually put together an aeroplane. Its features included wing flaps, a rear elevator, a tricycle under-carriage, a steerable nosewheel and a propeller. Its wingspan was 25ft.

There were many "flights". In some he was airborne for a few seconds, in others for a little longer. His aircraft was patented in 1906.

The Wright brothers employed skilled engineers and received government funding, whereas the introspective and taciturn Pearse worked in isolation and had no money or assistance. Like many who excel in a specific field, Pearse came to be appreciated for his genius only years after his death. During his life, neighbours labelled him Cranky Dick or Mad Pearse.

He was always secretive – his experiments with aeroplanes were unpublicised and had virtually no bearing on the history of air travel.

Pearse had a spell farming in Milton and travelled to Europe in 1918 to serve in the armed forces, though illness forced his premature return.

In 1921 he moved to Christchurch, where he built three houses. In the garage of one, at Woolston, he worked on what he called his Utility Plane. It had a tilting engine to allow vertical take-off and landing. Again he was ahead of his time. He worked on that plane for nearly two decades until it was finally patented in 1949.

Pearse, who never married, became ill soon after and spent his final years in Sunnyside Mental Hospital.

Though he died in obscurity, his imaginative audacity is saluted today. His Utility Plane was discovered in a house in Christchurch years after his death and is now displayed at Auckland's Museum of Transport and Technology. Remnants of his first plane are to be found there and at Timaru Museum. New Zealand Post has honoured Pearse several times, most notably in its 1999 Millennium issue. A Pearse monument has been built at Waitohi, near the site of that first flight.

Te Whiti

The Gandhi of the South Pacific

BORN: NEAR NGAMOTU, c1830. DIED: PARIHAKA, NOVEMBER 18, 1907.

Te Whiti-o-Rongomai III was the New Zealand version of Mahatma Gandhi and Nelson Mandela. He may have inspired Gandhi, the remarkable Indian leader, who learnt of Te Whiti from Irish travellers who had visited Te Whiti at Parihaka, where he lived. Gandhi was already committed to non-violence, but Te Whiti's story must have had special meaning for him.

Though Te Whiti was a Maori prophet and spiritual leader, his most significant role was as a pacifist in the face of inordinate provocation. He even encouraged men who had grown up as warriors to demand their rights using peaceful means. Soldiers intent on arresting or killing him were invited into his village and fed.

His parents were Hone Kakahi, of the Te Ati Awa tribe, and Rangi-kawau. He was educated by Maori elders, and by Lutheran missionary Johannes Riemenschneider, who taught him to read and write at the Warea mission school. Te Whiti learnt the scriptures and developed his devotion to the Bible. He was baptised, taking the name Erueti, which he later rejected. He always exhibited spiritual qualities, which were enhanced by his public-speaking skills and visions he claimed to have. He was about 1.78m (5ft 10in), strongly built and with piercing eyes. People naturally followed him. Te Whiti ran a flour mill at Warea. He may have fought in early skirmishes in the Taranaki land wars, but he soon renounced violence.

Te Whiti and his close relative, Tohu Kakahi (they married sisters and were both regarded as prophets), founded a settlement at Parihaka, near Mt Egmont. Maori from different tribes around New Zealand lived at the settlement, which became a haven for the dispossessed and disillusioned.

Both leaders were committed to non-violence, drawing on ancestral Maori as well as Christian teachings. By 1881 Parihaka was one of the largest Maori settlements in Taranaki, with 1300 inhabitants. Te Whiti believed Maori should be left to work out their salvation, that no land should be sold to Europeans and that because direct rebellion had failed, Maori should meet further incursions peacefully, by civil disobedience and non-violent obstruction. He maintained that there would be a day of reckoning, when all Europeans would voluntarily leave the country. A fund was set up at Parihaka in anticipation of this event and on the 18th day of each month Maori flocked to Parihaka to hear the prophet's words.

In 1879 the Government began surveying and preparing land for farmers in south Taranaki that it had confiscated 16 years earlier. Te Whiti's resistance policy proved surprisingly effective. He had the moral high ground – it is difficult to defend the systematic confiscation of three million acres of land. The policy left thousands homeless, but Maori defiance was deemed rebellion, punishable by imprisonment.

Te Whiti directed his men to put fences across the roads, plough across survey lines and roads and remove surveying pegs. Premiers George Grey and John Hall tried to negotiate, but would not concede Te Whiti's contention that the 1863 land confiscation was illegal. Eventually Native Affairs Minister William Rolleston signed a proclamation to raid Parihaka and on November 5, 1881, the peaceful village was invaded by 1600 members of the Armed Constabulary. The villagers allowed themselves to be arrested without protest. They greeted the charging cavalry with women and children in the front rank, singing and chanting and offering flowers.

Many were shipped off to Dunedin, where they worked in dreadful conditions as slave labour on roading projects such as the Otago Peninsula causeway.

At his trial in New Plymouth, Te Whiti was charged with "wickedly, maliciously and seditiously contriving and intending to disturb the peace". Te Whiti and Tohu were held in custody in humiliating circumstances for a year. During that time they were taken on a tour of the South Island in an attempt to impress them with developments Europeans had made there. They merely reiterated their demands for the return of their people's lands. They were returned to Taranaki in 1883. Tohu became more aggressive but Te Whiti continued his peaceful resistance. Te Whiti was jailed again in 1886, but, undeterred, steadfastly maintained his non-violent ways.

His symbol, the white feather, is still proudly worn in his honour by Te Ati Awa as an emblem of courage and peace.

A memorial to Te Whiti at Parihaka reads: "He was a man who did great deeds in suppressing evil so that peace may reign as a means of salvation to all people on Earth."

Richard John Seddon

The political giant

BORN: SCHOOL BROW, LANCASHIRE, JUNE 22, 1845.
DIED: SAILING FROM AUSTRALIA TO NEW ZEALAND, JUNE 10, 1906.

Dick Seddon was a towering figure in New Zealand, physically and metaphorically. "King Dick" was New Zealand's longest-serving Prime Minister. He was a boisterous, masculine figure who ate and drank heartily, and liked singing and dancing. He was 1.83m (6ft) tall and put on weight later in life, eventually tipping the scales at 127kg (20 stone). Seddon was an energetic and innovative man. He was also ceaseless in his desire for power and was a politician whose cunning was disguised by a perceived lack of polish – he dropped his "aitches" when he spoke, which caused contemporary critics and cartoonists much glee.

He was born in Lancashire, the son of school teachers, but struggled academically and left school at 12. He worked for some years in menial jobs on farms and in an iron foundry and was dismissed from one for agitation over pay. After a bout of smallpox, he sailed for Australia at 18 to try his luck in the Victorian goldfields.

Disappointed at his lack of success there, he sailed to Hokitika, where his mining ventures were more fruitful. He earned enough to be able to return to Melbourne in 1869 to marry his fiancée, Louisa Spotswood. The couple lived on the West Coast of New Zealand.

Seddon was immensely strong and shone as an athlete and a boxer, but politics always drew him. He was elected to the Westland Provincial Council in 1874, and gained a seat on the Westland County Council soon after. He became a publican and, in 1877, the first Mayor of Kumara, where he acted as an advocate in the goldfield warden's court, taking miners' cases when there weren't enough lawyers to cope. He struggled in business and narrowly avoided bankruptcy in 1878. The following year he became MP for Hokitika. He represented the constituency of Kumara from 1881-90, and then won the Westland seat, which he held until his death 16 years later.

Initially, Seddon's parliamentary career was undistinguished. His uncouthness and verbosity created a less-than-favourable impression. Things began to turn around when John Ballance's Liberal Party took office in 1891. Seddon held a number of portfolios, including Minister of Public Works, Mines and Defence. He was chosen over William Pember Reeves as the deputy Prime Minister and, when Ballance died in 1893, got the top job, outmanoeuvring his rival, Robert Stout, to assume the leadership on May 1, 1893. Seddon was New Zealand's first Prime Minister. Before him, the leader was called the Premier.

He was a curious mixture: domineering, dynamic, stubborn, populist, and, at times, conservative. He introduced the Old-Age Pensions Bill of 1898, but strongly opposed allowing women the vote. He was responsible for the introduction of a free-place system in secondary schools, for the Shops and Offices Act of 1904 and for the establishment of the State Fire Insurance Office. In 1899 he brought about the formation of the Liberal and Labour Federation of New Zealand.

Seddon was a strong imperialist, who supported New Zealand's entry into the Boer War and was at pains to maintain close links with Britain. He was keen for New Zealand to play an important role in the Pacific with its own tiny empire.

As well as being Prime Minister, Seddon was for much of his Prime Ministership the Minister of Labour, Education, Immigration, Public Works and Defence. He became the Native Minister in 1893 and in 1896 took over as Colonial Treasurer, handling the financial reins in a cautious, safety-first manner.

His autocratic nature was revealed in one early speech in the House, when he said: "A President is all we require." He further suggested that ministers be eliminated and that heads of department simply carry out instructions. Yet he kept in touch with his citizens. This was well-illustrated by his robust support of the first New Zealand rugby team's tour of Britain, in 1905-06.

He travelled incessantly around the country and overseas, and was a master at handling crowds and meetings. Seddon rewarded politicians who were loyal to him, and bullied those who were not, a factor in his retaining power through five elections. He died aboard the Oswestry Grange when returning from inter-government talks in Sydney.

Two towns were named after him, with his approval; Seddon, in Marlborough, and Seddonville, north of Westport. This colourful figure is not easily overlooked, even a century after his death – his prominent statue outside Parliament Buildings has come to signify the State's authority in New Zealand.

Peter Buck

Master of many trades

BORN: URENUI, TARANAKI, OCTOBER 1877. DIED: HONOLULU, DECEMBER 1, 1951.

Peter Buck was a man of many parts – doctor, athlete, politician, Maori leader, soldier, anthropologist – and excelled in all of them.

Buck, a popular, gregarious personality, had one special advantage as he made his way through adulthood. He was part-Pakeha, courtesy of his Irish father William, and part-Maori. Ngarongo-ki-tua, who raised him as her son, was descended from the Taranaki iwi Ngati Mutunga. In fact, Buck's birth mother was a relative of his mother named Rina. His mother was unable to bear children, so Rina lived with the family and bore William and Ngarongo a child. Buck, given the name of Te Rangi Hiroa by Maori elders, used his cross-cultural advantage to good effect.

After growing up in Taranaki and Wairarapa, Buck attended Te Aute College in Hawke's Bay from 1896-98 and excelled scholastically. He was dux of the school, captain of the athletics and First XV teams and a natural leader. Late in his school career he decided to study medicine at Otago Medical School, so set himself to learn Greek, which he did in 10 months. In 1904 he gained an MB ChB and became the first Maori doctor. He added an MD in 1910.

Never one to restrict himself to a single interest, he became a leading New Zealand athlete, winning national long jump titles in 1900 and 1903.

Buck worked briefly at Dunedin Hospital and at Sunnyside Mental Hospital, then as a locum in Greymouth, where, in 1905, he married Margaret Wilson. Their mixed marriage drew much comment. They never had children.

From 1905 Buck travelled the North Island with Maui Pomare, seeking to improve sanitation in small Maori communities. He moved into politics in 1909, winning the Northern Maori seat for the Liberal Party. He took responsibility for Native Affairs and became a Cabinet Minister. In 1914 he chose to stand for the Bay of Islands seat and was narrowly beaten.

Buck greatly distinguished himself during World War I. He argued for the right of Maori to go to war and in 1915 headed for Europe. He fought bravely at Gallipoli, earning a Distinguished Service Order, and fought in France and Belgium.

Back in New Zealand, he became the Chief Maori Medical Officer and then the director of Maori hygiene for the Department of Health. They were busy times, because of the influenza pandemic and because Buck battled hard to improve Maori sanitation and gradually reverse the Maori death rate.

He began taking more interest in Polynesian anthropology and, in 1923, presented a paper on Maori migration at the Pacific Science Congress in Melbourne, where he impressed Herbert Gregory, director of Hawaii's Bishop Museum. Gregory offered him a five-year research position, which Buck, after some misgivings, accepted.

He used the opportunity well, travelling extensively to museums in North America and Europe, and to the Pacific to study Polynesian migration patterns, with special attention on the Cook Islands and Samoa. One of the strengths of his work was its New Zealand perspective. He had the advantage of being treated like a brother while researching in the islands. Though he returned home in 1930, Buck was unable to secure a position that gave him the opportunities he was receiving in the United States. He went back to the museum, becoming its director in 1936.

Buck wrote prolifically. His books included *The Evolution of Maori Clothing* in 1928, *Vikings of the Sunrise* and *The Coming of the Maori*. He did line drawings to accompany his text.

He was given an honorary doctorate by the University of Hawaii for his "contribution to the knowledge of mankind". The universities of New Zealand, Rochester and Yale honoured him similarly.

He was knighted in 1946 and Sweden awarded him the Order of the Northern Star.

Despite the distance, Buck remained extremely proud of New Zealand. He had an abiding interest in Maori affairs and corresponded frequently with lifelong friend Apirana Ngata.

In 1948 Buck was told he had cancer and had three months to live. He stretched that to three years, during which he wrote four books and did a lecture tour of New Zealand in 1949. He died in Hawaii and his ashes were returned to the Okoki Pa, near Urenui.

Julius Vogel

The expansionist whose policies shaped a fledgling country

BORN: LONDON, FEBRUARY 24, 1835. DIED: LONDON, MARCH 12, 1899.

Julius Vogel spent only 18 years in New Zealand, but became one of its most important figures. His expansionist policies and drive helped to shape the fledgling country.

Vogel was born in London and, growing up in unhappy family circumstances, had a limited education. He relished the opportunity to join the rush to the Victorian goldfields in 1852. His life was to be full of experiments and bold schemes. Some proved disastrous, others succeeded, and many were hailed only after he died.

In Victoria, Vogel formed an importing business, then launched a gold-buying scheme. But he found most satisfaction in journalism, working for the *Melbourne Argus*, then editing the *Maryborough and Dunolly Advertiser* and establishing the *Inglewood and Sandy Creek Advertiser*.

He stood unsuccessfuly for the Victorian General Assembly in 1861, then headed to Otago, where the next goldrush was taking place. Again he was drawn to journalism. He worked for the *Otago Colonist* and in November 1861 became the first editor of the *Otago Daily Times*, a position he held until 1868. He became involved with the Chamber of Commerce, the Otago Club and the Otago Benevolent Institution.

Over-riding everything were his political aspirations. Pushing the Otago Separation Movement, which aimed for the political separation of North and South Islands, and free trade, he stood for Dunedin North and was elected to the House of Representatives in 1863. He also won a seat on the Otago Provincial Council, which he held for six years. In 1868 Vogel launched the *New Zealand Sun*. When it failed, he moved to Auckland and became general manager of the *Daily Southern Cross*.

Perhaps because he was partially deaf, Vogel was an unconvincing public speaker. But he was ambitious, had an inexhaustable fund of ideas and a forceful personality. He was not always popular, partly because he was so personally ambitious. "Brash and unscrupulous", was how one opponent characterised him. There may have been anti-Semitism in some of the antipathy towards him.

He formed an alliance with Willam Fox and they toppled Edward Stafford's government. Fox became the Premier, but Vogel, his Treasurer, had immense power. He advocated a stepped-up policy of immigraton, allied to massive borrowing to fund his extensive public works policies such as construction of railways, harbour facilities and parks. During the post-goldrush Depression, Vogel's policies stimulated the New Zealand economy and helped the country to develop. He had many other areas of responsibility, from Postmaster General to Minister of Immigration and Commissioner for Customs.

Vogel was Premier from 1873-75 and was knighted in 1875. He had another six-month stint as Premier in 1876, but his popularity waned, partly because he spent much time overseas, trying to establish or expand steamship, cable and economic links with the United States, Britain, the Pacific Islands and Australia.

He departed New Zealand in 1876, becoming agent general in London (the official appointed by the New Zealand Government to deal with the British Government in financial and other matters). He stood for Parliament on the Conservative ticket in 1880 and was well-beaten, then formed the ill-fated New Zealand Agricultural Company.

Vogel returned to New Zealand in 1884 and stood successfully for Christchurch North. He became Treasurer, then leader of the Opposition, but this time his policies of borrowing were seen as impractical at a time when the interest rate was far higher and the public was clamouring for retrenchment. Perhaps influenced by his strong-minded wife Mary, he introduced a suffrage bill in 1887. He was also an advocate of reconciliation with Maori.

He urged the expansion of the British Empire and imperialism in the Pacific, which he was confident would enhance New Zealand's commercial interests and political influence in the region. This aspiration is reflected in Allen Curnow's poetic reference to Vogel "howling 'Empire' from an empty coast". In 1888, Vogel sailed for England, never to return.

Vogel, who was inclined to be overweight, did not enjoy good health. He spent many years using a walker, then became wheelchair-bound. But he remained a clever thinker. In 1889 he wrote a novel, *Anno Domini 2000, or Woman's Destiny*. In it he envisaged a society in which women held many key roles – he was ahead of his time.

The Sir Julius Vogel Awards are presented annually for the best New Zealand fiction writing. His name is recalled through suburbs named after him in Wellington and New Plymouth and through Vogel House, which for decades was the Prime Minister's residence.

Maurice Wilkins

The scientist who helped unravel the mystery of DNA

BORN: PONGAROA, DECEMBER 15, 1916. DIED: LONDON, OCTOBER 5, 2004.

Maurice Wilkins, known as "the double helix man", played a central role in unravelling the mysteries of DNA, the essence of life. He helped revolutionise biology and medicine and his work has assisted police hugely in their hunt for criminals. Like fingerprints, DNA is unique to each person, and police can test it to establish guilt or innocence. Wilkins was his country's second great international scientist, after Ernest Rutherford, and, like many New Zealanders of his era, had to remain abroad to pursue his career at the highest level.

Though born in the Wairarapa, Wilkins spent his early life in Wellington. In 1923 his father, Henry, a doctor, took his family to England while he furthered his career. Maurice attended King Edward's School in Birmingham, then studied physics at St John's College, Cambridge. He gained a degree in 1938, and returned to Birmingham, where he became a research assistant to Dr John Randall in the Birmingham University physics department. Randall became a continuing influence in his life.

After gaining a PhD in 1940, Wilkins was seconded to the war effort, designing a powerful microwave transmitter that greatly improved Britain's radar capabilities. In 1943 he and other researchers from Birmingham moved to Berkeley, California, to work on the Manhattan Project, exploring nuclear physics. The result of their work was the atomic bomb, two of which were dropped on Japan in 1945. Wilkins said he hadn't comprehended the catastrophic possibilities of nuclear weapons. He became a strident opponent of them, and was the president of the British Society for Social Responsibility in Science. He was closely aligned to the Campaign for Nuclear Disarmament.

After the war Wilkins was briefly a physics lecturer at the University of St Andrews, Scotland, then moved to King's College, London, where he was a member of Randall's newly-formed Medical Research Council Biophysics Research Unit. This eclectic group became known as Randall's Circus.

Four leading scientists did most of the DNA research at King's College – Wilkins, British biophysicist Francis Crick, American geneticist Jim Watson and gifted young scientist Rosalind Franklin. People sometimes give one or more of them particular credit, but Wilkins said: "The discovery of the double helix was far more co-operative than what many people think."

Wilkins studied the genetic effects of ultrasonics, then switched to the study of nucleic acids in cells. He began x-ray diffraction studies of DNA and sperm heads. His discovery of a well-defined pattern in this material greatly enhanced knowledge of the molecular structure of DNA. He made it possible to photograph molecules and show the actual shape of DNA. His images of DNA were of unprecedented clarity and revealed that the DNA molecule was a double helix shape, like a gently twisting ladder.

Wilkins and Franklin had a testy relationship. "Everyone [at King's] was in informal groups, following up interesting things," Wilkins said. "As scientists go, Rosalind was perfectly normal, but our lab was very abnormal. It was productive, but was not what she was used to."

In 1950 Wilkins was assistant director of the Medical Research Council and in 1955 he became the council's deputy director. He was elected a fellow of the Royal Society in 1959 and, along with Crick and Watson, was honoured with the Albert Lasker Award by the American Public Health Association in 1960.

Franklin died of cancer in 1958 (almost certainly because of repeated exposure to x-rays), aged just 37, and so was not acknowledged when, in 1962, Wilkins, Crick and Watson were awarded the Nobel Prize in Physiology and Medicine for their contribution to the discovery of the DNA structure.

Wilkins was always extremely popular. He was private, humble and endlessly helpful. In 1959 he married Patricia Chidgey. They had two children. He spent his later years teaching at King's College, London, and, shortly before he died, wrote his autobiography, *The Third Man of the Double Helix*.

Though he remained in Britain, Wilkins always spoke fondly of New Zealand. He said his early years there were like "living in paradise" and the happiest of his life. He believed the opportunities for exploration and discovery that he received in New Zealand helped his later development as a scientist. "In the time of my parents, most people who came to New Zealand from Europe were the more enterprising people, the people who were stronger mentally. It takes a certain amount of imagination to make a life on the other side of the world, the same imagination it takes to climb the tallest mountain," he said.

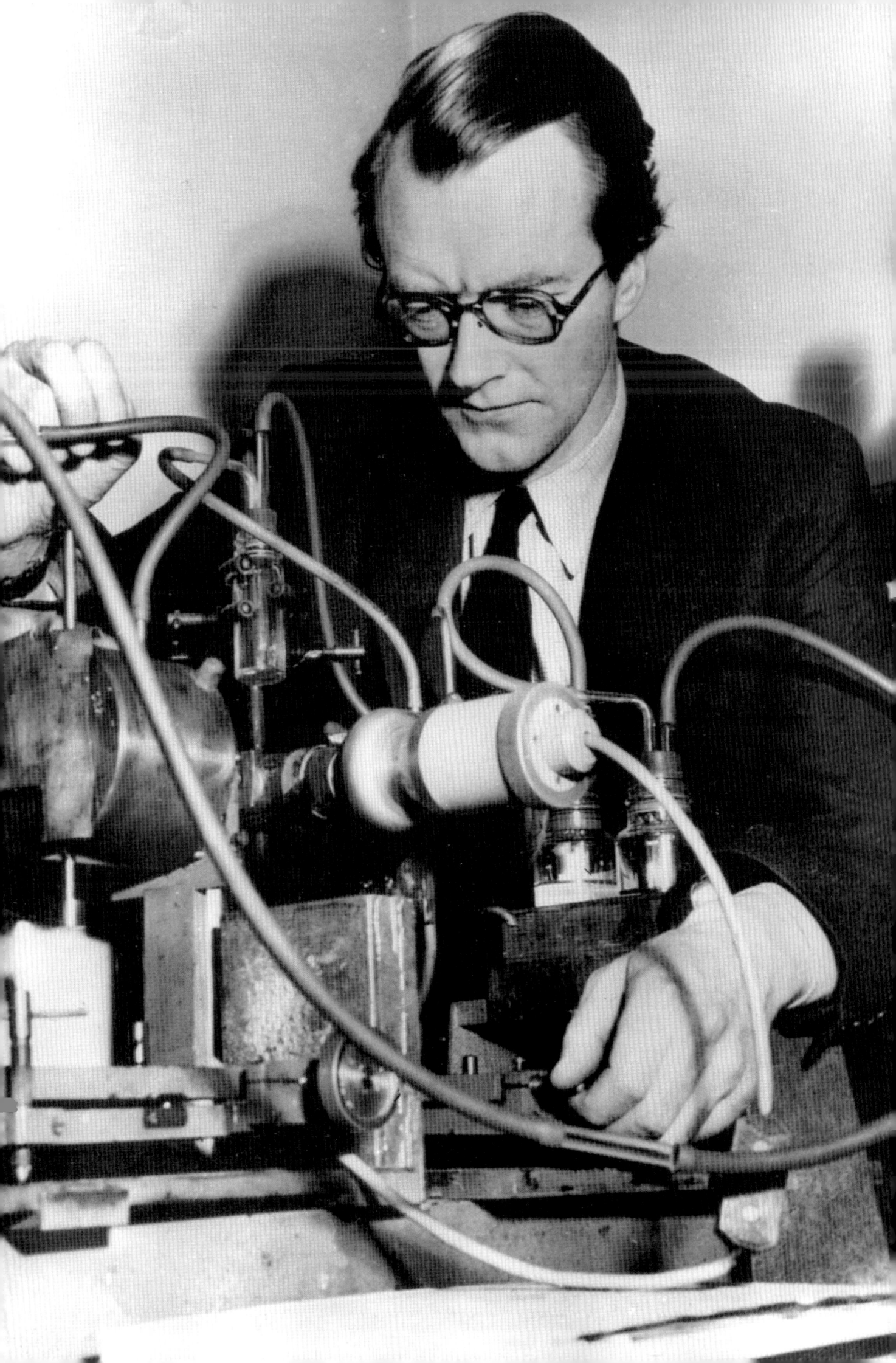

27 Helen Clark

Labour's First Lady

BORN: HAMILTON, FEBRUARY 26, 1950.

Helen Clark confirmed her status as one of most formidable politicians in New Zealand history when, in September 2005, she led Labour to a third successive election victory. Hers was the first Labour Government to win a third term for more than half a century. Clark was not New Zealand's first woman Prime Minister – National's Jenny Shipley beat her to that distinction – but she was the first woman elected to the position.

She was the oldest of four girls in a Waikato farming family and attended Te Pahu primary school and Epsom Girls' Grammar. Even before she graduated from Auckland University with an MA, it was clear that politics was going to be a central part of her life.

She lectured in political studies at Auckland University from 1973-75 and, after a year abroad on a University Grants Committee scholarship, from 1977-81. Clark became a member of the Labour Party in 1971 and from 1973-75 was president of the Labour Youth Council and a member of the Auckland Labour Regional Council. She stood unsuccessfully against Jack Luxton in the safe National seat of Piako in the 1975 election.

She climbed the Labour Party ladder quickly, being involved with the women's council and the party executive. In 1981, the year she married sociologist Peter Davis, she won the Mt Albert seat by 2861 votes from Warren Moyes, and has held it since.

When Labour, under David Lange, was re-elected in 1987, Clark was made Minister of Conservation and of Housing, and 17 months later she took on the complex Health portfolio. It was a tempestuous time for Labour because of the acrimony between Lange and Finance Minister Roger Douglas. Clark kept her head down. Lange later expressed disappointment at not receiving more support from her in the face of attacks from the Douglas camp, saying: "Helen was so dry she was combustible."

But Clark was a canny politician. In August 1989, aged only 39, she became Deputy Prime Minister when Lange resigned and was replaced by Geoffrey Palmer. Labour was bundled out of office in 1990 and lost again in 1993, after which Clark successfully challenged Mike Moore for the leadership. She has been the face of the Labour Party since.

She lost the 1996 election, the country's first under MMP, when Labour won 37 seats to National's 44. But in 1999 Clark swept to power, with Labour getting 49 seats to National's 39. Labour won again, even more comprehensively, in 2002, 52 seats to 27. In the 2005 election she defied many pollsters with a knife-edge victory, her party taking 50 seats to National's 48.

Though critics call her Minister of Everything because of her micro-management tendencies, Clark has been Minister of Arts, Culture and Heritage while Prime Minister. She has shown political astuteness in negotiating the challenges of MMP. She formed minority coalition governments with the Alliance in 1999 and with Jim Anderton's Progressive Party in 2002 and 2005.

Clark has become embroiled in various controversies while Prime Minister. She signed her name to a painting sold for charity that she did not paint (portrayed in the media as Paintergate), become involved in a row over genetic engineering before the 2002 election (Corngate), and was driven at high speed from Waimate to Christchurch in 2004, which resulted in driving offence convictions for some of the drivers in the motorcade. As an oblique criticism, political rivals often point to the fact that she has no children.

As a leader she has dealt severely with any whiff of scandal from her Ministers. Under her, Marian Hobbs, Phillida Bunkle, Dover Samuels, Ruth Dyson, Leanne Dalziel, John Tamihere, David Benson-Pope and Taito Phillip Field have been stood down.

Her Government has been criticised for being too accommodating to Maori, for pandering too much to beneficiaries and for over-taxing, and her alleged social engineering has been described by opponents as "Helengrad". On the other hand, she is immensely capable and thrives on the cut and thrust of political debate. She has won favour for her staunch adherence to New Zealand's anti-nuclear policies, for refusing to commit New Zealand to the war in Iraq and for fostering relations with some important trading partners, including China.

Clark has sometimes made statements that lacked tact and sensitivity. But she has courage to match her intelligence and it is likely that when her performance comes to be finally judged, she will rank among New Zealand's outstanding leaders.

Mabel Howard

The woman who shocked Parliament

BORN: ADELAIDE, APRIL 18, 1894. DIED: CHRISTCHURCH, JUNE 23, 1972.

The abiding image of Mabel Howard is of a feisty MP making her point by waving two pairs of bloomers in the House. The issue under debate, the Merchandise Marks Bill of 1954, was a relatively minor one, but Howard's gesture as she sought to emphasise the need to standardise clothing sizes, generated immense publicity.

That was always Howard's way. Not only was she never afraid to stand out, but she actively sought the spotlight. She made history in 1947, when she became New Zealand's first woman Cabinet Minister, and thereafter was never far from the headlines.

Howard spent her first nine years in Adelaide before her father Ted moved his three daughters to Christchurch on the death of their mother, Harriett. The family struggled financially for several years. Ted Howard was staunchly left-wing. He became an MP in 1908 and held the Christchurch South seat for Labour from 1919 until his death in 1939. Mabel inherited her father's political principles, and like him could be sharp-tongued and intolerant.

After attending Christchurch Technical College she began working for the Canterbury General Labourers' Union in 1911. In 1933 she became the union secretary, the first time in New Zealand that a woman had been appointed secretary of a male-dominated union. Through much of her pre-Parliament adult life, Howard worked as an office assistant. She hoped to succeed her father as the Christchurch South MP in 1939, but did not get the Labour Party nomination, possibly because she was seen as being too closely aligned to rebel MP John A Lee.

She threw herself into the war effort, working for the Canterbury Women's War Service Auxiliary, chairing the Christchurch Women's Active Service Club committee and serving on the St John Ambulance Association and the Christchurch City Council. In addition, she was confirmed an Anglican and served in the vestry of St Chad's parish in Linwood.

In 1943 she finally got into Parliament, by winning a by-election for Christchurch East. She became only the fifth woman to be elected to the New Zealand Parliament (the first was Elizabeth McCombs, for Lyttelton, in 1933). Howard became known as a forthright, passionate, courageous and somewhat erratic politician. She had a short fuse, but was capable of great generosity. Always a supporter of the down-trodden, she focused on social welfare, lobbying for better treatment for servicemen and women returning from the war, State-paid domestic help and equal pay for women. When Hilda Ross won the Hamilton seat for National in 1945, she and Howard formed an effective political friendship.

After being thwarted initially, Howard was elevated to Cabinet in 1947, taking responsibility for health and child welfare. She introduced several far-reaching health measures, including increased regulation of physiotherapists and occupational therapists, more teaching of obstetrics and gynaecology, and better care of the mentally ill. One scheme that failed was her plan to turn Burnham Military Camp into pensioner housing.

Only 1.5m (4ft 11in) tall and of rather rotund build, Howard was a colourful and flamboyant personality who even during her eight years in opposition from 1949 was an effective MP. She was extremely popular in her Sydenham electorate, introducing open-house Sundays, when she would deal with the needs of her constituents. People from all over the country would seek her help and she was extremely giving of her time. Howard never married and was obsessive in her love of cats. For many years she was the president of the SPCA's Christchurch branch.

With Labour back in power in 1957, Howard was made Minister of Social Security and given responsibility for the welfare of women and children and the Child Welfare Department. She did not get on especially well with Labour leader Walter Nash, but remained a popular public figure. Her election majorities were invariably among the largest in the country.

Throughout her parliamentary career she was capable of the outrageous gesture or statement that focused attention on her and made a point strongly. Once, discussing the issue of equal rights, she said: "I truly believe that men are just as equal as women in the work they do. I believe that a man should have equal chances with a woman." In 1959 she caused astonishment when she danced with pop star Johnny Devlin at a rock and roll party. Howard quit Parliament on reaching retiring age in 1969 and her health declined quickly thereafter. She suffered from dementia and ended her days in Sunnyside Hospital.

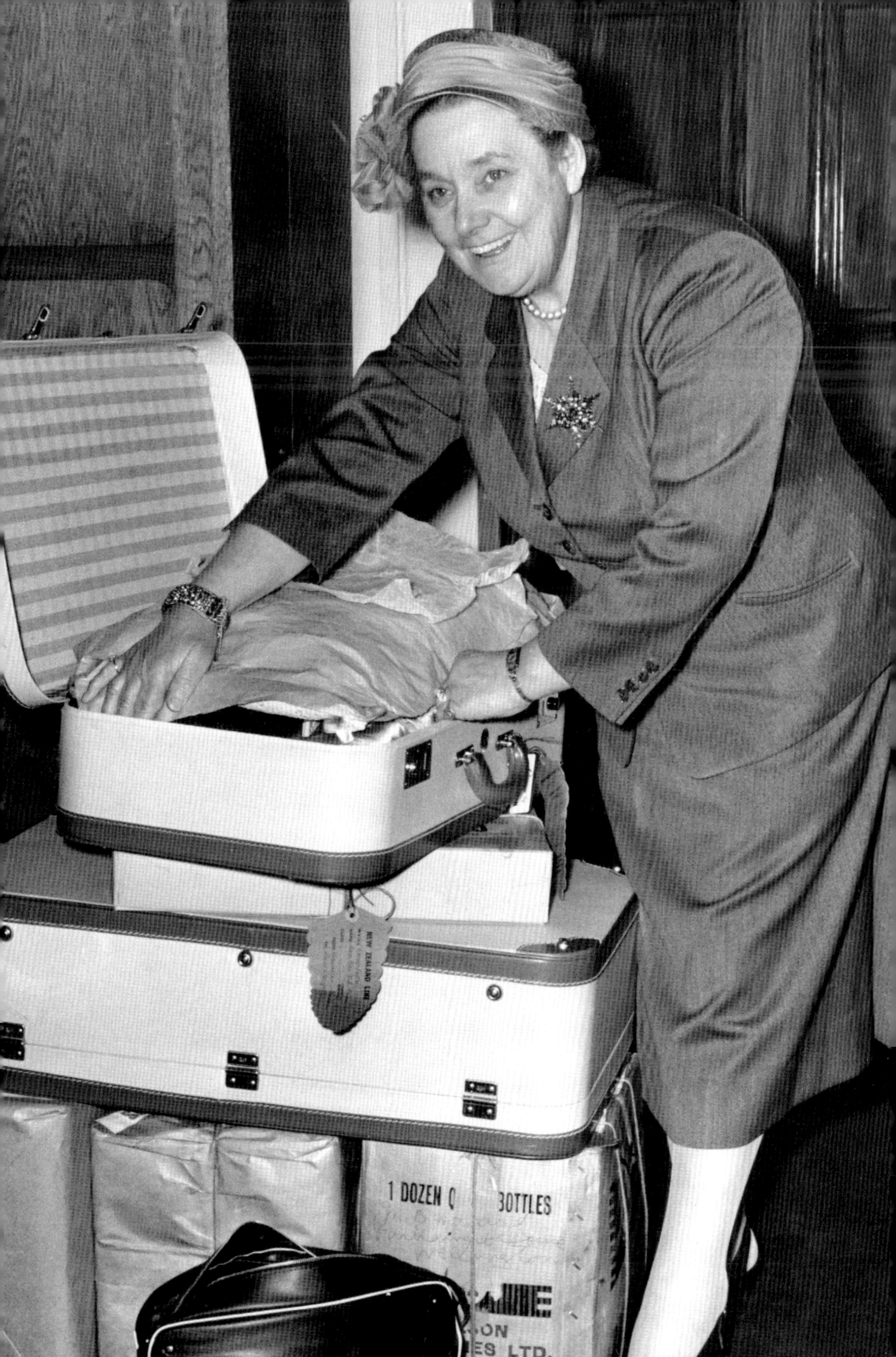

Bernard Freyberg

The soldier who became Governor-General

BORN: LONDON, MARCH 31, 1889. DIED: WINDSOR, JULY 4, 1963.

Bernard Freyberg was a heroic figure. A champion swimmer, a much-decorated soldier through two world wars, the first New Zealand-educated Governor-General. Though he was born and died in England and lived there for many years, New Zealanders regarded him as one of their own and were immensely proud of him.

Freyberg's parents moved from London to Wellington when Bernard was two. He attended Wellington College from 1897-1904, distinguishing himself mainly in sport. He won several national swimming titles, including, in 1906, the 100 yards, 880 yards and one mile championships. He was also a good water polo player. Though nicknamed "Tiny", he stood 1.83m (6ft) tall and had a strong build.

After considering a medical career, Freyberg turned to dentistry. He was admitted to the New Zealand Dentists' Register in 1911, practising briefly in Morrinsville, Hamilton and Levin. In 1912 he joined the New Zealand Territorials. Then came a change of direction – he became a ship's stoker and in 1914 headed to the United States and Mexico. At the outbreak of World War I he sailed for England.

Freyberg persuaded the First Lord of the Admiralty, Winston Churchill, to give him a commission into the Hood Battalion of the Royal Naval Division. After a spell on the Belgian Front he was sent to Gallipoli. Throughout the war, Freyberg fought with bravery and a constant disregard for his personal safety.

This was never better revealed than during the Gallipoli landing, when, amid heavy fire, he swam to shore and lit decoy flares to confuse the Turks, earning the first of four Distinguished Service Order medals. He was wounded twice before his division was evacuated in 1916.

On the Western Front his deeds, especially during the first battle of the Somme, were the stuff of legends. He was wounded four times during the fighting at Beaucourt, but led with courage and success through a drawn-out initiative that involved trench warfare and the taking of Beaucourt village and the capture of 500 prisoners. Freyberg was awarded the Victoria Cross. In 1917 he was given command of a brigade, making him at 28 the British Army's youngest general. By the armistice he had been wounded nine times. It was said later that there was hardly a part of his body unmarked by scars.

He became a general staff officer in the War Office and remained in Britain. In 1922 he married Barbara Jekyll, a widow with two children. They had one son. He dabbled with politics, standing unsuccessfully for the Liberals in the 1922 election and later putting his name forward as a Conservative candidate. Freyberg was ruled unfit for service for the British Army in 1937 because of a heart murmur, but was returned to the active list in 1939.

He was seen as a key figure by New Zealand's acting Prime Minister, Peter Fraser, who asked him to command the New Zealand Second Division and the Second New Zealand Expeditionary Force. It took Freyberg a while to win over the New Zealand soldiers because of his long-standing links with the British, but his care for those he was commanding, leadership qualities and courage eventually made him immensely popular among New Zealand soldiers. One of his subordinates described him as "a huge boy scout" and recalled him as "kind, considerate, compassionate, always ready to listen, always approachable".

Freyberg was given command of the allied forces during the 1941 Battle of Crete, after the frenetic retreat from mainland Greece. His tactics caused some consternation and the island was lost, but he retained Fraser's confidence. He later commanded the New Zealand Second Division in North Africa, which led Churchill to describe him as "the salamander of the British Empire". In the battle of El Alamein, in 1942, the New Zealanders played a vital part in the Allies' final breakthrough. Lieutenant General Freyberg, as he was then, turned his attention to the Italian campaign, which culminated in his troops entering Trieste in triumph on May 2, 1945.

Freyberg was appointed New Zealand's Governor-General in 1946 and filled the role until 1952, staying an extra year by special request. He was knighted in 1943 and in 1951 was elevated to the peerage, becoming Baron Freyberg of Wellington and Mustead (Surrey). In 1953 he was appointed Deputy Constable and Lieutenant-Governor of Windsor Castle.

His name is remembered in several ways – in Palmerston North by Freyberg High School and in Wellington by the Freyberg Building (with his bust outside) and Freyberg Pool.

Harold Gillies

The father of plastic surgery

BORN: DUNEDIN, JUNE 17, 1882. DIED: LONDON, SEPTEMBER 10, 1960.

Harold Gillies was a product of perfect timing. He was an artistically-minded person eager to be involved in medicine and was just shaping his career when World War I broke out. These factors combined to push him towards plastic surgery, with consequences that have become increasingly significant.

Gillies, the son of wealthy Dunedin parents – his father, Robert, was an MP – had the advantage of good schooling. He attended Wanganui Collegiate from 1895-1900, distinguishing himself academically and in sport. He was a prefect and captain of the First XI, and was regarded as a potentially outstanding cricketer. He attended Cambridge University in England from 1901, gaining a reputation as a fine scholar and a talented sportsman. Gillies became a good oarsman and fly fisherman and one of the best golfers in England.

He intended pursuing a career in otolaryngology (ear and throat surgery) and trained at St Bartholomew's Hospital, qualifying in 1908. For several years he made his way comfortably in London. He married Kathleen Jackson in 1911.

World War I was life-changing for Gillies. He received a commission with the Royal Army Medical Corps and was sent to Belgium. But at about this time he came into contact with two Frenchmen, Hippolyte Morestin, said to be the leading surgeon in Europe, and Auguste Valadier, who was experimenting with using tissue from other parts of the body to treat facial wounds.

Gillies could see immediately the possibilities of what we now call plastic surgery, and knew he had found his calling. Always personable and persuasive, and with a finely-honed sense of humour, he convinced the army of the need for plastic surgery for the thousands of soldiers being wounded in Europe. In 1916 he was given charge of the Cambridge Military Hospital at Aldershot. By the end of the war, he had seen 11,000 patients.

A talented artist – in 1948 his paintings featured in a London art exhibition – Gillies brought this skill to his surgery and was always concerned with the look, not just the health, of his patients. He would say proudly that his patients often looked better when he finished with them than before they were injured.

Gillies wrote *Plastic Surgery of the Face* in 1920. The British Medical Association said it was "one of the most notable contributions made to surgical literature in our day". From his Harley Street practice, Gillies established an international reputation. He was decorated by the Danish in 1923 for his work after the explosion of a Danish naval ship and years later the Norwegians honoured him for his work with their soldiers during World War II.

Always generous with his time – whether with patients or doctors seeking his advice – Gillies became extremely influential. He mentored Archie McIndoe and Rainsford Mowlem during the 1930s and the three of them led plastic surgery teams during World War II. Gillies also trained New Zealanders such as William Manchester, Frank Hutter and Joe Brownlee, who used their knowledge to good effect at home.

Gillies brought a lot of imagination to his work. He would sketch drawings of how he wanted his surgery to turn out and it was he who instituted the practice of incorporating specialists, such as dental surgeons, into his teams. During World War II Gillies established plastic surgery units around Britain. Rooksdown House, in Basingstoke, which he established, became the country's leading plastic surgery centre. Plastic surgery soon spread throughout the world. The Americans adopted it with much enthusiasm and in 1945 Burwood Hospital near Christchurch had a plastic surgery unit attached.

In 1946 Gillies became founding president of the British Association of Plastic Surgeons. Later the International Society of Plastic Surgeons made him honorary president. He became an honorary fellow of the Royal Australasian College of Surgeons and the American College of Surgeons.

Gillies performed the world's first sex-change operation, of a woman to a man, in 1945. In 1957 he co-wrote the authoritative *The Principles and Art of Plastic Surgery*. His wife died in 1957 and six months later he married Marjorie Clayton, his long-time surgical assistant.

He called plastic surgery "aesthetic reconstructive surgery" and said: "Within us all there is an overwhelming urge to change something ugly and useless into something more beautiful and more functional."

Gillies was knighted in 1930. In 1960, at 78, he was given a Special Honorary Citation by the American Society of Plastic and Reconstructive Surgery "for outstanding scientific contribution to the development of plastic surgery".

Kiri Te Kanawa

The diva who sang for royalty

BORN: GISBORNE, MARCH 6, 1944.

Kiri Te Kanawa became a celebrity in 1971 when she made her debut at the Royal Opera House, Covent Garden, as the Countess in *The Marriage of Figaro*. After her brilliant performance, she moved quickly to the forefront of international opera and became one of the 20th century's most famous sopranos, best-known for her repertoire of works by Mozart and Richard Strauss.

Though some English opera aficionados might not have realised it in 1971, she was already an experienced concert and recording artist, at home in front of the cameras and on stage.

Kiri Janette Te Kanawa was born to an unmarried couple (European mother and Maori father). They were extremely poor and already had a son, and after five weeks Kiri was adopted by a married couple in Gisborne (again, European mother and Maori father), Tom and Nell Te Kanawa.

Kiri's singing talent was obvious early and she was given every encouragement by her mother. The family moved to Auckland when she was 12, and from 1959-65 she was trained by renowned singing teacher Sister Mary Leo (whose other pupils included Mina Foley, Heather Begg and Malvina Major) at St Mary's Convent in Ponsonby.

From the early 1960s, Te Kanawa was winning important competitions in New Zealand and Australia. She finished second to Major in the Mobil Song Contest in 1963, and won it in 1965. She also won the John Court Aria Prize and the Melbourne *Sun* Aria. Australian music critic Linda Phillips said: "The winner has a luscious voice and a splendid histrionic sense. She is a very fine opera singer in the making."

Te Kanawa earned an arts council bursary to study at the London Opera Centre and departed New Zealand in style, with a packed farewell concert at the Wellington Town Hall. She has been based overseas since.

A career highlight was her singing *Let the Bright Seraphim* at the 1981 wedding of Prince Charles and Lady Diana, in St Paul's Cathedral, with a live audience of 600 million. In 2002 she performed at a gala concert at Buckingham Palace to celebrate the Queen's Jubilee.

She has not sung a full operatic role in New Zealand since the 1960s, but she has sung at the world's major opera houses, including the Metropolitan Opera in New York, Paris Opera, Sydney Opera House, the Royal Opera House in London and La Scala in Milan. She has also appeared at venues as varied as the Hollywood Bowl and Ayers Rock.

Her operatic repertoire includes major heroines of the Austro-German school – Mozart's Countess (*Le Nozze di Figaro*), Donna Elvira (*Don Giovanni*), Pamina (*Die Zauberflute*) and Fiordiligi (*Cosi fan tutte*), Strauss' Marschallin (*Der Rosenkavalier*), Countess (*Capriccio*) and the title role in *Arabella* – in addition to Italian roles such as Mimi (Puccini's *La Bohème*), Violetta (Verdi's *La Traviata*) and Elizabeth (Verdi's *Don Carlos*), and the French roles of Marguerite (Gounod's *Faust*) and Micalia (Bizet's *Carmen*).

On the concert stage she has joined the world's leading orchestral ensembles, such as Chicago Symphony, Los Angeles Philharmonic, London Symphony and Boston Symphony in recording performances of some of the major classical masterworks of the 19th century. In March 1994 she celebrated her 50th birthday with a concert at The Royal Albert Hall.

Te Kanawa has been at her best playing roles such as heroines and countesses. Her strong, rich voice has always made listening to her singing an emotional experience and her beauty and somewhat haughty manner are ideally suited to such parts.

Te Kanawa has maintained her links with New Zealand, returning occasionally to perform. In 1990 her concert in the Auckland Domain attracted a crowd of 140,000. At the dawn of the millennium she sang in a concert on a beach in Gisborne that was broadcast to 55 countries.

She was created a Dame Commander of the British Empire in 1982, and has honorary degrees from a dozen universities. She is also an honorary fellow of Somerville College, Oxford, and Wolfson College, Cambridge, and was invested with the Order of Australia in 1990. In 1995 she was awarded the Order of New Zealand.

Te Kanawa married Australian Desmond Park in 1967. The couple adopted two children, Antonia and Thomas, but divorced in 1997.

In 2003 she lent her name to the Kiri Te Kanawa Foundation, formed to support talented New Zealand singers and musicians.

Keith Park

Fearless in mind and duty

BORN: THAMES, JUNE 15, 1892. DIED: AUCKLAND, FEBRUARY 6, 1975.

Lord Tedder, head of the Royal Air Force, said of Keith Park in 1947: "If ever one man won the Battle of Britain, he did. I don't believe it is realised how much that one man, with his leadership, his calm judgment and his skill, did to save not only this country, but the world." It was often said of someone that he "had a good war". Well, Park had two outstanding wars and was aptly summed up as "fearless in mind and duty".

Park was born in Thames, the son of a Scotsman who was a noted geologist. He was educated at King's College, Auckland, and Otago Boys' High School. After working for the Union Steam Ship Company, he headed to World War I with the New Zealand Artillery in 1915.

He fought at Anzac Cove, Gallipoli, and then, after switching to the British Army, was wounded fighting on the Somme front.

He transferred to the Royal Flying Corps in December 1916 and quickly became known as an outstanding fighter pilot. He claimed 20 victims and was shot down once. By the end of the war he had been awarded the Military Cross, for "conspicuous gallantry and devotion to duty", and Bar, the Distinguished Flying Corps and the Croix de Guerre.

Instead of returning to New Zealand, Park stayed in England. He married Dol Parish in 1918 and remained involved in air defence. He served for periods in Egypt and in South America, and was an aide de camp for King George VI.

In 1938 he was promoted to Air Commander and became Hugh Dowding's deputy at Fighter Command headquarters. There was another promotion, to Air Vice Marshal, in 1940, when he was given responsibility for No 11 Group, the Fighter Command's main subdivision. Their job was to defend southern England and London against German advances.

But first there was the matter of co-ordinating the evacuation of 340,000 tired and hungry soldiers from Dunkirk, where they had retreated. It was a juggling act for Park who, never one to sit behind a desk, made many flying missions himself. Eventually the evacuation succeeded, though many troops felt it could have been accomplished more easily and with less suffering on their part.

Dowding and Park were the strategists for the Battle of Britain through 1940-41, with Park taking a daily hands-on role. He had to husband carefully the resources available and elected to defend rather than attack, a policy that was again criticised, but which eventually proved triumphant. Hitler finally abandoned Operation Sealion and turned his Luftwaffe attention to the Eastern Front. After the Battle of Britain, Winston Churchill made his famous statement: "Never in the history of human conflict, was so much owed by so many to so few."

Park, promoted once more, to Air Marshal, was made commanding officer of the Middle East and took charge of the defence of the strategic island of Malta. Having seen off the Germans and Italians there, he was sent to south-east Asia, and oversaw Burma's liberation from the Japanese.

Park retired from the RAF in 1946 and took a job representing the Hawker Siddeley Aircraft Company in Argentina. Then, finally, he went home, as the company's Auckland-based Pacific regional representative. He held this position from 1948-60.

He had many other interests. He was chairman of the Auckland International Airport committee, making decisions that resulted in Mangere Airport being opened in 1966. He served on the Auckland City Council from 1962-71 and was active in the New Zealand Foundation for the Blind, the New Zealand Epilepsy Association and the King George V Children's Health Camp in Pakuranga.

At 2m (6ft 5in), Park was a commanding presence, and he aged well, remaining upright and lively virtually until his death in 1975.

He was given a military funeral in Auckland and a memorial service in London. At the London event, Douglas Bader, one of his World War II critics, corrected the record when he said: "The Battle of Britain was controlled, directed and brought to a successful conclusion by the man whose memory we honour today."

Park was knighted twice. He was one of three war heroes – the others were Churchill and Lord Beaverbrook – who had locomotives named after them by Great Southern Railways in Britain. The Sir Keith Park IHC School in Mangere and the Auckland Museum of Transport and Technology were named in his honour.

Alan McDiarmid

The boy chemist who won a Nobel Prize

BORN: MASTERTON, APRIL 4, 1927.

A sign in Alan McDiarmid's study at the University of Pennsylvania read: "I am a very lucky person and the harder I work the luckier I seem to be." The point was made with humour, which was apt, and the message summed up McDiarmid's creed. He once said: "Success is knowing you have done your best and have exploited your God-given or gene-given abilities to the maximum. More than this, no-one can do."

McDiarmid was blessed with a brilliant, inquisitive mind, and used it to become a world-renowned scientist who won a Nobel Prize for Chemistry in 2000.

He was raised in the Wairarapa, the youngest of five children in a family struggling through the Depression. He attended primary school bare-footed and bathed once a week, in water shared by his brothers and sisters. Yet he felt he was fortunate that his childhood taught him the importance of sharing and being self-reliant.

After the family moved to Lower Hutt, McDiarmid attended Hutt Valley High School for three years from 1941, and was a contemporary of sports stars Ron Jarden and John Reid. He was an exceptional student, with a particular bent for chemistry. He would cycle to the Lower Hutt library, where, on the bottom shelf of the new book area of the children's section he discovered a blue-covered book called *The Boy Chemist*. He kept it for more than a year by continuous borrowing. The foreword of the 1924 book, written by Archie Collins, stated: "If you make the experiments in order, by the time you reach the tenth chapter you will have taken a fairly good course in Chemistry, and that will serve you well for all time."

McDiarmid left school at 16 and served for a time in the Air Training Corps. He was keen to get to Victoria University and became a part-time student. To pay his way, he worked in the university's chemistry department as a lab boy and became the live-in janitor at Weir House, the university hostel for young men.

After graduating with an MSc in chemistry, McDiarmid headed for the University of Wisconsin in the United States on a Fulbright Fellowship. He gained a PhD in 1953, majoring in inorganic chemistry, and won a Shell Scholarship that enabled him to study at Cambridge University, England, where he earned a second PhD.

A brief spell at the University of St Andrews in Scotland ended in 1955 when he was appointed an associate professor at the University of Pennsylvania in Philadelphia. He remained there throughout his working life. He became a full professor in 1964 and in 1988 became Blanchard Professor in Chemistry.

The research that really established his reputation was his discovery and development of electronically conductive polymers, or "synthetic metals". It was for showing how some plastics could conduct electricity that McDiarmid, American physicist Alan Heeger, who worked with him at the University of Pennsylvania, and Japanese chemist Hideki Shirakawa, won the Nobel Prize.

The discovery was not made in one blinding flash, but incrementally. A significant moment came in 1975, when McDiarmid was lecturing at Kyoto University. He visited Tokyo Institute of Technology and spoke with Shirakawa, who had done some impressive early research in the field of electrical conduction by polymers. McDiarmid invited Shirakawa to join him at Pennsylvania. There they made gradual progress towards the discovery that more than two decades later would culminate in the Nobel Prize. McDiarmid said: "We were fascinated by the science. We lived it, breathed it, slept it, dreamed it. Complete immersion. And at first people didn't necessarily believe what we were saying, but that slowly changed."

The consequences of their discovery have been far-reaching. There are opportunities in such diverse areas as rechargeable batteries, electromagnetic interference shielding, corrosion inhibition, flexible "plastic" transistors and electrodes. Their work has enabled computers to be made considerably smaller, yet work faster.

McDiarmid met his wife, Marian Mathieu, soon after he arrived at the University of Wisconsin. She died in 1990.

He has retained close ties with New Zealand, returning often on holiday. In recent times he has collaborated with colleagues at the Industrial Research Laboratories and at Victoria University, which in 1999 gave him an honorary doctorate. In 2001 the university created the Alan McDiarmid Chair in Physical Chemistry. That same year he was presented with the Rutherford Medal, New Zealand's highest science award. In 2002 McDiarmid became a Member of the Order of New Zealand.

Peter Blake

The Hillary of the seas

BORN: AUCKLAND, OCTOBER 1, 1948. DIED: MACAPA, BRAZIL, DECEMBER 6, 2001.

Peter Blake had the rare ability to take the nation with him on his expeditions. He was charismatic and inspiring, and New Zealanders basked in the reflected glory of his many triumphs. Though Blake, his wife Pippa and their two children lived in England, New Zealanders embraced him, and his tragic and violent death left the country stunned.

Blake came from a sailing family. His parents introduced their four children to the delights of sailing early. When he was eight, Peter already had his first boat, a P-class yacht named Pee Bee. He soon graduated to a Z-class dinghy. Auckland's Waitemata Harbour was his playground.

But Blake became more than a yachtie – he was an adventurer. He attended Auckland Institute of Technology, studying mechanical engineering, but from 1971, when he won the Cape Town to Rio de Janeiro race, he was on the lookout for a challenge. He won the Fastnet race off the England coast in 1979 and 1989, the Sydney to Hobart in 1980 and 1984 and the around-Australia in 1988.

In 1973-74 his life changed when he competed in the inaugural Whitbread around-the-world race on Burton Cutter. The boat didn't have the best of luck, but Blake's appetite had been whetted. He was back four years later aboard Heath's Condor. In 1981-82 he mounted his own campaign, skippering Ceramco New Zealand to third place. He returned with Lion New Zealand in 1985-86, and this time was second. Finally, in 1989-90, he did it when Steinlager 2 claimed line, handicap and overall honours on each of the race's six legs. After a triumph like that it was time to move on.

He set his sights on the Jules Verne Trophy, for non-stop around-the-world sailing. The aim was to get around the world in fewer than 80 days. His first attempt, in 1993, was halted when Enza hit a submerged object in the Southern Ocean. The following year he tried again with co-skipper Robin Knox-Johnston, and established a record of 74 days, 22 hours, 17 minutes.

By now Blake, tall, blond and moustachioed, was a national identity. His next goal was the America's Cup. Michael Fay, his campaign faltering, had pulled in Blake at the last moment to manage New Zealand's 1992 Cup challenge. NZL-20 reached the challenger final, before losing to Il More de Venezia of Italy.

In 1995 Blake had more time to prepare Black Magic's challenge, and what a job he did. With Blake also on board as a crew member, Black Magic crossed the line first in all but one race, beating oneAustralia 5–1 in the Louis Vuitton final, and then sweeping the final 5–0 against the San Diego Yacht Club's Team Dennis Conner. This contest really captured the imagination of New Zealanders. When it was publicised that Blake wore "lucky" red socks, hundreds of thousands of New Zealanders bought red socks, too. The proceeds helped fund the challenge. Blake was knighted in 1995.

Because Blake dealt so well with sponsors and had such a positive public image, his fierce competitive instinct was sometimes overlooked. He was organised, delegated well and always stressed that attitude was the key to winning.

Blake headed the 2000 America's Cup defence and had the satisfaction of watching Team New Zealand smash Italian challenger Prada 5–0 in the final. There were hints of a rift with his skipper Russell Coutts and some of the management and Blake decided to move on.

He assumed leadership of the Cousteau Society but formed his own organisation, blakexpeditions, soon after, with United Nations backing. The group's primary goal was to educate young people about the importance of maintaining the environment. Blake and his crew spent two months filming in Antarctica and then moved to the Amazon region, monitoring global warming and pollution.

One night, while they were moored quietly on the river, seven Brazilian bandits pulled alongside Blake's Seamaster, guns drawn. Blake charged up from below decks to confront the robbers and was shot twice and killed.

His death in such a manner was a terrible waste. Prime Minister Helen Clark, who had visited him in Brazil weeks earlier, described him as "our Hillary of the seas". blakexpeditions has continued and a number of Blake scholarships have since been announced.

Blake, or his teams, won three Halberg Awards. He was New Zealand Yachtsman of the Year twice and in 1994 was World Sailor of the Year, with Knox-Johnston. In 2002 he was awarded, posthumously, the International Olympic Committee's Olympic Order. He was inducted into the New Zealand Sports Hall of Fame in 2003.

Clarence Beeby

The visionary behind New Zealand's education system

BORN: LEEDS, YORKSHIRE, JUNE 16, 1902. DIED: WELLINGTON, MARCH 2, 1998.

In 1939 Clarence Beeby spelt out his vision for the New Zealand education system and then set about making it happen. His philosophy, groundbreaking for the time, has remained the cornerstone of New Zealand education.

Beeby, known to most as Beeb, was appointed Director General of Education by Peter Fraser in 1940 and was charged with implementing his egalitarian vision of education. Fraser and Beeby had previously explained what the government objective should be: "Every person, whatever his level of academic ability, whether he be rich or poor, whether he live in town or country, has a right to a free education of the kind for which he is best fitted and to the fullest extent of his powers."

Beeby was born in Yorkshire, and his family moved to Christchurch when he was four. He distinguished himself academically – he was dux of New Brighton School and one of Christchurch Boys' High School's leading scholars. He enjoyed debating and drama.

He became a Methodist lay preacher when he was 17 and in 1920 enrolled at Canterbury College, intending to study law. However, he soon changed his mind and decided to become a school teacher. He enrolled at Christchurch Training College, where he met Beatrice Newnham, whom he married in 1926. At training college, Beeby came under the guidance of Canterbury's first Professor of Education, James Shelley, who profoundly influenced Beeby's career choices and education philosophy.

Beeby graduated with an MA in 1924 and, on Shelley's advice, enrolled for a PhD at Victoria University, Manchester. He returned to lecture at Canterbury College in 1927. A visit to the United States and Canada in 1929-30, where he studied educational testing, remedial teaching, educational and vocational guidance and industrial relations, helped firm his ideas.

Though he was progressing well at Canterbury College, he was lured to Wellington, as the first director of the New Zealand Council for Educational Research. Beeby had a galvanising effect on the council. Chief among his many achievements was the standardisation for New Zealand conditions of an intelligence test.

Soon Beeby came to the notice of the Minister of Education, Peter Fraser. Beeby's belief that the education system suffered from too much centralisation and conformity and should be open to variety and experiment dovetailed with Fraser's.

Over the next two decades, Beeby drove many education changes, including developing School Certificate, reforming the University Entrance examination and forming the first committee on the teaching of reading. He pushed through new methods of teaching, a primary syllabus, manual training, arts and crafts training, changes to secondary teacher training, vocational guidance, school publications and the National Library service, and school visits to zoos and museums. He also began the policy of advancing students with their age group, rather than on ability. Beeby worked hard to reduce class sizes, though with wartime austerity and then rising birth rates, this proved extremely difficult.

His ideas generated much debate and in the 1940s "Beebyism" became a catch-cry for anything thought to be wrong with the revamped education system.

Beeby was director general for 20 years, but undertook many other projects during that time. In 1945 Fraser sent him to review educational arrangements in the Cook Islands, Niue, and Western Samoa. The following year, he led the New Zealand delegation to the first Unesco general conference in Paris. He returned to Paris as Unesco's Assistant Director General of Education in 1948-49. Beeby was back in Paris in 1960, serving three years as ambassador to France and as permanent delegate to Unesco. He was appointed to Unesco's executive board in 1960, and became its chairman in 1962.

After he left Paris, he worked in Harvard University's Graduate School of Education from 1963-67, and then for two years at London University's Institute of Education. Until 1987 he did consultancy work in countries as far-flung as Libya, India, Papua New Guinea, Indonesia, Malaysia and Tanzania.

Otago, Canterbury and Victoria universities conferred honorary doctorates on him, and the New Zealand Educational Institute made him a life member. The United States National Academy of Education elected him a foreign associate, and Unesco awarded him its Medal of the Silk Road of Dialogue. He was appointed a CMG and in 1987 he became one of the five foundation members of the Order of New Zealand, the country's highest public honour.

Beeby wrote *The Quality of Education in Developing Countries* in 1966 and his memoir, *The Biography of an Idea: Beeby on Education*, in 1992.

36 Jack Lovelock

An enigma who was our first great runner

BORN: CRUSHINGTON, WEST COAST, JANUARY 5, 1910. DIED: NEW YORK, DECEMBER 28, 1949.

Even decades after his death, there remains an aura of mystery about Jack Lovelock, the first New Zealand runner to win an Olympic gold medal.

He was a giant of athletics, one of only six runners to set world records for the 1500m and mile and win an Olympic 1500m gold medal. Lovelock and aviatrix Jean Batten were the most famous New Zealanders of the 1930s. Lovelock ensured his athletics immortality when, in front of Hitler at the 1936 Berlin Olympic Games, he ran a brilliant tactical race to win the 1500m in world record time. It was, he recorded in his meticulously-kept diary, "the most perfectly-executed race of my life".

Through the mid-1930s Lovelock scored a succession of big wins over the other leading milers of his time – Americans Glenn Cunningham, Archie San Romani and Bill Bonthron, Englishmen Jerry Cornes and Sydney Wooderson and Italian Luigi Beccali. Through it all he remained a rather aloof figure. He was an intensely private person, who masked his emotions and confided in few.

Lovelock was born on the West Coast in 1910 and as a youngster proved adept at a variety of sports, including, surprisingly, boxing. After leaving Timaru Boys' High School he attended Otago University. While there he gained a Rhodes Scholarship, and he departed New Zealand in 1931 to study medicine at Oxford University.

Lovelock's first major international athletics meeting was the 1932 Olympics, when he finished a disappointing seventh in the 1500m final. Thereafter, though, Lovelock's career was a tale of triumphs.

In 1933 he set his first world record. Representing Oxford-Cambridge at Princeton, he outclassed Bonthron and won the mile in 4min 7.6s, slashing 1.4s off Frenchman Jules Ladoumegue's world mark. The diminutive New Zealander floated effortlessly over the ground and when at peak fitness never seemed to strain. That record lifted him to celebrity status. Thereafter New Zealand newspapers recorded details about all his races and offered regular updates on his progress.

Lovelock, a shrewd analyst, decided the way to win major races was to outkick his opposition in the last lap, and he worked ceaselessly to improve his finishing sprint.

At the 1934 London Empire Games he ran down Cornes and Wooderson to win the mile gold medal. Then it was back to the United States for a much-touted Mile of the Century showdown in Los Angeles against Bonthron and Cunningham. Again, he had far too much pace over the last lap and won in 4min 11.2s. In 1935 he won another Mile of the Century duel against Cunningham, at Princeton.

Lovelock, a nervy character, was beset by doubts before the Berlin Olympics and flirted with the idea of running the 5000m instead of the 1500m. Finally New Zealand team manager Arthur Porritt told him to concentrate on the 1500m.

That Olympic final, on August 6, 1936, was a classic. The field was full of talent, yet Lovelock was in a class of his own. He took the lead with 300m remaining and opened a seven-metre gap that was never threatened. Radio broadcaster Harold Abrahams, a friend of Lovelock's, was beside himself, and his commentary has become as much a classic as the race itself. "Lovelock! Cunningham's second, Beccali third... my God, he's done it! Jack, come on! Lovelock wins... five yards, six yards... he wins! He's won! Hooray! Lovelock's passing the tape..." His time, 3min 47.8s, bettered the world record by one second and took middle-distance running into a new league.

Following his Olympic triumph, Lovelock won a three-mile title for the British Empire against the United States in London, then retired to pursue his medical career.

He made one fleeting return visit to New Zealand immediately after the Olympics and was fêted as he toured the country, visiting schools, making speeches and doing demonstration runs. In 1940 he was thrown from a horse and lay unconscious for an hour before being discovered. He suffered double vision and occasional dizziness for the rest of his life.

He and his wife moved to New York, where Lovelock was assistant director of physical medicine at the Hospital for Special Surgery. On December 28, 1949, eight days before his 40th birthday, he began having dizzy spells and telephoned his wife to tell her he would be coming home early. He was standing on the southbound platform of the Church Street subway station in Brooklyn when he suddenly pitched forward on to the tracks and was struck by an oncoming train, dying instantly.

Was it an accident or suicide? It was the final mystery of this enigmatic personality's life.

John Bedbrook

The biotech pioneer

BORN: AUCKLAND, MAY 2, 1949.

When John Bedbrook left Auckland in 1974 to attend Harvard Medical School, he intended to be away from New Zealand for a couple of years. More than 30 years later, the biotechnology pioneer is still living in the United States, where he is acknowledged as an expert in his field.

Biotechnology was born in the United States, growing out of advances in DNA technology. Bedbrook's early work at the biotech frontier included becoming the first person to isolate a plant gene, helping establish the first agriculture biotech company, and releasing the first genetically modified (GM) microbe to combat frost damage. Since then his work has crossed between commerce and biology – the development of GM products to improve crop productivity has increasingly captured his attention.

Bedbrook attended Papatoetoe High School, then completed a PhD degree in cell biology at Auckland University. As a Fulbright Scholar and fellow of the Anna Fuller Fund he did post-doctoral research at Harvard, where he learned new methods of DNA cloning. He moved to the Biological Sciences Department at Harvard and mapped the DNA of the chloroplast, the organelle responsible for photosynthesis in plants.

In 1978 Bedbrook attended Cambridge University, in England, as a fellow of the European Molecular Biology Organisation. With Dick Flavell, he studied the molecular structure of wheat and rye chromosomes. He also collaborated with the University of Warwick's John Ellis to isolate the gene in plants responsible for the conversion of atmospheric carbon dioxide into sugars.

The following year he moved to Canberra, to work for the Commonwealth Scientific and Industrial Research Organisation, developing systems for the genetic transformation of plants. At the same time he co-founded the Advanced Genetic Sciences biotechnology company, which aimed to steer the new developments in molecular biology towards agricultural applications. Bedbrook left Australia in 1982 to run the research department of Advanced Genetic Sciences, which in 1983 became the first plant biotechnology company to go public on the American securities exchange Nasdaq.

The company's first product, Snomax, a bacterial product used for enhancing ice formation, is used today for snow-making in ski resorts. Bedbrook established that genetically modified versions of this product could prevent freeze-damage in plants. This discovery formed the basis of the next product, Frostban, which in 1987 became the first genetically modified organism deliberately released into the environment, a watershed event for the biotech industry.

Advanced Genetic Sciences merged with DNA Plant Technology Corporation in 1988. Bedbrook became head of research and later company president.

One of the significant discoveries was the observation that gene expression in plants could be inhibited by RNA related in sequence to the target gene. This knowledge was used to develop flowers with new colours and the Endless Summer Tomato, so named because of its longer shelf life. The discovery became the basis of recent work in developing therapeutics for some human diseases.

Bedbrook left DNA Plant in 1997 to form and become chief executive of Plant Science Ventures LLC, a venture capital firm investing in biotechnology. In 1999 he moved to Maxygen as president of agriculture. Two years later the company spawned Verdia, of which Bedbrook became president and chief executive.

Verdia was successful in using DNA shuffling, a gene optimisation method, to develop genetic traits for weed, pest and disease control. In 2004 it was bought by Dupont, a $40 billion company with worldwide agriculture connections. Bedbrook became vice-president of research and development for Dupont's agriculture and nutrition business, a $7 billion enterprise.

Bedbrook is aware of the ethical dilemmas that GM presents to some people. He has urged his colleagues to be more active in moulding public opinion to ensure that GM food is understood to be just as safe as GM medicine. "People developing technology need to do something about the anti-GM sentiment," he says. "There is no controversy when genetic modification is used in curing diseases, but there is when it applies to food. Yet the benefits of GM technology for advancements in agriculture are enormous. The advancement of GM products is a foregone conclusion - GM corn, soybean, cotton, rice and canola are now planted on 190 million acres by seven million farmers in 18 countries. It is up to us to show the public the benefits and to allay fears."

Bedbrook makes regular visits to New Zealand to lecture and consult. Two of his four children attended New Zealand universities and live in Auckland.

James K Baxter

The gifted poet who challenged society

BORN: DUNEDIN, JUNE 29, 1926. DIED: AUCKLAND, OCTOBER 22, 1972.

When James K Baxter (he was Jim to friends, but was seldom referred to publicly without his middle initial) died, John Weir, who was to edit the posthumous *Collected Poems*, wrote: "When he died... he bequeathed to his countrymen a body of poetry remarkable in its range and achievement."

Baxter was many things – alcoholic, family man, baptised Anglican, Catholic convert, Pakeha-Maori, protester, commune leader – but above everything, he was a wonderful poet and that is his legacy. His disturbing reflections, delivered directly and with vivid imagery, often placed him at odds with New Zealand society.

He was born into a left-leaning Otago farming family. His father, Archie, was a conscientious objector during World War I, and wrote a moving autobiography, *We Will Not Cease*. The young Baxter displayed a talent for poetry – he wrote his first poem at seven.

The Baxters lived in London in 1937-38. On his return James attended King's High School and then, from 1944, Otago University. Though showing signs of the alcoholism that would plague him, he produced his first collection of poems, *Beyond the Palisade*, and won the Macmillan Brown prize for the poem *Convoys*. He was already an important new voice and his output was enormous.

Baxter spent some years working on farms and in factories and became much taken with a young Maori student, Jacquie Sturm, whom he met in Christchurch. They married in 1948. He continued in less-than-intellectually-taxing jobs, such as porter and freezing worker, and for a while was a *Christchurch Press* copy editor. He produced *Blow, Wind of Fruitfulness*, a much-admired second collection of his poems. *Landfall* editor Charles Brasch said of this book: "I go about repeating it to myself with joy and wonder that this should have sprung out of New Zealand."

Baxter was baptised an Anglican in 1948 and moved to Wellington, where he began study on a BA (completed in 1956) and worked briefly in an abattoir and as a postman. After attending Wellington Teachers' College, he taught at Epuni School from 1954. He was never an establishment figure, but he settled down somewhat, making an effort to be a conventional family man and joining Alcoholics Anonymous. When he left Epuni School in 1956 he worked for the Department of Education's school publications branch. This provided him with fertile material with which to attack bureaucracy in his writing.

More of Baxter's best work was published in *In Fires of No Return*, in 1958. He began writing scripts for stage plays and radio and converted to Catholicism. In 1958 he was awarded a Unesco fellowship that enabled him to visit Japan and India. The poverty in India made a huge impression on him, and his concern was reflected in his later work. *Howrah Bridge and Other Poems* was a success, but Baxter became viewed as increasingly anti-establishment. He campaigned against the Vietnam War, in his writing and with speeches, and became part of the 1960s protest movement. He returned to Otago in 1966, on a two-year Robbie Burns Fellowship at Otago University.

His marriage over, Baxter contemplated communal life and eyed the settlement of Jerusalem, on the Whanganui River. His goal was to "form the nucleus of a community where the people, both Maori and Pakeha, would live without money or books, worship God and work on the land". This was novel thinking for 1960s New Zealand.

Baxter arrived at Jerusalem in 1969. He grew a beard, dressed shabbily and walked about bare-footed. He took to calling himself by his given Maori name, Hemi. This image of Baxter is the one that often comes to mind, even though his time at Jerusalem was brief. The commune alarmed neighbours, who were concerned at the free-living environment and open drug use. When public opposition led to the commune's closure, Baxter commented derisively that there was no need for concern over the occupants, because they would soon be safe in jails and hospitals. In 1972 Baxter, who had neglected his health for years, died of a heart attack in Auckland.

Much of Baxter's work was published posthumously. He was one of New Zealand's most gifted and prolific poets, who managed to write memorably about contact between New Zealand people and the raw land. His verse plays, *Jack Winter's Dream* and *The Wide Open Cage*, are less well-known and he wrote some discerning critical essays about New Zealand literature.

For many people his life was appropriately assessed in a newspaper billboard after his death. It read: "James K Baxter – friend."

Fred Hollows

The wild colonial boy of eye surgery

BORN: DUNEDIN, APRIL 9, 1929. DIED: SYDNEY, FEBRUARY 10, 1993.

New Zealand claims Fred Hollows, but in truth he was a citizen of the world. He was a larger-than-life personality who spent many years in Australia, but whose humanitarianism benefited people from Africa to Asia.

Frederick Cossom Hollows grew up in a strongly religious family in Palmerston North. He earned a BA at Victoria University and contemplated a life in the clergy, attending Glenleith Bible College for a time. Eventually, though, he turned to medicine. After studying at the Otago University Medical School in the early 1950s he spent two years at Wellington Hospital, then worked as a house surgeon at Auckland Hospital from 1957-60.

In 1961 he decided to specialise in eye surgery and studied at Moorfields Eye Hospital in England, and then in Wales. His life path changed in 1965, when he became associate professor of ophthalmology at the University of New South Wales. He oversaw the teaching departments at the university, and at Prince of Wales and Prince Henry hospitals. He never lived in New Zealand again.

Hollows had a highly refined sense of justice. He was affronted at the treatment that Aborigines received, and when he discovered that a vast number of them suffered from eye diseases, caused by dirty conditions and poor health, he took action where he was able to offer most help – eye surgery. He pioneered the treatment of trachoma and in 1971 set up the Aboriginal Medical Service in Redfern, Sydney. There are now more than 60 such centres across Australia. The National Trachoma and Eye Health Programme, which he established in 1976, provided treatment to more than 450 remote communities.

He persuaded many volunteers, including doctors, to donate their time to the cause. In three years his team travelled all over outback Australia. They treated 30,000 people, performed 1000 operations and prescribed more than 10,000 pairs of glasses.

Hollows became known as the "wild colonial boy" of Australian surgery. It's true he had an abiding love of the bush, but the tag was even more apt because Hollows had such a short temper. He could be extremely impatient, determined never to let anyone stand in his way. As he said: "When I've seen an opportunity I haven't sat down and called a committee meeting... we've gone and done it."

Hollows' attention soon focused further afield and through the 1980s he travelled the world, establishing eye health programmes in struggling countries. "The rich should not live longer simply because they are rich and can afford treatment, and the poor should not die prematurely simply because they are poor," he said.

He visited Nepal in 1985, Eritrea in 1987 and Vietnam in 1991, and blindness prevention programmes were established in Asia, Africa and South America. For several years Hollows was a consultant to the World Health Organization.

He launched training programmes in under-developed countries to teach local technicians to perform eye surgery, and battled Western companies over the price of lenses, until the lenses were eventually provided at cost price in these countries.

Eritrea, one of Africa's poorest nations, became a special cause. He wanted to help the Eritreans build their own eye lens factory and asked Australians to support his dream. They donated more than $6 million. So he had a factory built in Eritrea to make cheap plastic eye lenses that could be used to fix diseased eyes. In 1991 he received honorary citizenship from Eritrea, which meant a great deal to him.

In his last few years Hollows knew he was dying of cancer, but he never slowed the pace of his work, and established the Fred Hollows Foundation. It has been estimated that more than one million people can see today because of initiatives instigated by Hollows and followed by his foundation.

Hollows received many honours, though that was never his motivation. He received an Advance Australia Award in 1981, but, appalled at what he described as blatant government lack of interest in eye care for Aborigines, refused to accept the Order of Australia four years later. In 1990 he was given a Human Rights Medal and was named Australian of the Year. He was Humanist of the Year in 1991.

Hollows was married twice, in 1958 to Mary Skiller, who died in 1975, and in 1980 to Gabi O'Sullivan. He became an Australian citizen in 1989.

Australians showed what they thought of Hollows by turning out in their tens of thousands for his state funeral service in Sydney.

Murray Halberg

Champion sportsman, generous human being

BORN: EKETAHUNA, JULY 7, 1933.

No-one personified the Olympic spirit of triumphing over adversity better then Murray Halberg. He was so badly injured playing rugby when he was 17 that it was feared he would die. After months of rehabilitation, he was left with a withered left arm and had to teach himself to do everything, from writing to eating, with his right hand.

From the embers of that disaster arose the courage of a champion. Halberg won the 1960 Olympic 5000m gold medal and Empire Games three-mile golds in 1958 and 1962. He was the first New Zealander to break four minutes for the mile, and was the first great athlete to emerge from the Arthur Lydiard stable. His tenacious example influenced not only New Zealand but world athletics.

Halberg had a lovely fluent stride, but did not look like a champion – he was not physically impressive like his famous contemporary, Peter Snell. He was shorter and rather sinewy, but he had incredible willpower. Rivals like Barry Magee and Bill Baillie said that he was the hardest opponent they faced in the home stretch.

Halberg was – or hoped he was – a budding cricketer before his accident, but was already starting to enjoy some success as a runner. The opportunity to watch the 1950 Auckland Empire Games fuelled his desire to succeed at sport. After his accident, his athletics talent was nurtured by Lydiard, with his revolutionary endurance training methods.

"Arthur meant everything to me," said Halberg. "If I'd never met Arthur I would never have become a top runner. I may have got as far as winning a New Zealand title, but that would have been it. Arthur's advice, encouragement and expertise enabled me to reach a much higher level, to become an Olympic champion. And that was the springboard that enabled me to use my name to launch the Halberg Trust for Crippled Children [now the Halberg Trust]. Arthur was my mentor, my guide, my guru."

Halberg ran competitively at the 1954 Vancouver Empire Games, a bit-part player in the drama of the Bannister-Landy Miracle Mile. Two years later, at the 1956 Olympics, he was overawed and ran poorly in the 1500m final. But by 1958 he was a great runner. He sprinted away from the field at Cardiff to win the Empire Games three-mile gold medal, and afterwards had a triumphant, if strength-sapping, tour of Europe.

In 1960 he was favoured to win the Olympic 5000m title. He and Lydiard decided on the same tactics he'd employed at Cardiff – sprinting clear with three laps remaining, then holding on. The tactic called for boldness and tenacity, and Halberg had both those attributes. He ran a 61-second 10th lap in Rome and established a 20-metre break. Could he hold it? Slowly the chasing pack, led by Hans Grodotzki, of Poland, closed in. Hunters targeting their prey. Except that Halberg refused to be caught. He mustered his remaining reserves to sprint down the final straight, snatching several quick looks behind. Finally he hit the tape, staggered a couple of yards, and collapsed, exhausted. He was an Olympic champion.

Halberg's gold medal came only a short time after Snell burst on to the world stage by winning the 800m. It was perhaps the greatest day in New Zealand sport.

For three more years, Halberg ruled middle-distance running. In 1961 he broke three world records (two-mile, 4 x 1 mile relay and three-mile) within 19 days. At Perth in 1962 he ran brilliantly to retain the Empire Games three-mile crown. He made the 10,000m final at the 1964 Tokyo Olympics, but was past his best and finished down the field.

There followed a spell of coaching, but by then he was pouring his energy into his trust. Inspired by the example of the Canadians, he relaunched the Sportsman of the Year dinner so that it became the focal point of an annual fund-raising campaign. (The term "sportsman" came to be seen as sexist, and in 1992 the occasion became known as the Halberg Awards, despite Halberg's lack of enthusiasm for the name.)

He has been a slightly reticent public figure, more than willing to front fund-raising campaigns, but otherwise generally shying away from too much publicity. However, there was no more popular decision than when he was knighted in 1988. It was public acknowledgement that here was not only a champion sportsman, but a rare human being. Halberg travelled with New Zealand's 2002 Commonwealth Games and 2004 Olympic teams as a mentor for the athletes.

Neil Finn

The dream's not over

BORN: TE AWAMUTU, MAY 27, 1958.

Neil Finn has become a giant of the New Zealand music industry, an internationally-acclaimed singer and song-writer, who is noted for the warmth and emotion of his work.

It was Tim Finn who provided Neil, his younger brother by six years, with the early inspiration to make a career out of music. At their Te Awamutu home they sang harmonies and performed for their parents' friends. When Neil was still at school he could hardly help but be impressed when watching Tim perform as lead singer in the group Split Enz. "I first saw Split Enz in November 1972, in Auckland, when I was a pimply schoolboy," said Neil. "That performance made a lasting impression on me. I went back to Te Awamutu and wrote 'Split Enz' on my pencil case. I was a fan."

Finn boarded at Sacred Heart College, Auckland, then attended Te Awamutu College. He honed his musical skills by performing in local prisons and hospitals. When he left college he worked as a hospital orderly in Auckland, but music drew him. He was well received as the support act for Split Enz's 1976 New Zealand tour and the following year formed a group called After Hours with Mark Hough, Geoff Chunn and Alan Brown. Then he was invited to replace the departing Phil Judd in Split Enz. Neil didn't need to be asked twice – he arrived in London to join the band in April 1977, the start of seven successful years with the group.

Neil contributed immensely to Split Enz, including writing *I Got You*, which catapulted the band to international stardom. It was the biggest Australian single of 1980 and was voted Song of the Year at the Australian music awards. He eventually shared lead singer duties and even led the group in 1983-84, after brother Tim had departed.

By 1984 Split Enz had run its course and Neil formed another group, the Mullanes (after his mother's maiden name), with Paul Hester, Craig Hooper and Nick Seymour. The Mullanes moved to Los Angeles in 1985, staying in a cramped North Hollywood home while seeking a record label. This inspired a name change to Crowded House. A record deal was secured with Capitol. At first their debut album, *Crowded House*, was snubbed by New Zealand radio, but propelled by *Don't Dream It's Over*, which reached No 2 in the US charts, it became a hit and the group was on its way. *Temple of Low Men*, Crowded House's next album, was also warmly received.

The wheel turned full circle in 1991 when Tim was invited to join Crowded House and was part of the *Woodface* album. The album was a hit in Britain, going triple platinum.

Crowded House's *Together Alone* was released in 1993. The band won the prized Q magazine award for Best International Act in 1994, but wound up after producing *Recurring Dream*, a best-of album. It went out in style, with a massive charity concert in Sydney in November 1996. The last song Crowded House played was *Don't Dream It's Over*. It was an emotional moment and reduced the band and many of the 100,000-strong crowd to tears.

Neil became involved in other projects. He worked with Eddie Rayner on Enzso (the symphonic orchestration of the Split Enz music) and with Tim on *Finn*, in which the brothers produced and played the instruments. In 2004 they produced a second album, *Everyone Is Here*.

After Crowded House, Neil was keen to go solo. He recorded *Try Whistling This* in 1998 and followed it with *One Nil*. This was remixed and released in North America as *One All* in 2002. Among his other projects were *7 Worlds Collide*, a live album/DVD of an evening at the St James Theatre, Auckland, and a contribution to the soundtrack of the movie *Rain*. Finn has also produced and recorded with other leading New Zealand artists, including Bic Runga, Dave Dobbyn and The Mutton Birds.

By any measure, Neil Finn is among New Zealand's most successful recording artists. In 2001, when New Zealand's top 100 songs of the past 75 years were named, he had nine entries, including *Don't Dream It's Over* (2), *I Got You* (11) and *Weather With You* (16, with Tim Finn). Split Enz had eight entries, Crowded House six.

Neil lived in Melbourne for 12 years but he and his wife Sharon, whom he married in 1982, have settled in New Zealand. They have two sons, Liam and Elroy. Liam formed the pop band Betchadupa.

Neil and Tim Finn were given international achievement awards at the 2005 New Zealand Music Awards.

Edward Gibbon Wakefield

Self-serving, but a man who got things done

BORN: LONDON, MARCH 20, 1796. DIED: WELLINGTON, MAY 16, 1862.

Few would describe Edward Gibbon Wakefield as an endearing personality, but his energy, imagination and reckless pursuit of success led to his becoming an important figure in the European colonisation of New Zealand.

Wakefield, a recalcitrant child, was expelled from several schools. His father, a farmer and land agent, wielded some influence and helped his son gain various minor diplomatic posts. Like the sons of many minor officials, the search for quick money was a lifelong driving force. Wakefield eloped with, and then married, 16-year-old heiress Eliza Pattle in 1816. The marriage made Wakefield rich. After she died in 1820 Wakefield turned his attention to scoring another financial windfall from marriage.

In 1826 he abducted 15-year-old schoolgirl Ellen Turner, the daughter of a wealthy manufacturer, and married her at Gretna Green. Her shocked parents located the pair in Calais, where Wakefield had holed up. The subsequent court case was sensational. Wakefield narrowly avoided being hanged, and was jailed for three years. His brother, William, and various accomplices were also jailed. The marriage was annulled.

While in Newgate prison, Wakefield wrote *A Letter from Sydney*, which was released in 1829. The book outlined his theory of colonisation, which aimed to create a vertical slice of English society in the new colonies. To Wakefield, the key was to set a "sufficient price" for the purchase of land for settlers.

On his release, Wakefield, realising he would never be considered respectable in England, looked abroad. He helped form the National Colonization Society, pushing colonisation as an answer to Britain's overcrowding and poverty, and played a role in the British colonisation of South Australia and Canada.

In the late 1830s he was Lord Durham's unofficial adviser in Canada – such appointments could never be official because of the nimbus of impropriety that surrounded him, though in 1842 he was elected to the Lower Canada Assembly.

His special preoccupation was with New Zealand, which he described in 1836 (16 years before setting foot there) as "the fittest in the world for colonisation… the most beautiful country with the finest climate". He established the New Zealand Association in 1837. The association soon engaged in disputes with the Church Missionary Society and the Colonial Office, both of which suspected it of being self-serving.

In 1838 the association became the New Zealand Company and, under William Wakefield's leadership, its first settlers were sent to Wellington, forcing William Hobson to quickly organise the Treaty of Waitangi on behalf of the British Crown. Other New Zealand Company settlements followed in Wanganui, Nelson and New Plymouth.

The British Government did not agree with Wakefield that the company should be given the rights of self-government within its settlements. In 1843 a group of company settlers from Nelson tried to pursue a dubious claim to the Wairau block, near Blenheim. When negotiations between the Ngati Toa chiefs and company officials became heated, firing broke out and there were several deaths on both sides. Wakefield's brother, Arthur, surrendered but was killed by Ngati Toa chief Te Rangihaeata, who was incensed by the death of his wife. This incident was the culmination of the arrogance and misunderstanding which typified New Zealand Company relations with Maori.

Undaunted, Edward Gibbon, in association with John Godley, planned a Church of England settlement in Canterbury in 1852. He finally made it to New Zealand himself, after years of long-range dealings.

Wakefield continued agitating for self-government, rather than New Zealand's status as a crown colony, and involved himself in national politics. He could make no progress with Governor George Grey, who had contempt for him, but in 1853 was elected to the House of Representatives and on to the Wellington Provincial Council. Wakefield was, briefly, a political power-broker, but there continued to be distrust of him. Key political figures, such as James FitzGerald and Robert Wynyard, were suspicious of him, despite his powers of speech and ability to persuade. FitzGerald said that the only security against Wakefield was to hate him intensely.

He had had several strokes in the 1840s and his health was erratic. In 1855 Wakefield fell ill with rheumatic fever. He resigned from his official posts and spiralled into depression, taking no interest in public affairs and seldom leaving his Wellington home on The Terrace.

There can be no doubting the impact of the Wakefield family. Brothers Edward Gibbon, William, Arthur, David and Felix, and Jerningham (Edward Gibbon's son), and Felix's sons, Oliver and Edward, were unloved but influential political figures of their time.

David Lange

Right man, right time

BORN: AUCKLAND, AUGUST 4, 1942. DIED: AUCKLAND, AUGUST 13, 2005.

David Lange was a man of his time. After the dictatorial leadership of Robert Muldoon, New Zealand was ready for a different sort of Prime Minister, and Lange was certainly that. He presided over one of the most innovative governments in New Zealand history.

Lange, a large man physically, was educated at Otahuhu College and graduated from Auckland University in 1966 with an LLB. After two years travelling overseas, he returned to tutor at Auckland University and completed an LLM. He worked as a lawyer in Kaikohe and then Auckland, and became well-known for his generosity, often taking cases for people who did not have the means to pay him.

Lange stood unsuccessfully for the Auckland City Council in 1974 and for Hobson in the 1975 general election. He got to Parliament in 1977, when he won the Mangere by-election. From there, Lange had a dazzlingly quick rise.

Within two years he was Labour's deputy leader. He challenged Bill Rowling for the party leadership in 1980 and lost narrowly, but in 1983 did replace Rowling. He was seen as Labour's counter to Muldoon.

With his quick tongue, Lange was comfortable in public and proved a charismatic leader. He had around him youngish, assertive politicians, such as Roger Douglas, Richard Prebble and Mike Moore, and this group planned a successful election campaign in 1984.

Labour won with a 17-seat majority and Lange, at 41, became New Zealand's youngest Prime Minister of the 20th century. The Lange Government undertook a radical restructuring of the country's economy. The architect was Finance Minister Douglas, but Lange gave him his head.

Lange, as Minister of Foreign Affairs, proved an eloquent advocate of Labour's nuclear-free policy. The highpoint was the televised Oxford Union debate in 1985, when he argued that "nuclear weapons are morally indefensible" with American Moral Majority leader Jerry Falwell. Lange's "I can smell the uranium on your breath" quip drew huge publicity. New Zealand's strong stance on refusing entry to its harbours of nuclear-armed or propelled ships caused its split from the Anzus alliance with Australia and the United States.

A superb, relaxed, pungent and at times self-deprecating speaker, Lange delivered some biting one-liners. Jim Bolger, he said, had "all the intellectual rigour of an amoeba" and Winston Peters was "the only Member of Parliament named after a concrete block, and I can understand that". He said United Party leader Peter Dunne's life was so dull that if it was re-run, he wouldn't be in it. He described a Secretary of Defence as equipped with wall-to-wall smarm that would make Lockwood Smith look like an untipped waiter. And he spoke of the difficulty of flying to the West Coast because the planes were smaller than he was.

Labour won the 1987 election with an increased majority, though the results were bizarre. Labour did better in traditional National areas, but struggled in previously strong Labour seats. During the early years of the Lange Government, the "yuppie" culture flourished and investment companies prospered, but that all changed with the October 1987 sharemarket crash. In 1987 Lange took on the education portfolio and ushered in the Tomorrow's Schools programme of reforms.

Gradually, Lange's Labour team fell apart. He separated from his first wife, Naomi (nee Crampton) to live with his speech writer, Margaret Pope, whom he later married. When Douglas proposed a radical flat income tax, Lange got twitchy about the pace of the reforms, saying it was time "for a cup of tea".

He was strongly criticised by Prebble, who he sacked. This led to Douglas' resignation. Lange stood down as Prime Minister in August 1989, becoming Attorney-General. Lange's troubles within his own party were not reflected in his performance in Parliament, where he was endlessly entertaining. He remained in the House until 1996, but in his final years there gradually drifted away from the hustle and bustle of political life.

After leaving Parliament he became a national rugby league and motor sport administrator.

Lange was beset by health problems. He'd had a stomach stapling operation to help shed weight. But in 2002 it was announced that he was having chemotherapy for a deadly protein disorder, amyloidosis. He died three years later, soon after having a leg amputated. His memoirs, *My Life*, were published only days before his death and were notable for their strong criticism of many of his former Cabinet colleagues.

Lange was made a Companion of Honour in 1990 and was appointed a Member of the Order of New Zealand (ONZ) in 2003.

Rob Muldoon

The feisty Nat who changed the face of politics

BORN: AUCKLAND, SEPTEMBER 25, 1921. DIED: AUCKLAND, AUGUST 5, 1992.

Few New Zealand politicians have polarised opinion as Robert Muldoon did. He was Prime Minister and Minister of Finance from 1975-84, and, with his feisty, combative nature, changed the face of New Zealand politics.

Muldoon was the last New Zealand Prime Minister who fought in World War II and grew up at a time when Britain was still referred to as "Home". For someone so outspoken, he could be extremely conservative, perhaps best seen in his statement upon becoming Prime Minister that he hoped to leave New Zealand "no worse off than I found it".

He was educated at Mount Albert Grammar and, after serving in the army, became an accountant. In 1947 Muldoon joined the Junior Nationals and he stood unsuccessfully for Parliament in 1954 and 1957.

In 1960 he became one of the new wave of National MPs in Keith Holyoake's Government. He was to represent Tamaki for the next 31 years. Muldoon's forceful personality, energy and ability stood out and by 1963 he was Under-Secretary to the Minister of Finance. Even then he was known as "Piggy", though the tag's origins remain unclear. He gained much exposure in 1967 when he oversaw the introduction of decimal currency.

He was Minister of Tourism in 1967, but had loftier ambitions and was soon promoted to the key Finance portfolio. Muldoon was never afraid to express his views, even crossing the floor to vote with the Opposition over abolishing the death penalty.

When Holyoake resigned he was replaced by Jack Marshall, but Muldoon felt he would be a better leader and offered Marshall only muted support. Using his ability in front of the television cameras to rally public support, he supplanted Marshall in 1974. In the following year's elections, Muldoon and his fellow "Young Turks" swept to power, demolishing Bill Rowling's Labour by 55 seats to 32.

Muldoon was a vigorous, abrasive and even cruel campaigner, but built a huge following among a group that became known as "Rob's Mob". On one occasion he snuffed out a challenge to his leadership by going on television and appealing successfully to his "Mob" for support. He became increasingly autocratic and desperate to retain power, and narrowly won the 1978 and 1981 elections, despite the repercussions of the 1970s energy crisis and Britain's entry into the EEC. The 1981 election was fought against the background of that year's divisive Springbok tour, which Muldoon had refused to stop.

He ruled his Cabinet, brooking little criticism, and was feared by many colleagues. Television viewers became accustomed to his grim humour, rough handling of interviewers and cackling laugh. He was also a master at the quip. Asked about New Zealanders migrating to Australia, he said they were raising the IQ of both countries. His reaction after the infamous underarm cricket incident: "It was appropriate that the Australians were wearing yellow."

On the international stage he was uneasy and controversial. His sharp tongue upset many overseas dignitaries. He had a habit of creating enemies among African leaders and did himself no favours by his derisive reference to United States President Jimmy Carter as "a peanut farmer".

The tide eventually turned against Muldoon, and by the early 1980s the New Zealand economy was in poor shape. He imposed wage and price controls and borrowed massively, partly to fund the Think Big projects. There were positive initiatives, too, such as the Closer Economic Relations programme with Australia.

Faced with declining support within his own caucus he called a snap election in 1984. He was well-beaten (56 seats to 37) by David Lange's new-look Labour, and took defeat badly. There was one final and, in retrospect, farcical controversy. While Muldoon was still technically Prime Minister, a currency crisis occurred. By convention, the caretaker government would defer to the incoming government. However, Muldoon stubbornly refused for some time Lange's requests to devalue the dollar.

Though he was supplanted as National leader by Jim McLay, Muldoon remained in Parliament another seven years, often criticisng his own party and looking increasingly disenchanted. Still, he remained an icon to some, especially the elderly.

Muldoon was an exceptionally fast and decisive worker and delved into many projects, even while running the country. He wrote five books, hosted a radio talkback show, did television advertisements and even took the role of the narrator in the stage production of *The Rocky Horror Show*.

In 1983 Muldoon became the only New Zealand Prime Minister to be knighted while in office.

Thomas Edmonds

The businessman who rose to the top

BORN: POPLAR, LONDON, OCTOBER 13, 1858. DIED: CHRISTCHURCH, JUNE 2, 1932.

In 1879 a disgruntled customer walked into Thomas Edmonds' small grocer's shop on the south-west corner of Randolph St and what is now Edmonds St in Christchurch and asked if his new baking powder would improve her scones. He assured her they would be "sure to rise". The subsequent rising-sun-with-cakes image on Edmonds baking products has become New Zealand's most colourful and recognisable trademark.

Edmonds wrote the biggest-selling book in New Zealand history. *Edmonds Cookery Book* was published in 1907. It comprised 50 pages of "economical everyday recipes and cooking hints". Its phenomenal success continues and the updated, enlarged version, with recipes on everything from pavlova to hokey pokey, remains an essential item in a vast number of New Zealand kitchens. It has been reprinted dozens of times and sales have topped 3.5 million. Many spin-off Edmonds cook books have also been produced.

Edmonds grew up in London, where he worked for the Allen and Sons confectionery business, gaining experience in mixing various powders. He married Jane Irvine (they shared the same birthday) in June 1879 and they immediately set off for New Zealand on the Waitangi.

In Christchurch he "drifted into making my own baking powder". He found that New Zealand women were complaining that the imported variety of baking powder gave variable results. With his business struggling, he turned his attention to making a New Zealand baking powder. The results were spectacular and more than 125 years later Edmonds baking powder is an institution, a reliable product that, as its creator claimed, makes cakes rise. Edmonds spent about three years perfecting his baking powder while his wife tended to the shop. Finally he went around his neighbourhood asking customers to try it out, an early form of the money-back guarantee.

In the early 1890s Edmonds moved his now-flourishing business to Ferry Road. By 1912, it was producing more than one million tins of baking power a year and by 1928 that number had risen to 2.5 million. Even after Edmonds went into semi-retirement he remained chairman of the private company that bore his name. He also maintained a connection with the Australian Cream of Tartar company that supplied the raw material for the baking powder.

Edmonds became one of Christchurch's leading citizens, a person of great generosity. Christchurch Mayor Daniel Sullivan said at his funeral: "The death of Mr Edmonds removes from our midst one of the most philanthropic citizens we have known." He left a legacy of buildings and parks that were bequeathed in the hope that they would encourage others to help make Christchurch the beautiful Garden City that the pioneers had planned.

In 1923 Edmonds commissioned an elaborate garden to be built around his newly-opened factory in Ferry Road. The garden and factory, which are featured on the cover of the cookbook, have delighted generations of visitors, winning many awards in civic beautifying competitions. The site has proved consistently popular for outdoor wedding photography.

After the city council acquired a major portion of the original Edmonds Factory Garden, the building was demolished in 1990, though the garden was retained and enhanced.

Edmonds and his wife celebrated the 50th jubilee of their residence in Christchurch in 1929 by building a band rotunda and shelter on the north bank of the Avon River, between Colombo and Manchester Streets. On the south bank he gave a clock tower with telephone and letter-box. He arranged for an area of Cambridge Terrace that he had designed, in the vicinity of the rotunda, to be named Poplar Crescent, after his birthplace.

Known for his honesty in business dealings, Edmonds treated his huge staff well and engendered a family atmosphere. During the Depression, his Christchurch factory was the first in New Zealand to introduce a 40-hour/five-day working week.

He travelled to Sydney to see the opening of the harbour bridge in 1932. Shortly after his return Edmonds, who had always enjoyed good health, began suffering heart problems. He died soon after. An indication of Edmonds' standing in Christchurch was that after his death the flags of the Municipal Chambers and the electricity department flew at half-mast. Thomas and Jane Edmonds had eight children.

These days Edmonds products – there have been more than 200 down the years – are made in Auckland by Bluebird Foods. In 2004, to mark the 125th anniversary of the Edmonds business, the Edmonds Heritage Scholarship was set up to help with study in Christchurch within the heritage field.

Colin McCahon

The modernist who enhanced cultural nationalism

BORN: TIMARU, AUGUST 1, 1919. DIED: AUCKLAND, MAY 27, 1987.

As with many great painters, Colin McCahon's talent seemed to be more appreciated after his death than during most of his life. When the *Urewera Mural*, one of his most famous paintings, was stolen from the Aniwanawa Visitor's Centre in 1997, it became a highly-publicised political stunt. But even without the publicity surrounding the theft, McCahon's work has escalated in value over the past two decades and he is regarded internationally as an artist of rare ability.

His most significant works are wall-sized paintings with a dark background, overlaid with religious words in stark white. His paintings generate considerable controversy, but few question his talent or pre-eminent position in the history of modern New Zealand art.

Colin John McCahon was born in Timaru, but was raised in Dunedin and Oamaru. Art was an early passion and the family were regular visitors to the Dunedin Art Gallery. McCahon received private art tuition from Russell Clark. On leaving Otago Boys' High School, he worked in a furniture store until 1937, when he enrolled at the Dunedin School of Art and prospered under the guidance of Robert Field, who had recently arrived from England and had ideas about the use of colour that were most unusual at the time.

McCahon's painting career began in 1939. He became a member of The Group, a set of Christchurch-based artists, and showed his work at their exhibitions for the next three decades. He married Annie Hamblett, a talented artist, in 1942, but while McCahon chased seasonal work – as a labourer, gardener or fruit-picker in Wellington, Christchurch and Nelson – they did not always live together. His painting continued to develop, though for years he received a somewhat frosty reception from many in the art world.

He was influenced by other artists, notably Gaugin, and benefited from his overseas travels. Most importantly, he spent four months studying art in the United States in 1958, after which his painting changed – it became larger, more loosely painted and more abstract. In 1953 he began work at the Auckland City Art Gallery, becoming the deputy director before his departure in 1964. He was not the easiest person to get along with, being inclined to be intolerant of those who disagreed with him, and had drinking problems that developed into alcoholism.

McCahon was the first major New Zealand artist to see the decorative potential of words and numbers. His most celebrated use of this technique was the 1954 *I am*. He had always been drawn to religion. His best-known early religious work was *I Paul to You at Ngatimote* in 1946, the first of many paintings in which he placed events from Christ's life in a New Zealand setting.

His modernist approach caused lively debate and he was always disappointed by the lack of comprehension of his work. Still, there were regular McCahon exhibitions in Wellington, Dunedin and Auckland, and he found that Auckland artists were more accepting of his ideas than the more conservative painters in the South Island.

McCahon's *Northland Panels*, which he began working on in 1959 on his return from the United States, became pivotal to his art's future direction. A painting of considerable size, it consolidated McCahon's habit of presenting a landscape in several facets, each reflecting a different aspect of the same scene, yet together forming a whole. The panels are painted on unstretched canvas hung like wall hangings, giving the effect of being less finished or less academic than was appropriate at the time.

He produced some of his best work in the late 1950s and 1960s. Besides the *Northland* drawings, there were *The Wake* and *Tomorrow will be the same but not as this is*. Then came a series of paintings called *Gate*, which represented a way through the nuclear weapons threat. McCahon began his large *Waterfall* series in 1964, the year he began lecturing on painting at the Elam School of Fine Arts.

For a number of his works, McCahon drew on Maori history, language and tradition, as in the *Parihaka Triptych*, *The Shining Cuckoo* and the *Urewera Mural*.

McCahon was a significant contributor to the cultural nationalism that sprang up in New Zealand from the 1930s. New Zealand, he said, was "a landscape with too few lovers".

He was a pioneer in other ways, too – he was New Zealand's first and arguably greatest modernist, particularly in his landscape work, and one of the first New Zealand painters to make a living from his work.

Colin Murdoch

The lateral thinker who saved millions of lives

BORN: CHRISTCHURCH, FEBRUARY 6, 1929.

Colin Murdoch, a Timaru man to whom millions around the world owe their lives, says his inventions have required equal parts knowledge, experience and lateral thinking. He might also have added perseverance, because at times Murdoch has been so far ahead of his time that authorities have not grasped the importance of his work.

He grew up in Christchurch, where, despite a natural talent for chemistry, he struggled at school because he was dyslexic. He was always an inquiring and inventive boy – at 10, to his mother's horror, he discovered how to make gunpowder. When he was 13 he won a Royal Humane Society medal for saving a drowning man at the New Brighton estuary.

Like his father, he became a pharmacist, though later he was drawn to becoming a veterinarian and eventually he used his extraordinary talent to revolutionise medical and veterinary science.

Murdoch's first patented invention was the filled disposable plastic syringe, in 1956. He was just 27, and when he presented his concept to the New Zealand Health Department and other government authorities they scoffed at him, calling such a syringe, which he felt should replace the standard glass syringe, "too futuristic". Today its importance is unquestioned.

As Murdoch said: "Dangerous bacteria and viruses were transferred from one patient to another by doctors who used improperly-sterilised reusable glass hypodermic syringes and needles to inject other patients. It is impossible to comprehend the catastrophic consequences of this situation if such practices were still occurring today. Diseases of such ultimate incurability and virulence as the HIV and the Aids virus, hepatitis A, B, C and most, recently, a new D form... and TB to name just a few. Instead of now having to care for, and contain, the several million infected people throughout the world who have Aids, the numbers could well be 30 or 40 per cent of the entire population."

His syringes have had other immense benefits, too. For example, diabetes sufferers, with their need for regular injections of insulin, would be lost without them.

Murdoch created several versions of the syringe. In the early 1970s he produced the disposable automatic vaccinator syringe, of which half a billion are sold every year in the United States alone.

One of his major breakthroughs was the tranquilliser gun, in the 1960s. Murdoch was seeking a more effective vaccinator for animals and this led to a gun that would fire darts with velocity and speed, but reasonably quietly. Always a hands-on inventor, Murdoch spent much time in hunting situations in Africa modifying and perfecting his tranquilliser gun, which quickly became standard use around the world. In 1979 it was used on a human, by the Armed Offenders Squad during a hostage situation in Auckland.

In 1966 Murdoch had three inventions patented – a silent burglar alarm, a new heat-detection device for fire, and a new electrical wiring system. He then combined them to produce the silent burglar and fire alarm, which could trigger phone calls to the local fire or police station.

Another of more than 40 patented inventions, and one of his most significant, was the child-proof cap for medical containers, which he produced in 1976.

His company, Paxarms, formed in 1961 to market tranquilliser guns, continues to flourish. It now produces a variety of animal-based equipment for remote injection, as well as equipment for the removal of tissue from a variety of species. Tasman Vaccine, the Australian-based company that marketed and sold his syringes, made huge profits.

Murdoch is just what many would imagine an inventor to be, in that he would wake in the middle of the night and immediately have to jot down his latest thoughts. Often he would be found at his kitchen table, ruler and pencil in hand, making preliminary sketches. He has lived an exciting life, travelling extensively. He has narrowly avoided being in planes that have crashed or been hijacked and has survived life-threatening fires and typhoons. His inventions have not made him particularly wealthy. As he stated once: "Patenting an invention gives you the right to sue, but not the money to do so."

However, he has been recognised globally. At the 1976 World Inventors Fair in Brussels, Murdoch won three gold medals and a bronze. He has been similarly honoured by the New Zealand Design Council. In 2000 he was made a member of the Order of New Zealand.

Archie McIndoe

The maestro who worked miracles with the Guinea Pig Club

BORN: DUNEDIN, MAY 4, 1900. DIED: LONDON, APRIL 12, 1960.

It was the human side of Archie McIndoe that made him so special. Not only was McIndoe one of the world's great plastic surgeons, but he was inordinately helpful in his patients' rehabilitation. He remained in contact with them long after their treatment finished, and it was not unusual for him to lend his former patients money or attend their weddings.

McIndoe grew up in Dunedin. His father, John, owned a printing firm and his mother, Mabel, was a popular singer and artist. After attending Otago Boys' High School, McIndoe studied at the University of Otago, qualifying as a doctor in 1924.

He had a stint as a house surgeon at Waikato Hospital, and was then awarded a fellowship to the Mayo Clinic at Rochester, Minnesota. He graduated with an MSc at the University of Minnesota in 1927, then spent three years as assistant surgeon at the clinic.

The lure of England was strong, though, and in 1930 he travelled to London, where he was disappointed to discover that there was no job awaiting him. His cousin, Harold Gillies, the doyen of plastic surgeons, came to his assistance. Gillies pointed him towards a career in plastic surgery, offering him a position as his assistant at St Bartholomew's Hospital and making him a partner in his private practice.

McIndoe passed his Fellow of Royal College of Surgeons exams in 1932. His first permanent appointment in England was as general surgeon and lecturer at the Hospital for Tropical Diseases and the London School of Hygiene and Tropical Medicine. But it was as a plastic surgeon that he was to make his reputation.

In 1938 McIndoe was chosen as a consultant in plastic surgery to the Royal Air Force and at the outbreak of World War II he became the surgeon in charge of the pioneering plastic and jaw injury centre at the Queen Victoria Hospital, East Grinstead.

He established what became known as his Guinea Pig Club and had incredible success helping war victims with horrific war injuries, not only fixing their faces, but remaining involved in their lives. The down-to-earth McIndoe made such an impression with his friendly, compassionate manner that decades after his death, Guinea Pig Club patients still met annually to salute the memory of the man they called "The Maestro". He referred to his patients as his "boys" and showed tremendous concern for their well-being, working exceptionally long hours. It was said that "he gave many new life and the courage to face it".

McIndoe also managed to get the East Grinstead community involved in his work. Recovering pilots tended not to mix in the community because of their disfigurement and their need for so many operations – McIndoe operated on some of them 30 times. Two of McIndoe's good friends, Neville and Elaine Blond, assisted in developing community support so that pilots did not feel ostracised. The Blonds persuaded some families to accept the recovering pilots into their homes as guests. Appropriately, when a burns centre was opened at Queen Victoria Hospital in 1961, it was called the Blond-McIndoe Unit.

McIndoe was a man of vision. He once said: "The next great era in surgery will be when we learn how to transplant tissue from one person to another. I foresee the day when limbs, kidneys, lungs and even hearts will be surgically replaced."

His efforts were recognised in many ways. He became vice-president of the Council of the College of Surgeons, and president of the British Association of Plastic Surgeons. He was made a Hunterian Professor in 1939 and the Bradshaw Lecturer in 1958 (when his subject was facial burns). He helped found the British Association of Plastic Surgeons. The American College of Surgeons made him a fellow and he was knighted in 1947. McIndoe married twice, to Adonia Aitken, of Dunedin, in 1924 and, shortly after that marriage was dissolved in 1953, to Constance Belcham.

One of his most famous patients was Richard Hillary, a fighter pilot who was badly burnt in a crash during the Battle of Britain. Hillary, who was later killed in action, wrote a graphic account of his dealings with McIndoe, whom he categorised as inspirational, in *The Last Enemy*. That book was the basis of a Stuart Hoar play called *The Face Maker*, which was staged in Christchurch in 2001, with Mark Hadlow playing McIndoe.

Samuel Marsden

The driving force behind Christianity in New Zealand

BORN: FARSLEY, YORKSHIRE, JULY 28, 1764. DIED: WINDSOR, NEW SOUTH WALES, MAY 12, 1838.

Samuel Marsden was the driving force behind the establishment of Christianity in New Zealand in the early 19th century and an important influence in the early European settlement of the fledgling country.

Marsden's parents were Wesleyan Methodists, and after a grammar school education he eschewed a business career to devote himself to the Christian ministry. He became a student at Magdalene College, Cambridge, in 1790. Three years later he was appointed assistant chaplain of New South Wales. He was ordained early in 1793 and married Elizabeth Fristan a month later – they were to have eight children – then set sail for Australia. It was a difficult voyage on a convict ship, but his zeal won over his fellow travellers and he was soon conducting services and giving sermons.

Marsden settled well in Sydney, where he lived at Parramatta. He began buying land – he eventually owned more than 3000 acres – and became a successful farmer. In 1795 he was appointed a magistrate and soon after he became Superintendent of Government Affairs.

He was promoted to chaplain of the colony in 1800 and began to concentrate more on apostolic labours. In 1804 he became local agent for the London Missionary Society's Pacific operations. Gradually his attention turned to Maori – he often accommodated Maori in his house and one of his early visitors was the powerful Rangihoua chief Te Pahi.

Marsden returned to London in 1807 and convinced the Missionary Society to extend its mission to New Zealand. However, the reputation of Maori as cannibals deterred most would-be missionaries from travelling to New Zealand and recruitment was not easy. In 1809 Marsden left London aboard the Ann. Nga Puhi chief Ruatara was also aboard and during the eight months he spent with Marsden, he taught him much about Maori customs and the rudiments of the language.

It proved difficult to get boats to stop at New Zealand, so Marsden bought his own ship, the Active. His first trip to New Zealand was in December 1814. There were graphic tales of previous European visitors being killed and eaten by Maori. But Marsden, who never lacked courage, spent his first night in the Bay of Islands sleeping beside Maori warriors. He had early success at Matauri Bay, when he persuaded Ngati Uru and Nga Puhi to make peace. On Christmas Day, 1814, he gave what is believed to be the first formal Christian religious service in New Zealand.

Marsden supervised the affairs of the mission from Sydney for the next 24 years and returned to New Zealand for visits in 1819, 1820 (when he spent nine months exploring the upper North Island), 1823, 1827, 1830 and 1837. He dealt with many of the leading Maori of his time, including Hongi Hika, Ruatara and Korokoro. Te Rauparaha visited him in Sydney in 1830.

In 1815 Marsden had a seminary built at Parramatta for the instruction of young Maori and many New Zealand chiefs and sons of chiefs stayed there. In New South Wales his relentless acquisition of land – he employed a large number of people, including Maori, to work on his farms – caused resentment and he also had many disagreements with the Governor, Lachlan Macquarie. His reputation was sullied when he was dismissed as a magistrate in 1822 after allegations of legal impropriety.

In difficult circumstances, Marsden did well in New Zealand, though there were few converts to Christianity until the 1830s. He intervened to try to restore peace between warring Maori tribes, and he bought land on which to establish schools, churches and farms, and built a strong relationship with pioneer missionary Henry Williams, in whom he vested much authority. Marsden's final trip to New Zealand, in the company of his daughter Martha, became a triumphant procession through Northland.

Despite his Australian reputation as "the flogging parson", the evidence suggests that the Marsden who was seen in New Zealand was a more generous and dynamic person. Besides his efforts to introduce Christianity to New Zealand, Marsden made a notable contribution to the eventual British occupation of New Zealand. It was Marsden who urged the appointment of a British Resident with proper authority, to whom Maori could appeal for redress.

In 1907 an impressive cross in honour of Marsden was unveiled in the Bay of Islands. It bears this inscription:

ON CHRISTMAS DAY, 1814
THE FIRST CHRISTIAN SERVICE IN
NEW ZEALAND
WAS HELD ON THIS SPOT
BY THE REV. SAMUEL MARSDEN

Peter Fraser

The great war-time leader

BORN: FEARN, SCOTLAND, AUGUST 28, 1884. DIED: WELLINGTON, DECEMBER 12, 1950.

History has been kind to Peter Fraser, whom some now regard as New Zealand's finest Prime Minister. He led the country from April 1940-December 1949, the longest span of a Labour Prime Minister, and showed his greatness during World War II.

Fraser was born in the Scottish highlands. Reading was always a passion. He devoured the works of British socialist writers Keir Hardie and Robert Blatchford and throughout his life could quote extensively from a vast range of writers. This ability was hard-won, because even when young he suffered poor eyesight and wore thick spectacles. In his last years he was nearly blind.

In 1910 he was lured to New Zealand by the progressive nature of the young country. Pat Fraser, as he was known then, arrived in Auckland in 1911, an earnest, gangly young man. Working as a wharfie, he was soon involved in union affairs. He joined the New Zealand Socialist Party and was Michael Savage's campaign manager when Savage stood for Auckland Central.

Fraser was a militant unionist, who represented the Federation of Labour during the bitter 1912 miners' strike at Waihi. He moved to Wellington in 1913 and helped found the Social Democratic Party. He was involved in more strike action, was arrested and bound over to keep the peace, which helped persuade him that better progress could be made through appropriate parliamentary action.

In 1916 Fraser was part of a small group that created the Labour Party. World War I was under way and though not a pacifist, he opposed conscription that did not embrace wealth as well as manpower. He was jailed for 12 months for advocating repeal of the conscription laws. On his release he edited the *Maoriland Worker* and the *New Zealand Worker*, both Labour Party organs.

Fraser entered Parliament in 1918, representing Wellington Central. He held the seat until 1946, when it was renamed Brooklyn. He was a man of immense energy. He became Labour Party president in 1920 and served on the Wellington City Council from 1919-23 and 1933-36. In 1919 he married Janet Munro. It proved to be an endearing and sustaining association.

During Labour's long spell in opposition, Fraser became noted for his oratory and debating skills, his mastery of parliamentary procedure, his vast knowledge and his stamina. He helped devise much of the party policy.

Labour swept to power in 1935 and Fraser became Prime Minister Savage's deputy, taking the key portfolios of education and health. He made access to secondary school education a priority and in 1938 pushed through the Social Security Act. Few politicians had his single-minded focus or matched his 17-hour work days.

Savage became very ill and Fraser assumed virtual leadership of the Government in 1939. One battle he won was in evicting the increasingly recalcitrant John A Lee from the party.

Fraser became Prime Minister on Savage's death in 1940 and represented New Zealand with tenacity and insight at war meetings in Europe, the Middle East and the United States.

He insisted that New Zealand retain control over its forces, and equipped General Freyberg, commander of the Second New Zealand Expeditionary Force, with a charter, committing him to report to, and secure the agreement of, the New Zealand Government on major undertakings involving New Zealand troops.

When Japan entered the war Fraser decided to keep New Zealand forces in the Middle East, rather than following Australia and recalling them to the Pacific.

Fraser's strengths were amplified by the war. He had remarkable command of detail, the courage to make difficult decisions and the confidence to operate on the international stage. At the formation of the United Nations in San Francisco in 1945 he was an outstanding figure, pressing the rights of small nations, opposing the veto power accorded the five great powers and playing a leading part in shaping the trusteeship powers of the United Nations charter.

In 1946 he took the Native Affairs portfolio, which he renamed Maori Affairs. This had long been an area of interest to him.

Labour lost power in December 1949 and Fraser became leader of the Opposition. Worn out by years of relentless work, his health failed and he died a year later.

Fraser was never held in the same public affection as Savage and his contemporaries have identified his failings – he was badly-organised, inconsiderate of others, rarely able to forget or forgive a grievance and prone to bully. But when the full range of his achievements is assessed, he has a secure place among New Zealand's great men.

John Clarke

The comic genius who showed New Zealand how to laugh at itself

BORN: PALMERSTON NORTH, JULY 29, 1948.

Nearly 30 years after moving to Melbourne, John Clarke still has New Zealanders coming up to him on the street and barking, "Get in behind!" Clarke's Taihape cow-cocky persona, Fred Dagg, struck a chord in the mid-1970s and became the most popular comedy character in New Zealand history.

Fred Dagg's Greatest Hits achieved gold status the day it was released and within three weeks the record's sales totalled 85,000. The first two editions of *Fred Dagg's Yearbook* sold out before the book was released. He did a six-month national tour in 1976, performing in front of packed houses every night. Fred Dagg was a public figure for less than four years, but his unique appearance, and some of his expressions, are timeless. He showed the country how to laugh at itself.

John Clarke, the comic genius who invented the character, grew up in Palmerston North, then Wellington. He attended Scots College until an abrupt parting of the ways in his sixth form year. He has had little complimentary to say about the school since. At Victoria University he dabbled in a variety of subjects – law, arts, economics – but never got near a degree. It was an important time though, because he became part of the university revue, and, appearing regularly at Downstage, honed his acting talents. Others at the university then included Paul Holmes, Sam Neill and Ginette MacDonald, all of whom went on to make a splash in the entertainment world.

After a spell of OE in England, Clarke returned to a variety of jobs, including shearing, driving a van, labouring and working as a clerk for the NZBC. Along with Holmes and company, he appeared in *Buck House* in 1974, playing the part of Ken Giles.

His breakthrough came at the end of 1973, when, as Fred Dagg, he appeared on the *Gallery* current affairs programme. Dagg's flat, deadpan delivery and simplistic view of the world made him a cult hero, and his trademark black singlet and gumboots quickly became haute couture.

Some of the Dagg skits have become classics. In an early one, he was duck shooting on a traffic island outside the DIC building in Lambton Quay when interviewer David Exel approached him and asked what he was doing. "Get in behind," Dagg growled. Soon he gave viewers the hayseed flea race, his radical solution to the energy crisis and his take on daylight saving.

Fred Dagg made regular appearances on *Gallery*, *Nationwide* and *Tonight at Nine*. A Fred Dagg comedy show pilot, *The Wonderful World Of*, drew rave reviews, but the programme never got off the ground. Some politicians didn't take kindly to his jibes – the Labour Government got huffy about him for a while in 1974, though Prime Minister Bill Rowling later appeared in a skit in the pilot. Television New Zealand did not seem to know how to react to the Dagg phenomenon. Two staff members quit when Dagg appeared on current affairs programmes. It was only his overwhelming popularity that kept him on screen until the end of 1976.

By then he'd appeared on *Country Calendar* and announced that he had six sons, all called Trevor. There had been many variations on the theme – *The Naked and the Dagg*, *Moby Dagg*, *Wuthering Dagg*, *A Dagg at My Table*. After his record was released he had half the country singing, "You don't know how lucky you are". Clarke was Television Personality of the Year in 1974 and 1975, and in 1976 was New Zealand Entertainer of the Year.

Getting little encouragement from TVNZ ("I was removed for committing satire," he said), Clarke headed to Australia in 1977 and proved just as big a hit there. *The Gillies Report* and a long-running satirical contribution to *A Current Affair* were both critically acclaimed. Clarke has continued to entertain, with programmes like *The Games*, an edgy television comedy series leading up to the Sydney Olympics. He has worked on radio, written books and acted. He understands comedy well, but is all the funnier because of his sharp observations of life.

His wife, Helen, whom he married in 1973, is Australian. They have two daughters. The Fred Dagg character has never been reprised, but in 1996 there was an indication of Dagg's continuing appeal when Clarke wrote *A Dagg Tale*, a collection of his satirical writings. The book sold out twice.

It is a significant feature of Clarke's humour that his mockery of sensitivities or excesses in New Zealand and Australian life has been accepted and enjoyed in both countries.

Ettie Rout

The free spirit who was born too soon

BORN: LAUNCESTON, TASMANIA, FEBRUARY 24, 1877. DIED, RAROTONGA, SEPTEMBER 17, 1926.

In 1922 Ettie Rout wrote to her friend, English novelist H G Wells: "It's a mixed blessing to be born too soon." That sentence summarised the life of this remarkable woman. She was a pioneer and liberal thinker who was reviled by the establishment during her lifetime, but is appreciated now for her courage and vision.

Ettie Annie Rout was born in Tasmania, but when she was seven her family (she had a twin sister and a younger sister) moved to Wellington. She was an outstanding scholar – she was the top student in the Wellington Education Board's 1891 examination. When the family moved to Christchurch, she attended Gilby's shorthand and typing classes, and again shone.

Throughout her life, Rout was a barrier-breaker. She became one of the first government-appointed shorthand writers working in the Supreme Court and on commissions of inquiry. In 1904 she began her own public typing business, and did reporting for the *Lyttelton Times*. She quickly gained a reputation as a free spirit – she disdained the customary corset and dressed in short skirts, or in men's boots, jacket and trousers. She was an inveterate cyclist who amazed people with her energy.

Rout was always a confirmed socialist. She became involved in the labour movement in 1907 and three years later set up and edited the *Maoriland Worker* with the New Zealand Shearers' Union.

During World War I Rout formed the New Zealand Volunteer Sisterhood, inviting women to travel to Egypt to care for New Zealand soldiers. Her idea was unpopular with the Government, but she sent a group of 12 women to Cairo in 1915. The women cooked and worked in hospitals. Rout arrived in Egypt in 1916 and was appalled to discover the soaring venereal disease rate among soldiers. Rather than make a moral judgment, she concentrated on treating and preventing the illness. She urged the issue of prophylactic kits and the establishment of inspected brothels, though neither idea received the backing of the New Zealand Medical Corps officers.

Determined to fight the venereal disease problem she went to London, where, after consulting medical experts, she produced her own prophylactic kit, containing calomel ointment, condoms and Condy's crystals. She sold these at the New Zealand Medical Soldiers Club in Hornchurch.

Rout's safe-sex initiatives drew a confused reaction. The New Zealand Expeditionary Force distributed her kit to soldiers going on leave, but gave her no credit. Worse, for the rest of the war, New Zealand newspapers were banned under war regulations from mentioning her, under threat of a £100 fine. The Cabinet was appalled at a suggestion she had made in a letter to the *New Zealand Times* calling for kits and hygienic brothels. Yet her letter was instrumental in Defence Minister James Allen approving kit issue.

Women's groups railed against Rout. She was depicted as an evil woman who supported "vice". Lady Stout led a deputation imploring Prime Minister William Massey to close Rout's Hornchurch club. Undeterred, Rout went to Paris, where she stepped up the tempo of her campaign. As troop trains arrived from the front she stood on the platform of the Gare du Nord, greeted the New Zealand and Australian soldiers with her customary kiss on the cheek and handed out cards recommending the brothel of Madame Yvonne, who had agreed to run her establishment hygienically.

Rout ran a Red Cross depot in Villers Brettoneux in 1919-20 and was awarded the Reconnaissance Française medal. In 1920 she married physiotherapist Fred Hornibrook in London. She kept busy, writing, among other books, *Sex and Exercise* and *Safe Marriage*, which was banned in New Zealand, but published in Britain and Australia.

She returned home only once. After travelling around New Zealand in 1926 she committed suicide in Rarotonga, self-administering a quinine overdose.

Rout split public opinion all her life. The New Zealand Returned Soldiers' Association sent her a post-war tribute of £100, but this gesture was not publicised. After her death the Press Association described Rout as "one of the best-known New Zealand women", but could not bring itself to say why. The French called her "the guardian angel of the Anzacs", but in the House of Lords she was described as "the most wicked woman in Britain".

Happily, her work has been seen in context in recent times, and she is now widely admired. When the New Zealand Aids Foundation's Christchurch office was relocated to Montreal Street in 1988, it was named The Ettie Rout Centre.

Arthur Lydiard

The coach who revolutionised athletics training

BORN: AUCKLAND, JULY 6, 1917. DIED: HOUSTON, UNITED STATES, DECEMBER 11, 2004.

Arthur Lydiard was New Zealand's most influential sports figure. Other coaches have produced champions, but none had the influence on the public, sporting and non-sporting, that Lydiard did, through his personality and vision. During a lifetime packed with achievement, the revolutionary athletics coach:

- Guided four New Zealanders, including running legends Peter Snell and Murray Halberg, to Olympic athletics medals.
- Introduced jogging to the world. He promoted jogging as a form of improving health in the early 1960s and then watched the concept take off in the United States and elsewhere.
- Revamped ideas on cardiovascular rehabilitation so that exercise was a key.

Forceful, articulate and inspirational, Lydiard changed world thinking on training methods. He would help anyone who asked, and that included swimmers, canoeists and rugby players. He coached all around the globe and became one of world athletics' leading figures.

Lydiard, who grew up a stone's throw from Eden Park, was not particularly interested in athletics as a youngster. The All Blacks were his sports heroes. He used to smoke – "We all did; we didn't know any better" – and was not averse to a few beers. He played rugby and thought a jog around the park during the one practice evening a week constituted solid training.

Then he joined the Lynndale Athletics Club and discovered a book by English coach Michael Webster called *The Science of Athletics*. "Webster was very progressive," said Lydiard. "He felt that because men could run one lap in under 60 seconds, they would be able to run four in under four minutes if they were fitter and stronger. He advocated heavier training than was normal then." With typical enthusiasm, Lydiard took Webster's theories a step further. There followed years of experimenting, and Lydiard used himself as the guinea pig. In some weeks he ran 400km – a marathon in the morning, another at night – as he flogged himself to discover what his body could stand.

In 1950, aged 32, Lydiard represented New Zealand in the Auckland Empire Games marathon, placing 12th on a stifling day. But he earned far more renown for his coaching than his running. He guided athletes like Ernie Haskell, Lawrie King, Colin Lousich and Bill Rodger, who generally lived nearby, to national titles and records. After them followed Halberg, Barry Magee, Bill Baillie, Ray Puckett, Jeff Julian, Snell and John Davies, all champions proud to call themselves Arthur's Boys.

His methods were revolutionary – training every day and totalling 100 miles [more than 160km] a week. Halberg recalls: "There were fantastic scare stories circulating. We were told that Arthur would burst our hearts. I never doubted his methods. He was inspiring and he made sense. Soon the records starting coming, and that's the best incentive."

Curiously, Lydiard, acclaimed around the world, did not receive the same approbation at home. He was overlooked as a coach for the 1960 and 1962 Olympic and Empire Games teams, and it required public subscriptions to get him to those games to help his athletes.

By 1965 Lydiard was seeking new challenges. He'd worked for the Rothmans Sports Foundation, travelling the country talking about athletics. Now he began to view more enthusiastically some lucrative overseas offers he was receiving. He had coaching stints in Mexico, Finland (where he had huge success), Denmark, Australia and Venezuela. He lectured in every corner of the world, from the old Soviet Union to Japan and the United States. One of his books, *Run For Your Life*, was reprinted repeatedly and in 25 languages.

Lydiard returned to New Zealand with his Finnish wife, Eira, and while working for Winstones in the 1970s, set up what became known as the Winstone Walks, into the Waitakere Ranges. These introduced thousands to the delights of bush-walking.

In 1974, when he was one of the coaches of the New Zealand athletics squad at the Christchurch Commonwealth Games, he helped Dick Tayler to a famous victory in the 10,000m. Lydiard was also an assistant coach of the 1990 New Zealand Commonwealth Games team, but he was 72 then, and his best years had been lost to New Zealand athletics.

After that, ironically, honours were heaped on him. He was inducted into the Sports Hall of Fame, was awarded an Order of New Zealand medal, was recognised at the Halberg Awards for service to sport, and, in 2003, was finally made a life member of Athletics New Zealand.

Lydiard, aged 87, was still lecturing when he died during a speaking tour of the United States.

Kupe

The voyager who discovered Aotearoa

Kupe, the most revered figure in Maori mythology, is said to have discovered New Zealand. Stories that have been passed down the generations for more than 1000 years offer differing accounts of his activities.

Kupe was a great chief of Hawaiki (Tahiti). His father was from Rarotonga and his mother was from Rangiatea (Ra'iatea). These were the three islands over which his power extended.

There are many versions of his historic journey from eastern Polynesia to New Zealand, but generally the outline is similar. Kupe's fishermen were unable to catch any fish because their bait kept being taken by a vast number of octopi. The chief culprit was a huge octopus, Te Wheke, the pet of a man named Muturangi.

Kupe requested that Muturangi stop his pet from enticing the octopi to the fishing grounds, but Muturangi ignored him. Kupe sought guidance from the island priests, who told him that he would have to kill the giant octopus or his men would never have any success with their fishing.

So Kupe made elaborate plans to hunt Te Wheke. Two waka headed across the ocean. In one, named Matahorua, was Kupe, his wife, Hine-i-te-aparangi, their daughters, a navigator named Reti and several dozen men. In the second waka, named Tawhirikura, was Ngake (sometimes referred to as Ngahue), Kupe's brother-in-law, and another large group.

Te Wheke led them a merry dance all the way across the ocean. Finally land was sighted. Hine-i-te-aparangi is credited as the first to sight the land – a huge, long, stationary cloud on the horizon. She is said to have exclaimed, "He ao! He ao!" ("A cloud! A cloud!") Legend states that it was from this exclamation that the name Aotearoa (ao = cloud, tea = white, roa = long), commonly translated as Land of the Long White Cloud, was derived.

Having arrived near Muriwhenua (Northland), Kupe followed the giant octopus south along the east coast. He stopped for a long time at Hokianga to search for food and to rest, while Ngake continued in pursuit of the octopus. When Kupe resumed sailing, he linked again with Ngake at Rangiwhakaoma (Castlepoint). The octopus escaped after being trapped for a time in a cave and Kupe and Ngake chased it to Te Kawakawa (Cape Palliser, the southern-most point of the North Island), and then to the mouth of Te Whanganui-a-Tara (Wellington Harbour). There were further stops at Hataitai (the Miramar Peninsula) and Owhariu (Ohariu), west of Wellington on Cook Strait. They named the two islands in Wellington Harbour Matiu and Makaro after two of Kupe's daughters. (They are now Somes and Ward islands).

Kupe sailed to Porirua Harbour and then to Mana Island, where Hine-i-te-aparangi and her daughters disembarked. Kupe and Ngake went out together in search of the octopus. They made a course for Te Wai-pounamu (the South Island). Once they got to Awa-iti (Tory Channel) they saw the giant creature and killed it.

Some versions have it that Kupe then returned home. But others suggest he sailed south, to see what resources the South Island offered and whether there were any inhabitants. He went down the west coast of the South Island to the Arahura River, just north of what is now Hokitika, and discovered pounamu, or greenstone. Continuing south, he finally reached the tail of the South Island. After a brief time exploring, he left the land to the penguins and seals and set out for home.

Kupe sailed north by way of the West Coast, reuniting with his family along the way. When he got to the Whanganui River he paddled up as far as Kau-arapawa, about 25 kilometres inland from what is now Wanganui, in search of people, but saw only birds. On he sailed, around the coast to Patea and then north to Hokianga. After a feast there, Kupe placed the lands under tapu and, leaving behind his two dogs, returned to Hawaiki.

Once home, Kupe reported the discovery, telling of a distant cloud-capped land. He described mountain ranges, fertile plains, healthy vegetation, rivers, birds and fish. He gave directions on how to get to this land, describing the direction ("to the right of the setting sun") and suggested the most suitable month to travel was Tatauuru-ora (November).

Despite entreaties that he return to New Zealand leading a large group, Kupe was adamant that he would not go back. However, Maori legend has it that it was Kupe's precise navigational directions that enabled later migrants to make the journey, most notably the Great Fleet of the 14th century.

Te Puea Herangi

The greatest Maori woman of her time

BORN: WHATIWHATIHOE, PIRONGIA, NOVEMBER 9, 1884. DIED: NGARUAWAHIA, OCTOBER 12, 1952.

Te Puea Herangi is often called Princess Te Puea. She despised the title, which was bestowed on her by Pakeha. It hints that she gained influence because of a hereditary title and ignores the momentous social, cultural and educational work she undertook. It was said of her that she led Tainui from the darkness into the light. Wearing her trademark working clothing, white headscarf and gumboots, she said of herself: "I work, I pray, I sleep, and then I work again."

She was a grand-daughter of the second Maori king, Tawhiao, and was educated by Maori elders still bitter at their treatment during the 1860s land wars. She became an exuberant, headstrong young woman who had several romances, including one with a Pakeha, which led to her being shunned by her people.

When Mahuta, Te Puea's uncle, became king he called her to duty. She returned to Mangatawhiri in 1910, determined to create a centre for Kingitanga (the King movement). She sealed her support among Tainui during World War I when she opposed the Government's conscription policy, allowing men not wishing to enlist to live on her farm at Mangatawhiri. When the authorities took the men to the Narrow Neck training camp, Te Puea would encourage them by sitting outside the camp in clear view.

In 1920 she oversaw the purchase of 10 acres on the banks of the Waikato River. This land, which had been confiscated by the Crown, was of spiritual significance to Tainui. She then moved her people from Mangatawhiri to Ngaruawahia to build a new marae, Turangawaewae, "a place to stand".

Te Puea, who was funny, outspoken, persuasive and inspiring, was intent on restoring the status of her people and, with her organisational skills, energy and discipline, her vision became a reality. Kimikimi, the dining hall, was opened in 1923, and other buildings followed over the next 15 years. To help pay for the work, Te Puea formed the first fund-raising kapa haka. The Te Pou O Mangatawhiri troupe toured first in 1922.

She travelled widely to supervise Native Affairs Minister Apirana Ngata's land development schemes, thereby building an economic base for her people. In 1940 she and her husband, Rewi Tumoko Katipa, bought a farm close to the marae and provided work for a generation of Maori.

Te Puea's friendship with Ngata and Prime Minister Gordon Coates meant she was in frequent contact with Government officials as she set about forming a true partnership between Maori and Pakeha. Te Puea invited politicians to Ngaruawahia, which assisted mutual understanding. In 1937 she was made a CBE. She always remained her own person. After initially supporting the Waitangi centenary celebrations, she bypassed them when she felt Tainui had been slighted. She opposed conscription again in World War II. "Look Peter," she said to Prime Minister Peter Fraser, "it's perfectly simple. I'm not anti-Pakeha. I'm not pro-Germany. I'm pro-Maori."

She showed her pragmatic side when she accepted Fraser's offer of £5000 per year in perpetuity to Tainui as compensation for the 1860s land confiscations. She did not consider the price fair, but realised it would allow her people to pursue vital economic and educational goals and, importantly, it vindicated her people's stance.

In 1919, during the influenza epidemic, loss of life among Tainui was severe and many children were orphaned. Te Puea gathered them, made her community responsible for their care and took some into her home. She made herself responsible for the group's education. Her strong social conscience was revealed also in her attitude towards women's organisations – in 1951 she became the Maori Women's Welfare League's first patron.

Te Puea observed a personal form of the Pai Marire faith that blended Maori beliefs with elements of church and Hebrew doctrine. After early antagonism, she came to welcome other faiths to the marae, and was especially close to the Methodist church leaders. She worked alongside Harold Turbott, the Minister of Health, to tackle the high mortality rates caused by typhoid and tuberculosis among Maori, and was a strong opponent of alcohol and smoking.

When Te Puea died the BBC devoted a broadcast to her memory. Obituary writers hailed her as "the greatest Maori woman of our time".

Today, for one week a year, celebrations are held at Turangawaewae to mark the coronation of the Maori queen. The ceremonies range from a diplomatic reception in a dining hall that can seat 1200 to cultural performances on a vast stage by the river. They are a fitting fulfilment of Te Puea's vision and unstinting labours for her people.

John Walker

The third of New Zealand's great middle-distance champions

BORN: AUCKLAND, JANUARY 12, 1952.

John George Walker, the third of New Zealand's great Olympic 1500m champions and mile world record-holders, shares the same pedestal as his predecessors, Jack Lovelock and Peter Snell. He was one of a trio of superb New Zealand athletes who emerged at about the same time, and, with Dick Quax and Rod Dixon, blazed a trail around the running tracks of Europe.

During his 18-year international career, Walker:
- Won the 1976 Montreal Olympic 1500m gold medal.
- Became the first person to break 3min 50s for the mile, setting a world record of 3min 49.4s at Gothenburg in 1975.
- Set a 2000m world record that lasted a decade.
- Ran more than 100 sub-four minute miles, the first person to reach that milestone.
- Won three Commonwealth Games medals.
- Was New Zealand's Sportsman of the Year twice.

As a youngster, Walker showed more ability at tennis than running, but once he was taken in hand by athletics coach Arch Jelley, his natural talent emerged. By 1972 he was the national 800m champion and missed selection for that year's Olympics by a whisker. Tall, strong and with a mane of flaxen hair, he became a glamour figure of track and field. His first sub-four minute mile was at Victoria, Canada, in July 1973, when he blitzed a B section field and stamped himself as a potential champion.

The New Zealand public realised how good he was at the 1974 Christchurch Commonwealth Games, when he earned the 800m bronze medal and chased home Filbert Bayi in a sensational 1500m final. Bayi ran 3min 32.2s to break Jim Ryun's world record. Walker, at 3min 32.5s, was also under the old record.

In 1975 Walker was supreme. He ran eight sub-four minute miles and won them all. The big one, of course, was at Gothenburg, on August 12, when he thrilled 11,000 spectators with a mind-boggling display of power and speed and cracked the magic 3min 50s barrier. That changed Walker's life forever. He was besieged by the world's sports media and became track and field's brightest star. The following year, though beginning to be hampered by a leg problem that eventually required an operation, Walker was again in a class of his own. He rates his 2000m world record of 4min 51.4s at Oslo that year as the best race of his career.

In the 1500m event at Montreal, Walker, in a field weakened by the African boycott, was always the man to watch. After a slow early pace in the final, he grabbed the lead with 300m remaining (the same point Lovelock had begun his famous finishing burst 40 years earlier), and had enough in hand to hold off Ivo Van Damme and Paul-Heinz Wellmann. His immediate reaction? "Relief. Then came the joy. They can break your world records, but they can never take away your Olympic gold medal."

That was his career peak, though he set a New Zealand all-comers' record of 3min 50.6s at Auckland in 1981, ran 3min 49.08s for the mile in 1982 and completed his 100th sub-four minute mile on his home track at Mt Smart in 1985. He endured better than any previous middle-distance athlete. He took a silver medal behind Steve Cram in the 1982 Brisbane Commonwealth Games 1500m and flirted, with moderate success, with the 5000m at the 1984 Olympics and 1986 Commonwealth Games.

In 1990 he contested the 1500m at the Auckland Commonwealth Games, only to be tripped early in the final. After the race, his international swansong, he did a victory lap at the invitation of the gold medallist, Englishman Peter Elliott.

There was a mixed reaction to Walker in New Zealand. While everyone admired his running ability – he was named Sportsman of the Decade for the 1970s – some felt he was too opinionated and outspoken.

Overseas he was adored at all the circuit stops in Europe and was a special favourite at London's Crystal Palace.

When Walker announced in 1996 that he was suffering from Parkinson's disease, the news was nearly as big in Britain as in New Zealand. Walker, in typically candid fashion, spoke of his illness and then said he wasn't going to spend the next 20 years moping. He said he was too busy getting on with life. He and his wife Helen, who have four children, run an equestrian shop just south of Auckland. He has maintained his links with athletics as a television commentator and has served on the Manukau City Council.

Tim Finn

The creator of Split Enz

BORN: TE AWAMUTU, JUNE 25, 1952.

As a boy, Brian Timothy Finn considered becoming a priest. Instead he dropped his first name and became a rock star, whose appeal has spanned more than 30 years. He is the brother of the equally well-known Neil Finn and because they collaborated so often, in rock bands Split Enz and Crowded House and in producing their own duo records, the temptation is to consider them as one entity. That does neither justice.

Tim Finn's early musical inspiration was drawn from a number of sources. He grew up during the era of the Beatles. He took piano lessons from a Catholic nun in his home town of Te Awamutu. Tim and Neil, who is six years younger, would often sing together to their parents' friends and during family holidays at Mount Maunganui. Their mother, Mary, was a continual source of musical encouragement.

At Sacred Heart College, a Catholic boarding school in Auckland, Tim's interest in music grew. He attended Auckland University in 1971-72, ostensibly to study philosophy and English for a BA, but he found the music room, Room 129 of the O'Rorke student hostel, more of a lure and enjoyed jamming there with his friends Mike Chunn, Robert Gillies, Philip Judd and Noel Crombie. Study paled when compared to music and Finn quit university and formed a group called Split Ends. It became Split Enz when they toured Australia in 1973.

It was heady stuff, because Finn was just 20 when Split Enz was formed. The band produced an eclectic mix of music, ranging from art rock to vaudeville, punk to pop. The original music, plus a striking visual presentation, caught the public's imagination. For the next 12 years, Finn was the group's lead singer. He invited brother Neil to join the group when Judd departed in 1977. The band produced nine albums and two live albums, and did much to put New Zealand on the international rock music map, producing a string of hits, including *I See Red*, *Poor Boy*, *I Hope I Never*, *Six Months In A Leaky Boat* and *Dirty Creature*, all written by Tim. The most notable of Split Enz's albums was *True Colours*, which was hailed in Australia and Britain in 1980.

Finn, a highly-strung personality prone to bleak periods, married English dancer Liz Malam in January 1981, but nine months later the marriage collapsed and he had a nervous breakdown. Years later he remarried Marie Azcona. They have two children.

In 1984 Finn left Split Enz, partly because of the success of his first solo album, *Escapade*. He moved to London for several years. Probably the best-known, if not the most musically satisfying, song on *Escapade* was *Fraction Too Much Friction*. Several more solo albums followed – *Big Canoe* (1986), *Tim Finn* (1989), *Before and After* (1993), *Say It Is So* (2000) and *Feeding the Gods* (2001) – but none matched the success of *Escapade*.

However, Finn enjoyed plenty of other musical triumphs. In 1987 he wrote the soundtrack to the movie *Les Patterson Saves The World*.

At Neil's invitation he joined Crowded House for their third album, *Woodface*, but departed soon after during their European tour. In 1995 he combined forces with Andy White and Liam O'Maonlai, releasing an album called *Altitude* under the group name ALT (their first initials).

Also in 1995, Finn was commissioned by New Zealand Cricket to mark its 100th anniversary with a song and produced *Runs in the Family*. In 1996 he contributed to *Enzso*, Eddie Rayner's album of orchestrally-arranged Split Enz songs.

His most successful work was in collaboration with brother Neil. The Finn brothers released *Finn* in 1995. In 2004 they produced a second album, *Everyone Is Here*. Finn made an extremely successful tour of New Zealand with Bic Runga and Dave Dobbyn in 2000. *Together in Concert* was released soon after.

When a vote was taken in 2001 to find the best New Zealand songs of the previous 75 years, Tim Finn scored extremely well – *Six Months in a Leaky Boat* (6), *Weather With You* (16, with Neil Finn), *I Hope I Never* (25) and *I See Red* (28) all made the top 30 and he had eight in the top 100. Split Enz had eight songs in the top 100, Crowded House six.

True Colours, an exhibition at the museum in Te Awamutu, has been dedicated to Tim and Neil Finn. The brothers were given international achievement awards at the 2005 New Zealand Music Awards.

John A Lee

From Labour Party pin-up boy to exile

BORN: DUNEDIN, OCTOBER 31, 1891. DIED: AUCKLAND, JUNE 13, 1982.

John A Lee – he is seldom referred to without the initial, though close acquaintances called him Jack – was perhaps the most famous New Zealand socialist of his time. He had two advantages over his rivals: he was a brilliant communicator, and he lived until he was 90. When his bitterest opponents were long dead, Lee was still "setting history straight".

Lee had a grim childhood. His parents fought constantly and split soon after he was born. There was a lot of alcohol and gambling in the Lee household, but no money. "Grinding poverty" was how Lee recalled his childhood living conditions. He was in constant trouble as a boy. He rarely attended school and was soon engaged in petty crime. One magistrate labelled him "incorrigible" and sent him to Burnham Industrial School. Lee was forever attempting to escape and eventually succeeded, living as a swagman for some years. At Raetihi he was arrested for breaking and entering and theft, and was sent to Mount Eden Prison for a year.

Lee, always a prolific reader, showed increasingly socialist tendencies after his release. When he enlisted in the New Zealand Expeditionary Force in 1916, he was tagged "Bolshie Lee". He was an outstanding soldier, winning the Distinguished Conduct Medal in 1917 for single-handedly capturing a German machine-gun post at Messines. The following year he lost his left arm fighting at Mailly-Maillet.

He returned to New Zealand in July 1919 and married Mollie Guy, who was to provide him with massive support throughout his political life. Lee poured his energies into the New Zealand Labour Party and the New Zealand Returned Soldiers' Association. The Labour Party used Lee as a symbol of what it offered. Criticised because of its anti-conscription and anti-war stances, Labour happily hauled out its one-armed war hero.

Lee entered Parliament in 1922, representing Auckland East. He proved a fiery, charismatic MP, who concentrated on foreign affairs and defence and was always willing to debate Labour Party policy. His career stuttered in 1928 when he lost his seat, and he and Molly ran a hotel in Rotorua for a time. However, he returned to Parliament in 1931, controversially earning the Grey Lynn nomination over sitting MP Fred Bartram.

The Depression brought out the passion in Lee. He fought for import and exchange controls and protection for local industry, and wrote *Children of the Poor*, which became a seminal book.

When Labour swept to power under Michael Joseph Savage in 1935, Lee expected a Cabinet post, but Savage, suspicious of him, offered only an insignificant under-secretary role. The following year he was included on Cabinet finance and defence committees and tackled both areas with zest.

Lee's vision and energy were revealed when Savage entrusted housing to him in 1936. He instituted a socialist housing scheme, which in three years resulted in 3440 good-quality State homes being built. By 1939 Lee had developed a huge following. He mastered the medium of radio, spoke movingly at public rallies and helped ensure Labour's big election win that year. Lee earned the biggest majority in the country.

However, thwarted again politically by the Labour hierarchy, he became an unmanageable party maverick. He criticised Labour's leaders for steering too central a line, and became the Labour left's champion. His particular target was Finance Minister Walter Nash, whom he accused of being financially conservative.

Savage fell gravely ill and Lee brought matters to a head by writing an article called "Psychopathology in Politics", which implied Savage was of diminished capacity and unable to do the job of Prime Minister. It placed Lee beyond the pale. Savage recovered briefly and, saying that Lee had made his last two years a "living hell", moved with his deputy, Peter Fraser, to get rid of him. On March 25, 1940, Lee was expelled from the party, by 546 votes to 344.

Lee formed the Democratic Labour Party, but it did not win a seat in the 1943 election. That was the end of Lee politically, but he lived for another four decades.

He established Vital Books in 1950 and became a successful bookseller and publisher. He continued to write, and his political memoirs, *Simple on a Soap-box* (1963), sold well.

Lee died in 1982. He was an ardent socialist, a compelling speaker and a feisty personality. But his writing made the most indelible impression.

Some described Lee the author as New Zealand's Charles Dickens because, with a bitter experience of the conditions he described, he focused so evocatively on the under-privileged.

James Wattie

The man who gave us baked beans and frozen veges

BORN: HAWARDEN, NORTH CANTERBURY, MARCH 23, 1902. DIED: MANGATERETERE, JUNE 8, 1974.

James Wattie never lost the common touch. Even when he had built his canned food company into a massive concern, with extensive overseas interests, he remained modest, generous and accessible to all his staff. His is the ultimate New Zealand success story.

He was born into a farming family with Scottish roots. His parents moved from North Canterbury to Nelson, then to Marlborough and finally to Hawke's Bay. After leaving primary school in 1915 Wattie took a job as a telegraph messenger, but his chances of promotion faded when he failed his medical because of a cataract in his right eye.

He turned to accountancy, becoming a junior clerk for the Hawke's Bay Farmers' Meat Company at its Whakatu office in 1916, and beginning an accountancy correspondence course. Wattie progressed well. By 1924 he was an accountant for Roach's, one of Hawke's Bay's biggest department stores. The following year he became secretary of Hawke's Bay Fruitgrowers and in 1928 became the company's manager.

In 1934 Wattie and a young accountant named Harold Carr decided to investigate the possibility of establishing a food canning factory. They appealed to local pride, leased property from Hawke's Bay Fruitgrowers and quickly returned a profit. Before long J Wattie Canneries was producing a variety of canned fruits and vegetables. Wattie was the company's managing director and Carr its secretary.

Wattie was a clever boss, always looking to stay abreast of changes and never afraid to spend money to modernise or diversify. He even set up a research unit. He was a firm believer in the value of publicity and had a good feel for the market. He developed the business overseas and had success supplying New Zealand, American and British military forces with dehydrated food during World War II.

In 1947 Watties began quick-freezing vegetables, a significant advancement for a canned food company. By then the company was dominating the New Zealand food processing industry.

Watties expanded into Gisborne in the early 1950s. The boss's two sons, Gordon and Ray, took senior management positions, with Gordon managing the Gisborne factory and Ray the Hastings factory. By then Watties foods were household products in New Zealand. Watties provided thousands of jobs locally and stimulated the regional economy. The fertile Heretaunga Plains provided the ideal land for such a business.

Wattie made almost annual trips overseas, seeking new markets and modern methods. He was an extremely well-liked boss, who for many years knew all his staff by name. He thought nothing of sitting in the staff cafeteria and chatting to all and sundry and would work anywhere in his factory when required. His popularity was illustrated when in February 1962, at the height of the processing season, a fire destroyed two-thirds of his Hastings factory. His staff worked around the clock and within 50 hours the factory was back in production. They were pleased to help the man who generated such goodwill.

The company continued to expand through a series of mergers. In 1968 it combined with General Foods Corporation and the following year with Cropper-NRM, New Zealand's biggest flour miller. In 1971 Watties Industries was formed, with James Wattie as its chairman and managing director. It was a leading player in New Zealand industry.

Wattie was a Hawke's Bay legend. He and his wife Gladys – they married in 1925 – were well-liked figures who were involved in all manner of clubs and societies. Watties was a public-minded company that sponsored the New Zealand book-writing awards for many years, and James Wattie quietly funded medical research and education and contributed to organisations such as the Plunket Society. Horse breeding and racing were a special passion for Wattie and one of his horses, Even Stevens, won the 1962 Melbourne Cup.

Though he was troubled by health problems, including a heart attack while in London in 1962, Wattie stayed closely involved with his company until his death. More than 2000 people attended his funeral.

Watties has continued to grow, becoming part of the Goodman Fielder Wattie Group, a giant corporation within Australasia, and linking with the multinational Heinz Group to become Heinz Wattie.

Wattie's name is recalled for many reasons, not the least of which are the Sir James Wattie Memorial Visiting Professorship for the Advancement of Medical Science and the Sir James Wattie Memorial Youth Trust. Wattie, who was knighted in 1966, was one of the inaugural inductees into the New Zealand Business Hall of Fame in 1994.

William Hamilton

Jet-boat inventor

BORN: ASHWICK, JULY 26, 1899. DIED: FAIRLIE, MARCH 30, 1978.

William Hamilton is one of New Zealand's most famous inventors. His creations ranged from earth-moving machinery to an air-conditioning plant. But his lifetime of achievement took him into many other fields, including farming, motor racing and, his best-known accomplishment, developing the jet-boat.

Charles William Feilden Hamilton, known as Bill, was educated at Christ's College, Christchurch. He moved to Irishman Creek Station after he left home in 1921. It was a sheep farm in the heart of the Mackenzie Country and was where much of the early development of his inventions was carried out. Hamilton soon discovered that he was more suited to designing heavy earth-moving machinery than to tending the needs of sheep, and the land gave him the opportunity to exploit his mechanical genius. It was at Irishman Creek that he established his first workshop, the forerunner of the Hamilton group of companies.

At the age of 23 he visited England, where he not only met his future wife Peggy, but also bought an old Sunbeam car. In 1925 he drove the Sunbeam in the New Zealand 50-mile Motor Cup race at Muriwai Beach. During a historic day's racing he set an Australasian speed record for five miles of 100.3mph, becoming the first New Zealander to top the 100mph barrier. In 1928 Hamilton won the flying mile at Oreti Beach, Southland, stretching his national speed record to 109.9mph (177km/h). He returned to England in 1930 and enjoyed further motor-racing triumphs, gaining national recognition.

Boats were always Hamilton's primary fascination, from when he was a boy on his father's farm at Fairlie. The boats were modest affairs, canoes mainly, constructed of bamboo rods and old pieces of canvas. But they floated and Hamilton revelled in piloting his frail vessels down the streams near his home. "It was great going down, but what a job I had getting the darned things back up again," he said. "They weighed about 22 pounds and I could hardly manage to carry them. I dreamed of a miracle to propel me upstream in comfort through the shallow water."

Hamilton experimented at first with an airboat that relied on an externally-mounted engine and an aeroplane propeller to push it across the water. "I soon discarded that scheme... It was too noisy and did not manoeuvre well enough." Years of trial and error followed before the first Hamilton jets-boats were constructed in 1954. He experimented with various forms of tunnel boat, then with a retractable water propeller and an air screw. "The biggest advance we made was to get the jet stream out of the back of the boat, rather than underneath it. We perfected units which became capable of pushing a boat through water at up to 60 miles an hour [70km/h]."

The jet-boats became world famous, never more so than in 1960, when three of them completed the first run up the Grand Canyon of the Colorado River in the United States.

Surprisingly, Hamilton did not consider the jet-boat his greatest invention, only the one that made him most famous. He was always particularly proud of his 1927 invention of a tractor-drawn scoop. He needed electricity for his homestead and workshop, so designed and built the scoop to construct a dam to provide water for a 17.5-kilowatt hydro-electric plant. He went on to build several such scoops and used them in construction contracts throughout New Zealand.

As World War II approached, Hamilton constructed airfields and roads for the Government. In 1935 he was awarded a contract to build the first Hermitage aerodrome. In 1939 a large building was erected on his farm. Inside it, 17 men, working two shifts a day, began producing munitions. Soon he opened a similar plant at Fairlie.

By 1945 he was able to establish a business, C W F Hamilton, in Christchurch, with £30,000 capital. He opened in central Christchurch, but soon moved to Middleton, where he built an engineering factory on a 20-acre site and eventually employed 500 workers. Bulldozers, scrapers, hydraulic machinery and the intake gates for many of the country's hydro-electric power schemes have come from these premises.

For a time, the pipe-smoking Hamilton, always looking for adventure, contemplated becoming a pilot. His enthusiasm was undented even after a tragic accident in 1936, when he was a passenger in a plane that struck a mast in a storm near Wellington airport. The pilot was killed but Hamilton emerged unhurt.

Hamilton was knighted in 1974.

Norman Kirk

Big Norm, the champion of ordinary New Zealanders

BORN: WAIMATE, JANUARY 6, 1923. DIED: WELLINGTON, AUGUST 31, 1974.

Norman Kirk was Prime Minister for only 21 months, but left an indelible mark on New Zealand. In his brief time as New Zealand's leader he achieved much and gave promise of more.

Kirk came from a working class family that struggled during the Depression years. They lived first in Waimate, then Christchurch. Kirk did not have much formal education and left school at 12. He had a variety of menial jobs, including roof-painter, gas welder, fitter and turner, cleaner and part-time fireman. He worked on the railways and even in a goldmine.

In 1943 he married Ruth Miller and the couple moved north to Katikati, where Kirk was a boiler engineer at a dairy factory. The Kirks stayed in Katikati until 1948, when they bought a section at Kaiapoi. Kirk became an engine driver at the Firestone factory in Papanui, cycling to work to save money. He built his own house, including digging a 70-foot well by hand.

Already Kirk was attracted to politics, having joined the Labour Party in 1943. In 1953, at 30, Kaiapoi elected him New Zealand's youngest mayor. He set his sights on national politics, and unsuccessfully sought the Hurunui seat in the 1954 election. However, in 1957 he won Lyttelton, by 567 votes. He remained the Lyttelton MP until switching to Sydenham in 1969. Kirk was a strong electorate politician. His electorate encompassed the Chatham Islands and he took that responsibility seriously, to the extent that he is still revered in the Chathams.

It was easy to warm to Kirk. He was a big man – he eventually weighed 128kg (21st) – with sparkling eyes, a ready smile and a sharp wit. He was a commanding speaker, with a voice that could be stentorian or gently persuasive. He excelled in the House and signalled his ability during his maiden speech, when he dealt in impressive depth with New Zealand's place in the world.

Kirk stood for the Labour deputy leadership in 1962, losing to Hugh Watt. The following year he became Labour president. He toppled Arnold Nordmeyer as Labour leader in 1965. At this point he had been in Parliament only seven years, yet was both Labour president and leader. He worked assiduously and no-one read and researched more deeply. Kirk vigorously promoted the welfare state, supporting government spending on housing, health, employment and education. As such, "Big Norm" was the champion of ordinary New Zealanders.

He described Labour's philosophy as "a social programme that will promote the housing of our people, protect their health, and ensure full employment and equal opportunity".

Under Kirk Labour lost the 1966 and 1969 elections. The 1969 result was especially galling, but it energised Kirk. He lost weight, let his hair grow and dressed better. A large, distinguished man emerged, with a shock of silver hair. In 1972 Labour, campaigning on the "It's time for a change" slogan, swept to power with a 23-seat majority.

Kirk was photographed at Waitangi in February 1973 holding the hand of a small Maori boy. The picture symbolised a new era of racial partnership and is the strongest image of Kirk's short time as Prime Minister.

International affairs were a particular strength. Kirk deviated from previous New Zealand policy by recognising China, cancelling the 1973 Springbok rugby tour because of South Africa's apartheid policies, and focusing world attention on French nuclear tests at Mururoa by dispatching the frigate Otago to be a "silent, accusing witness". He formed strong links with black Africa, Asia and the Pacific.

In a series of appearances abroad – the United Nations, the Washington Press Club, Commonwealth Prime Ministers meetings, and in South-East Asia – he made a deep impression with his eloquence, breadth of knowledge, idealism and pride in New Zealand.

In its first year his government enjoyed a record surplus, but high oil price rises fuelled inflation and by 1974 New Zealand was struggling economically.

Kirk had never enjoyed great health – he suffered from goitre in his 20s and failed his army medical. His workload increased when he became Prime Minister and he rarely took holidays. In 1973 he developed heart problems, then, when he had his painful varicose veins attended to, blood clots developed.

On August 28, 1974, Kirk entered a private hospital in Island Bay. He died three days later of "congestive cardiac failure", aged 51. His death was followed by an outpouring of grief at home and abroad.

Bill Gallagher

His electric fence took farming into a new era

BORN: HAMILTON, MAY 17, 1911. DIED: HAMILTON, AUGUST 8, 1990.

Bill Gallagher's gift to farming – electric fences – spun out of his efforts to control a pesky horse in the 1930s. While on his Waikato farm he was bothered by a horse named Joe, which would scratch itself on the family car. Gallagher applied his inventive mind to the problem and decided to electrify the car. Every time the horse rocked the car, a triggering device would send a current through the car, and the horse. The problem was soon solved.

Adapting that simple solution, Gallagher soon discovered that it was possible to control farm animals by administering electric shocks through fences. That development radically changed farming pasture management practices in New Zealand and in more than 100 other countries.

Alfred William Gallagher (known as Willie and later Bill) was the oldest of six children born into a farming family. His parents farmed at Horotiu, near Hamilton, until 1920, when they moved to Papamoa, in the Bay of Plenty. After leaving Te Puke District High School at 15, Bill worked on the family farm. In 1927 his parents' marriage ended and the farm management was taken over by Bill and his brother, Henry.

Gallagher married Millie Murray in 1936 and they moved to a new farm at Horsham Downs, near Horotiu. Soon after came the breakthrough with electric fencing. It suited Gallagher. Though he was a farmer, he was happier solving problems and was at heart an engineer.

The electric fence proved a cheap alternative to the standard post, wire and batten fencing. However, there was a problem. It was illegal to use the mains power supply, as he did initially, so he developed a battery-powered design. It quickly became evident there was a ready market for electric fences.

In 1940 Gallagher sold his farm and moved to Hamilton. During World War II, after a brief stint in Wellington, he worked for the Colonial Ammunition Company in Hamilton and subsequently for a farm machinery repair business.

After the war his business expanded rapidly. Initially the Gallaghers – Bill, and two brothers, Henry and Viv – worked from a garage at Bill's house, where they made gas producers and electric fences. Then they moved to a bigger workshop and soon there were eight employees. A spinning top-dresser was designed, and the company also produced cow bails, hay barns and cattle-stops.

In 1950 Bill went into business on his own. He was always a boat lover and from 1949-58 he was heavily involved in boat building and commercial fishing, though not with any notable financial success.

A big breakthrough for him came in 1961, when a law change made it legal to run electric fence energizers off the main electricity supply. Soon the old battery-model electric fences had been vastly modernised. Within two years Gallagher Engineering had been established as a limited liability company. By 1964 the company had made more than 20,000 electric fence units and 2600 top-dressers.

Bill's two sons, John and Bill junior, played an increasingly prominent role. Much time was spent improving the electric fence, but other agricultural machinery, such as forage harvesters and rotary hoes, was produced.

Gallagher Electronics was established as a separate company in 1974. The Gallaghers' businesses continued to grow, partly because of Bill Gallagher's salesmanship and emphasis on quality, but also because of his sons' creative marketing and drive. Bill junior had opened up the Australian market in the 1960s and, after that, overseas sales mushroomed.

In later years Gallagher senior became known as "the Admiral". He had strong Christian principles, detested swearing and would not allow alcohol on his work premises. With his lively sense of humour he was a popular boss, and was so generous with staff bonuses and pay increases that sometimes the company bottom line suffered.

He remained a company director until 1989, but increasingly devoted time to other projects. He invented a hoist for transferring hospital patients between bed, bath and wheelchair, and redesigned the boiler system and installed emergency lighting at the Assisi Home and Hospital in Matangi. Gallagher served on the board of the first Presbyterian Church in Frankton for more than 30 years, was a JP and a member of the Masonic Lodge. In 1990 he was awarded an MBE.

By the early 1990s the original Gallagher Engineering had become uneconomic, largely because of the removal of farm and export subsidies, and was sold, but the Gallagher Group, run by Bill junior, has continued to expand and now has several hundred employees.

Michael King

The writer who explained New Zealand to New Zealanders

BORN: WELLINGTON, DECEMBER 15, 1945. DIED: MARAMARUA, MARCH 30, 2004.

The deluge of tributes to Michael King as a writer and a person when he died were in stark contrast to the criticism he received earlier in his career for daring to write about Maori history. King is now acknowledged as one of New Zealand's finest historians, the natural successor to Keith Sinclair. But he went through times of anguish along the way.

King and his second wife, Maria Jungowska, died in a horrific car crash south of Auckland. Ironically, and even more sadly, he had just received a medical clearance after months of chemotherapy treatment to ward off throat cancer.

Despite his versatility and industry, King had struggled for decades to progress financially. Even when he was acclaimed for his writing, he seldom made much money from his work. Then he had *The Penguin History of New Zealand* published in 2003. It proved to be stunningly successful, running into several reprints in a short time. Soon after, King was awarded one of the Prime Minister's inaugural awards for literary achievement, and with it $60,000. He had financial security at last, which made the car crash all the more tragic.

King grew up near Paremata Harbour, just north of Wellington. His father, Lew, an advertising pioneer, and mother, Nellie, raised him as a practising Catholic. He attended Sacred Heart College in Auckland when the family moved north briefly, and then boarded at St Patrick's College Silverstream when they returned to the capital. As a boy he loved reading, was keen on rugby, and found himself drawn to the study of Maori history.

After gaining academic qualifications – a BA at Victoria University in 1967 and an MA at Waikato University the following year – he was employed as a reporter for the *Waikato Times*. He became the newspaper's Maori news roundsman and approached his job so studiously that he soon had far more knowledge than his employers had need of. This led to his first book, *Moko: Maori Tattooing in the 20th Century*.

Though he was a journalism teacher at Wellington Polytechnic for three years, he was a full-time writer by the mid-1970s, earning an income by producing books, newspaper and magazine articles, and contributing to radio and television programmes. His most notable television work was the 1974 documentary series *Tangata Whenua*. But writing books was his passion.

Initially he focused on Maori stories, including biographies of Te Puea Herangi, Whina Cooper and John Rangihau, and other historical perspectives.

Though the level of his research was outstanding, it didn't take long for the criticism to begin. Who did he think he was, a Pakeha, trying to define Maori history? What gave him the right? He was accused of being an "academic raider".

It troubled him, to the extent that he wrote *Being Pakeha: an Encounter with New Zealand and the Maori Renaissance* in 1985, in which he endeavoured to explain his position. He followed it up in 1999 with *Being Pakeha Now – Reflections and Recollections of a White Native*.

Eventually the criticism faded away. There was no better answer than more work of the highest quality. His range widened. He wrote about the sinking of the Rainbow Warrior, Moriori history and the Chatham Islands, and produced definitive biographies of Apirana Ngata, Frank Sargeson, Janet Frame and (with Michael Bassett) Prime Minister Peter Fraser. He dealt with Catholicism in New Zealand in his 1997 book *God's Farthest Outpost*, and, of course, there was his seminal *History of New Zealand*.

King wrote or edited 39 books, winning nearly every writing scholarship available, including the prestigious Mansfield fellowship to Menton in 1976.

Along the way he made an incredible number of friends. He encouraged other writers through his links with the Frank Sargeson Trust, and through personal contact. King won the Watties Book of the Year award twice and won prizes for history, journalism and literature.

King was the quintessential Kiwi, who, when asked what made him what he was, said: "The flavour of my New Zealand culture includes the following ingredients: a strong relationship with the natural world, intensified by the sea, boating, fishing, camping and tramping; an engagement with the history of that land which began with boyhood encounters with Maori, whaling and battlesites around Paremata Harbour and north Wellington; a relationship with the literature of the country."

King had two children by his first marriage, to Ros Henry. He and Jungowska, who were married in 1988, lived in Opoutere, on the Coromandel Peninsula.

Frances Hodgkins

The Dunedin painter who became world-renowned

BORN: DUNEDIN, APRIL 28, 1869. DIED: DORCHESTER, DORSET, MARCH 22, 1947.

Though Frances Hodgkins is perhaps New Zealand's most celebrated painter, her career bloomed only when she moved to England in her 30s. Hodgkins painted from an early age – her father William was a very competent amateur artist who founded the Otago Art Society – but it was many years before she was saluted as an artist of world renown. A continuing thread throughout her career was her single-minded desire to improve her work, and her willingness to seek advice.

Hodgkins was an enthusiastic teenage artist. She had works exhibited in Dunedin and Christchurch in 1890 and took lessons from Girolamo Nerli, an Italian painter resident in Dunedin, who had an approach to landscape and portraiture that was uncommon at the time.

Through the 1890s Hodgkins built a following by sketching for the *Otago Daily Times and Witness* and *NZ Illustrated Magazine*. She attended Dunedin School of Art and Design, gaining first-class passes. In 1895 she won a New Zealand Academy of Fine Arts prize for *Head of an Old Woman*. Hodgkins taught art privately for several years and, with her sense of humour and engaging personality, proved a popular teacher.

She left New Zealand in 1901, following a path trodden by many contemporaries, including Dorothy Kate Richmond, Margaret Stoddart and Grace Joel. She enrolled at London Polytechnic and formed a close friendship with Richmond.

Hodgkins' *Fatima*, a large watercolour, was hung at the Royal Academy of Arts in 1903, the first time a New Zealander had been so honoured. She sent work for exhibition to New Zealand and their sales supplemented her income. She and Richmond returned to New Zealand in 1903 and she became engaged briefly to Thomas Wilby, an English writer she had met on the return trip. While she had many male friends thereafter, she never married.

In 1906 Hodgkins left New Zealand and travelled extensively through Europe, living in Paris for four years. She had exhibitions at several cities, including, in 1907, her first in London, at Paterson's Gallery.

She thrived in Paris, where she dabbled with oil-painting, though she continued to work principally in watercolour and guache, an opaque form of watercolour. There were exhibitions at the Salon in Paris and she held watercolour classes at the Académie Colarossi – the first woman to be appointed to this prestigious school's staff. She even began her own school for watercolour in Paris.

During a second trip to New Zealand, in 1913, she had several exhibitions and her use of colour and unusual compositions were viewed as modern and original and created a stir.

For many years Hodgkins' subject matter hardly changed – she generally painted people, and rural or sometimes street and harbour scenes – but she became increasingly renowned for her choice of an unusual tonal range of colours.

She was never afraid to experiment and in her 60s began working more with oils. *Spanish Shrine*, *Self Portrait: Still Life* and *The Courtyard in Wartime* were among her better-known oil paintings. She became part of the avant garde set of English artists, most of whom were decades younger. In 1931 she began an association with the Lefevre and Leicester galleries that lasted for the rest of her life. She represented Britain at the Venice Biennale in 1940.

By World War II Hodgkins, in her 70s, was in declining health. Yet she continued to paint until 1946, finding her subject matter in Dorset, around Corfe Castle village, where she had a studio. In 1946 the Lefevre Gallery held a popular Hodgkins exhibition of 64 paintings and 17 drawings, ranging from 1902 to 1946.

When Hodgkins died in 1947 her reputation was still undervalued in New Zealand. In 1949 her *The Pleasure Garden* became a cause célèbre. A group of Christchurch citizens bought the watercolour and gifted it to the city council, which rejected it repeatedly as "too modern". For many art historians the council attitude epitomised the conservatism of public taste and the event became a watershed in New Zealand art history.

In 1969 the Queen Elizabeth II Arts Council organised a Frances Hodgkins centenary exhibition. It was the first time a comprehensive selection of her work had been seen at home.

Hodgkins' impact on New Zealand artists should not be understated. Colin McCahon, speaking of his childhood in the 1920s, said: "There was one painting in the [Dunedin Public Art] Gallery I loved above all else – Frances Hodgkins' *Summer*. It sang from the wall... strong and kind and lovely."

George Nepia

The prince of All Black fullbacks

BORN: WAIROA, APRIL 25, 1905. DIED: RUATORIA, JUNE 27, 1986.

George Nepia rivals Colin Meads and Jonah Lomu as the most famous All Black. He was the sturdy 19-year-old Maori who played at fullback in every match of the so-called Invincibles 1924-25 team's tour of Britain and France. He had minimal experience at fullback before that tour, but grew into the position so quickly that even now some bypass the claims of Billy Wallace, Bob Scott, Don Clarke and Christian Cullen and opt for Nepia as the prince of All Black fullbacks.

He almost won selection for the 1935 All Black team to Britain. When he missed, he turned to rugby league, enjoying two fruitful years in the paid ranks in England. He had a special charm, a magic that drew others to him. He was too popular, too charismatic, to be shunned, as were others who switched to league, and was readmitted to rugby union by dint of a war amnesty. When he retired he took up refereeing. He was always at or around rugby.

As a carefree boy heading to college, Nepia hopped off the train with his mates at Hastings, instead of continuing to Te Aute College, where he had been enrolled. He attended Maori Agricultural College and received guidance from American Elder Moser. With his gridiron background, Moser instilled in Nepia the secrets of tackling and torpedo kicking.

Nepia made his representative debut in 1921, aged 16, and got his break playing the Te Mori Rose Bowl match between Southern and Northern Maori in Auckland. At the insistence of Maori identity Ned Parata, he switched from first-five to fullback. He seldom played anywhere else after that. Though Nepia knew little about fullback play when the Invincibles tour began, he responded magnificently. He was 1.75m (5ft 9in), weighed 82.5kg and exuded solidity. His courageous diving at the feet of onrushing forwards, fantastic punting and uncompromising tackling made him a sensation in a team of superstars.

Famous English writer Denzil Batchelor summed up the admiration Nepia drew: "When I hear others debating who will play at fullback for the Kingdom of Heaven versus the Rest, I turn to stone. It is not for me a question of whether Nepia was the best fullback in history. It is a question of which of the others is fit to loose the laces of his Cotton Oxford boots." Batchelor graphically described Nepia's playing style as "a panther slinking behind its prey".

During the 1920s he was a key figure in Norman McKenzie's record-breaking Hawke's Bay Ranfurly Shield team. In 1927 Nepia moved north to eke out a living from a rugged piece of farmland outside Gisborne. Because he was a Maori he was ineligible for the 1928 tour of South Africa, and little was heard of him for years. During the Depression, survival, not rugby, was the priority for Nepia, as he cared for his wife Huinga and their four children.

He returned to rugby in 1935 and toured Australia with the New Zealand Maori team, playing superbly. Then he switched to rugby league and, on the day the All Blacks lost the third test, and the series, against the 1937 Springboks, Nepia helped the Kiwis to a historic win over Australia.

He returned to play rugby after the war, making his last representative appearance in 1950, at 45 years, 158 days, a New Zealand record. He had the longest first-class career in New Zealand rugby history. In that final match his son, George, also played.

After his retirement, Nepia became a living legend. He courageously led the anti-South Africa tour marches through the 1950s, two decades before public feeling turned strongly that way. He maintained that one of the proudest moments of his life was in 1986, when he was made an honorary life vice-president of the South Africa Rugby Board. Another memorable occasion was in 1982, when he returned to Wales and walked on to Swansea's St Helen's ground, 58 years after he'd played there. The crowd stood to him, first in silence, and then in wave after wave of applause.

Nepia was a fine singer and had a best-selling record, *Beneath the Maori Moon*. He sang it at a huge public meeting in Wellington in support of "No Maoris, no tour".

Nepia was always incredibly popular. Nothing was too much trouble for him, and he had a unique giggly, high-pitched laugh. Younger New Zealanders saw why Nepia was so special when he was the subject of a 1986 *This Is Your Life* programme, which drew record ratings.

James Fletcher

The engaging immigrant who built an empire

BORN: KIRKINTILLOCH, SCOTLAND, MARCH 29, 1886. DIED: AUCKLAND, AUGUST 12, 1974.

James Fletcher, one of 13 children in a struggling Glasgow family, intended emigrating to Canada. However, an untimely bout of pneumonia forced him to change his plans and instead he headed for Dunedin. In time Fletcher's energy, optimism and daring led to his becoming one of the giants of New Zealand business.

Soon after his arrival in Dunedin in 1908 Fletcher had become one of the city's rising figures in the building industry. He had a short spell as the foreman of a building firm, then formed a house-building partnership with Englishman Albert Morris. They often tackled projects that pushed the limits. Their company built the St Kilda Town Hall and Knox College, but ran into trouble when building the Dunedin swimming baths – the pool had to be closed soon after its grand opening while Fletcher tried to figure out how to stop the water leaking.

At about the time that Morris quit the company, William, Andrew and John Fletcher joined their brother. The business became Fletcher Brothers and opened a branch in Invercargill. The family connection was to be extended over future generations. Fletcher married Lottie Cameron in 1911. Two of their three children, John and Jim, became principals in the business.

In 1916 Fletcher set his sights further afield. He won a tender to build the Auckland city markets, then started building in Wellington. By 1919, not content with simply running a national construction company, Fletcher began buying or establishing businesses related to the building industry. Fletcher Construction, as it had become, soon owned, or was associated with, a joinery factory, a brick-making concern, a concrete-production business, a marble quarry and, most important, some timber mills. The company headquarters was moved to Auckland.

Fletcher was avaricious in his thirst for technological knowledge. He read widely and his company often used equipment that was only just being introduced overseas.

Even through the Depression years of the 1930s, Fletcher Construction thrived. It helped to rebuild Hawke's Bay after the 1931 earthquake, and took on major building projects such as Auckland University College of Arts, Chateau Tongariro, Auckland Civic Theatre, Wellington Railway Station and the Dominion Museum.

One of the company's strengths was Fletcher's personality. He was outgoing and engaging, and mixed easily with everyone. He formed friendships with leading politicians of his day, including Peter Fraser and Walter Nash, and committed his company to building hundreds of State houses. This scheme took a long time to become financially viable, but eventually Fletcher made money from it. In 1940 the company was publicly listed as Fletcher Holdings, with James Fletcher its executive chairman.

However, Fletcher became more involved in other matters, as part of the Government's domestic World War II effort. He was appointed Commissioner of Defence Construction, Superintendent of Military Works and Controller of Shipping and, at his insistence, reported directly to Prime Minister Fraser. He was effective in pushing through projects with tight deadlines – a camp for 20,000 American marines was built north of Wellington in six weeks, and at Cornwall Park, Auckland, a hospital of 122 buildings was completed in 16 weeks.

Fletcher was knighted soon after he returned to private business. By then his son Jim (often called JC) was taking a leading hand in the company, and in 1950 became the managing director. Father and son worked with the National Government to establish the Tasman Pulp and Paper Company. James Fletcher became chairman of Tasman, which, after teething troubles, became a profitable company and a big foreign exchange earner.

Fletchers continued to expand, establishing Fletcher South Seas in Samoa and also getting a footing in Australia. James Fletcher decided to build a steel-making facility and, having studied overseas trends, opted to produce steel from scrap metal rather than using iron-sands. It proved an astute decision. Fletcher retired as chairman of Fletcher Holdings in 1967, and became founder president.

Besides his company interests, Fletcher was keenly involved in horse-breeding and racing. He established the Alton Lodge stud near Te Kauwhata. The stud produced many champions, including 1952 Melbourne Cup winner Dalray.

Fletchers continued to thrive after its founder's death, becoming Fletcher Challenge after merging with the sprawling Challenge Corporation. At the time of the merger it was the biggest New Zealand business, amounting to almost 10 per cent of the capitalisation of the New Zealand share market. After Jim Fletcher stood down, Ron Trotter and then Hugh Fletcher (Jim's son) ran the company.

67 Suzanne Aubert

New Zealand's Mother Teresa

BORN: LOIRE, FRANCE, JUNE 19, 1835. DIED: WELLINGTON, OCTOBER 1, 1926.

Not for nothing is this remarkable Frenchwoman known as New Zealand's Mother Teresa. Steps are being taken to have her canonised.

Marie Henriette Suzanne Aubert, the daughter of a well-off Lyons family, was introduced early to the Marists, but it was the curé of Ars, Abbé Jean Marie Vianney, who influenced her most, especially in spiritual matters. A childhood accident that left Aubert disabled for some years contributed to her lifelong empathy with the underprivileged, suffering and deformed.

In 1860, after nursing in the Crimean War, she sailed to New Zealand with Bishop Pompallier and other Catholic missionaries. Thus began more than 60 years of determined and unrelenting work by Sister Mary Joseph Aubert on behalf of society's less fortunate. She was an inspiring person, who was not afraid to cross authority. She had disputes and fallings-out with various church, bureaucratic and political figures, but her over-riding concern was always the care of the underprivileged.

Mother Aubert, as she became known, is recalled chiefly because of the religious order she founded, the Daughters of Our Lady of Compassion. But that hardly does justice to her life's work.

In Auckland through the 1860s, when working in an orphanage, she was pivotal in the establishment of the Nazareth Institution, a pioneering school for Maori girls. She did missionary work among Maori people in Northland, Hawke's Bay, and, from 1883, at Jerusalem on the Whanganui River. While at Jerusalem she expanded her work to care for unwanted and neglected Pakeha children. Her work encompassed teaching, nursing and religious studies. Mother Aubert became fluent in Maori and, in 1879, published a Maori-language prayer book and catechism. In 1885 she wrote *New and Complete Manual of Maori Conversation*, which deals with grammar and includes an extensive vocabulary. She also began to market Maori herbal remedies, entering an agreement with Kempthorne, Prosser and Company's New Zealand drug agency.

In 1899 she moved to Wellington, where she set up St Anthony's soup kitchen in Buckle Street. Mother Aubert and other Sisters of Compassion began visiting the ill and the poor. To support their work, they begged for alms, using baskets and prams to collect clothing, food and home utensils. Mother Aubert opened St Joseph's Home for Incurables in Buckle Street in 1900. Most patients were unmarried elderly men who had no family and were chronically ill.

She also established a day-care nursery, a revolutionary concept. She recognised the pressure on widows, deserted wives and other women who were trying to earn money while caring for their children. Women were able to leave their children in the sisters' care from 7am–6pm.

In 1907 Mother Aubert opened a larger institution for young children, Our Lady's Home of Compassion, at Island Bay. Children were transferred from Jerusalem and soon more illegitimate children, plus others who were physically and intellectually handicapped, arrived. The sisters also nursed children suffering from acute illnesses, including paralysis and tuberculosis. In 1910 Mother Aubert extended her work to Auckland, establishing St Vincent's Home of Compassion.

Mother Aubert travelled to Rome in 1913, seeking pontifical approval of the Daughters of Our Lady of Compassion, and a transfer of jurisdiction from Archbishop Redwood to herself as superior general. In April 1917 she gained permission from Pope Benedict XV. The Sisters of Compassion, as it is commonly known, remains New Zealand's only indigenous order.

Her work was pursued without regard to religious or political affiliations. She refused to restrict her activities to Catholics, telling benefactors seeking to place such a condition on donations that her work was the "salvation of souls, not the sanctification of Catholics". The Sisters of Compassion responded to a variety of local needs, from Maori mission work to the care of the elderly and sick.

Unemployment, child neglect, illegitimacy, family desertion, disease and lack of education left many children and adults in desperate straits, and she was always ready to help. She had rare determination, imagination, energy and confidence. She was extremely polite, but would never give in on a matter of principle.

She was a member of the St John Ambulance Association and the New Zealand Society for the Protection of Women and Children, and had links with the Plunket Society.

Mother Aubert became a much-loved national figure. When she died in 1926, aged 91, her funeral, attended by politicians and church leaders of many denominations, was described as the largest held for a woman in New Zealand.

Charles Heaphy

The adventurer with many strings to his bow

BORN: LONDON, 1820. DIED: BRISBANE, AUGUST 3, 1881.

Charles Heaphy is best recalled because of his paintings of New Zealand scenes in the mid-19th century. But he was a multi-talented individual, a prominent architect, surveyor and draughtsman, a courageous soldier, and a politician.

Heaphy, whose father, Thomas, was a capable painter, grew up in an affluent family and worked in London as a draughtsman until he entered the Royal Academy at 17. Two years later the New Zealand Company employed him as an artist and surveyor and he sailed to New Zealand on the Tory, arriving at Queen Charlotte Sound. He painted *Kakariki, from Ship Cove* and *Teawaiti*, his first major work in New Zealand, and several of the prominent Maori leaders in the area, including Te Rauparaha.

He was sent to Wellington to be a surveyor and drew extensively, including *Thorndon Flat and Part of the City of Wellington* in 1841. After a year spent travelling between Wellington and Nelson, with surveying trips to the Chatham Islands and Taranaki squeezed in, he returned to London. Much to the New Zealand Company's delight, he was a zealous backer of life in New Zealand. He wrote *A Narrative of a Residence in Various Parts of New Zealand* and provided supporting artwork to tempt would-be migrants.

Soon Heaphy was on his way back to New Zealand. He proved to be an incorrigible adventurer. There were two big expeditions around the South Island, one up the Buller River and the other, with Thomas Brunner, a strength-sapping five-month trek around much of the South Island.

Though able and versatile, Heaphy never made much money. His often parlous financial state was of concern throughout his life, despite all the get-rich schemes he dabbled in. Having failed to make a proper living as a farmer near Nelson, he shifted to Auckland in 1848, becoming a draughtsman for the colonial government's Survey Office. Three years later he married Catherine Churton. They never had their own children, though they adopted a boy and a girl.

Heaphy founded the Auckland Society of Arts and assisted with the first geological survey of Auckland. In 1851 he produced the massive Auckland town plan, which included names of original Crown Grant purchasers.

Heaphy was Commissioner of the Goldfields at Coromandel, travelled to the New Hebrides and Norfolk Island with Governor Grey and Bishop Selwyn, did surveying work around the northern part of the North Island and, in 1859, enlisted in the Auckland Rifle Volunteers, being commissioned to lieutenant in 1863. He was a fearless soldier, especially during the Invasion of Waikato, and in 1864 became the first British colonial soldier to be awarded a VC. He was part of a group that was attacked by Maori at Waiari, near Te Awamutu. Though hit by a volley of bullets from point-blank range, he continued to advance in order to help two fellow soldiers. When he could make no further progress, he stayed to direct fire against the Maori and prevent them moving in to kill the soldiers.

Heaphy had a spell as the Government's chief surveyor for Auckland, and in 1867 was elected to the House of Representatives for Parnell. He stayed busy, investing in and managing a gold mine in Thames, again without any real financial benefit. He resigned from the General Assembly to become Commander of Native Reserves, but by then his health was failing.

He suffered from chronic rheumatism and looked prematurely aged. After a couple of years as a Native Land Court judge he went to Queensland in 1881, to try to recover his health. He died in Brisbane and was buried in Toowong Cemetery. In 1961 the New Zealand Government marked his grave with a soldier's plaque.

Heaphy was resourceful and energetic, but rather soured on his life in New Zealand in his later years, possibly because of the huge demands placed on him as a surveyor. Earlier he had been noted for his humour and cheerful optimism. His watercolours provide an important but very personal record of early New Zealand. His 1841 *Mt Egmont from the Southward* is possibly the most remarkable, and the exaggeration of the familiar cone-shaped peak is so bizarre that his interest in stylization gets the better of his interest in realism. He is considered by some as a propagandist, whose works were designed to beguile potential settlers.

The Heaphy River, which rises in the Tasman Mountains in Buller, was named after him by Brunner in 1846, and the Heaphy Track has become a popular 70km walking trail through Nelson Forest Park.

Alfred Reed

Pioneering publisher and inspirational wanderer

BORN: HAYES, MIDDLESEX, DECEMBER 30, 1875. DIED: DUNEDIN, JANUARY 15, 1975.

Alfred Reed had a personal creed that began: "I believe in the gospel of work, of laughter and of goodwill to men; in the power of choice between good and evil." If anyone lived up to his beliefs it was Reed, and they served him well – he lived to 99 and was a strikingly happy, fit and active person.

Reed is recalled for two reasons: the publishing house he formed; and his marathon walks when well into old age. His strong Christian beliefs underpinned his life.

He was born near London and when he was 11 his father James, a brickworks owner of varying fortunes, moved his family to New Zealand. The Reeds did not find things easy in their adopted country, travelling from Wellington to Auckland and then to Parahaki, near Whangarei, in search of employment. James Reed eventually found work in the kauri gumfields and was joined by Alfred for a time.

But Alfred, though he had only limited schooling, was bright and ambitious. He taught himself shorthand and, after moving to Auckland at 19, typing. This enabled him to find a position with the New Zealand Typewriter Company. Within months the company sent him to run its Dunedin branch. Thus were planted the seeds of a flourishing career as a publisher and writer. In 1899 Reed married Isabel Fisher, whose family he had lived with previously in Auckland. Both were devout Christians and members of the Wesleyan Methodist Church. Reed became a lay preacher and was for years a Dunedin Sunday school superintendent.

In 1902 Reed bought the New Zealand Typewriter Company, which by then was operating only in Dunedin. He began importing religious material for Sunday school, built a mail order business dealing in religious literature and, in 1907, formed Sunday School Supply Stores.

He had a couple of years away from publishing during World War I, when he joined the 21st Reinforcements. He spent most of his time at the Trentham and Featherston military camps, where his clerical skills made him a valuable member of headquarters staff. Otherwise he gradually expanded his religious supply business into an important publishing firm.

In 1925 Reed's nephew, Alexander Wyclif Reed (known to most as Clif), joined him and A H Reed Publishers became A H and A W Reed. The company logo, the raupo (a New Zealand reed), became extremely well-known. Their first major book-publishing venture was *The Letters and Journals of Samuel Marsden*, produced in 1932. The following year they jointly wrote and published *First New Zealand Christmases*.

Though they continued to produce religious publications, A H and A W Reed became publishers of many types of New Zealand books, especially travel, sport and history.

Alfred Reed "retired" in 1940, but it was an active retirement. He remained on the company board until 1960 and wrote prodigiously – he wrote 44 books, mainly about his walking expeditions and provincial histories. Reed's last book, *The Happy Wanderer*, was published on his 99th birthday.

Some of his walks lasted months, amazing for a person who as a 12-year-old nearly lost a leg because of osteomyelitis. All along the way people would clap him, toot from cars, bring him cups of tea and keep him company. Classes of schoolchildren would gather to watch the sprightly old man walk happily through the country. He became a folk hero. At the age of 85 he walked from Cape Reinga to Bluff. At 86 he walked from East Cape to Cape Egmont. At 88 he traversed the South Island. At 89 he walked from Sydney to Melbourne. In his 80s he climbed Mt Ngauruhoe, Mt Egmont and Mt Ruapehu.

Reed had many interests. He was an experienced lecturer and broadcaster and visited hospitals regularly. He was also an eager collector of books, autographs and medieval manuscripts. His book collection, based around the works of Charles Dickens and Samuel Johnson and a large assortment of Bibles, became extremely valuable. In 1948 he donated it to the Dunedin Public Library, which now boasts a Reed Room.

In 1938 Reed, his wife and his sister formed the Alfred, Isabel and Marian Reed Trust for promoting Christianity, education and literature. Reed contributed handsomely to the trust for the remaining 36 years of his life.

He was knighted in 1974, when he was 98. In 1957 a scenic reserve near Parahaki was renamed the A H Reed Memorial Kauri Park and in 1974 a walking track on Mt Cargill was named after him.

Frank Sargeson

The writer who captured New Zealand working-class vernacular

BORN: HAMILTON, MARCH 23, 1903. DIED: NORTH SHORE, MARCH 1, 1982.

Frank Sargeson was one of New Zealand's finest short story writers, the first after Katherine Mansfield to be critically acclaimed at home and abroad. But success didn't come easy for Sargeson, who laboured for years to get his work published. He had a gift, but it required perseverance and resilience before it flowered.

Sargeson was born Norris Frank Davey and grew up in a middle-class Hamilton family. After leaving Hamilton High School in 1920 he set out to become a lawyer, working in a solicitor's office while studying law.

His uncle, Oakley Sargeson, owned a sheep farm in the King Country, and he had a significant impact on Davey, who appreciated his sense of humour and understated view of life. After a row with his mother – one of many blow-ups with family and friends – Davey moved to Auckland, where he redoubled his efforts to qualify as a solicitor.

A turning point was his 1927-28 trip to Europe. He thrived on life in London, visiting galleries, museums and the theatre, and travelled around the Continent. He also made his first attempt at writing for publication, but abandoned *Journal of a Suicide* as too dull and lifeless.

Back home, Davey worked for the Public Trust in Wellington. He wrote many poems and stories, but could not get any published. In 1929 he was arrested after a series of homosexual encounters. They were not his first – he had had homosexual liaisons in England and in New Zealand before that. He received a two-year prison sentence, suspended on condition he lived on his uncle's farm.

His writing activity increased, but nothing was published until *In France, Along the Road*, dealing with part of his journey around Europe, ran in the *New Zealand Herald* in May 1930. He worked long hours to complete a novel, *Blind Alleys*, but could not find a publisher. By now Davey was calling himself Frank Sargeson – he made it official in 1946 – partly, he claimed, in protest at his family's bourgeois values, but more likely to conceal his criminal conviction. In 1931 Sargeson settled in the family bach in Takapuna. He met former horse trainer Harry Doyle and they remained partners and friends until Doyle's death in 1971.

The Australian Woman's Mirror and some Auckland newspapers began publishing his work, but it was a 500-word fictional sketch, published in the radical periodical *Tomorrow* in 1935, that set him on his way. *Conversation with My Uncle* revealed what was to become the classic Sargeson style, quiet but sometimes stinging narrative, and dialogue that conveyed accurately the laconic and often slangy accents of New Zealand working-class vernacular.

Sargeson's writing career prospered. He had several collections of his works released and wrote prodigiously. *The Making of a New Zealander* was joint winner of the 1940 Centennial Literary Competition's short story section. His work was published in Sydney, London and the United States, besides New Zealand. Many of his books were also translated into other languages. His writing centred on ordinary New Zealanders doing ordinary things and he focused mainly on the period between the world wars, especially the Depression years.

Sargeson enjoyed mixing with other leading writers, including Rex Fairburn, Robin Hyde, Jane Mander, Oliver Duff and Denis Glover. He mentored aspiring writers, such as Janet Frame and Maurice Duggan. Frame spent two years living on his Takapuna property and wrote *Owls Do Cry* there.

Sargeson's first full-length novel was *I Saw in My Dream*, published in 1949. By then he had become a national figure. He suffered from surgical tuberculosis and was on an invalid's benefit, but the Government converted it to a literary pension, which he drew until he qualified for the old-age pension.

Through the 1950s Sargeson concentrated on writing plays, though not with great success. He revived his career in the 1960s with *Collected Stories 1935-63*, and wrote a novel, *Memoirs of a Peon*, plus several successful short stories and short novels. In the 1970s he produced three volumes of his autobiography, *Once is Enough, More Than Enough* and *Never Enough!* He became well-known around Takapuna. Invariably sporting a beret and with a canvas haversack slung over his shoulder, the bearded, bespectacled Sargeson was often stopped by people eager for a chat.

His health eventually broke down, but he wrote until almost the end. *Conversation In a Train*, a collection of his critical writings, was published in 1983, a year after he died. The Frank Sargeson Trust was established in 1987. It has preserved the house in which he lived and wrote, and sponsors writers' scholarships.

Roger Douglas

The man who shaped New Zealand's modern economy

BORN: AUCKLAND, DECEMBER 5, 1937.

Roger Douglas was a controversial but pivotal figure in New Zealand history. Though he had trade union roots and his family were long-time Labour Party members, the radical economic restructuring he introduced when he became Minister of Finance in 1984 was anything but left-wing. Many Labour supporters accused him of betrayal. On the other hand, Douglas's policies attracted interest and accolades from financial commentators, theorists and politicians throughout the world.

There is still debate about Douglas's reforms, but what is undeniable is their importance in New Zealand history. His policies were known as Rogernomics. How many political figures in New Zealand have a movement named after them? Douglas, educated at Auckland Grammar, gained an accounting degree at Auckland University. He became company secretary of Bremworth Carpets and was involved in Red Seals, the family health food business.

His interest in politics was whetted by a three-year stint on the Manukau City Council. Politics was in the blood – his father, Norman, was a long-time MP for Auckland Central (they served six years together in Parliament), and his family's Labour Party connections stretched back to the days of Keir Hardie and Ramsay MacDonald in England.

Douglas entered Parliament as the member for Manukau in 1969 and stamped himself as well-organised and energetic. After only three years he was promoted to Cabinet by Norman Kirk, becoming the youngest Cabinet Minister for nearly half a century.

While in Opposition through the late 1970s he developed his monetary theories to such an extent that in 1980 he released an alternative Budget, written while he was shadow Minister of Transport. This led to Labour leader Bill Rowling dismissing him from the Opposition front benches. Later that year he produced a book called *There's Got To Be A Better Way*.

Douglas was one of a group – along with the likes of Mike Moore, David Caygill, Trevor de Cleene, Michael Bassett and Richard Prebble – who hitched their wagon to rising Labour star David Lange, and supported his supplanting Rowling as leader.

When Lange led Labour to a storming election victory in 1984, he made Douglas Minister of Finance. New Zealanders hardly knew what hit them. Douglas implemented perhaps the most radical changes in New Zealand's economic history. He devalued and floated the dollar and altered the structure of the public and private sectors, trying to eliminate the over-regulation of the Muldoon years. He slashed subsidies and trade tariffs, imposed a goods and services tax and privatised public assets. These policies were regarded as a betrayal of Labour's left-wing policy platform, and were massively unpopular with party members.

Unfazed, Douglas, if anything, increased the pace of his reforms. For some time Lange let him run his own show, despite plaintive pleas from Labour stalwarts. The 1987 election was won with an increased majority, though tellingly Labour did poorly in its traditional strongholds and Douglas even struggled in Manurewa, which he had previously held comfortably.

Finally, in the aftermath of the October 1987 sharemarket crash, Lange baulked when Douglas proposed introducing a flat tax rate, and a stand-off took place between the two most powerful members of the Government. When Douglas backer Prebble was sacked, Douglas resigned his portfolio in December 1988.

However, his colleagues wanted Douglas on board and he was voted back into Cabinet after six months, though Lange demoted him by giving him only the Immigration and Police portfolios. Shortly after, Lange stood down and was replaced as Prime Minister by Geoffrey Palmer, and then Mike Moore, neither of whom returned Douglas to the finance job.

Douglas quit Parliament in 1990. In 1993 he and Derek Quigley formed the right-wing Association of Consumers and Taxpayers, which, once the introduction of MMP was announced two years later, became the Act New Zealand political party. Douglas had a brief spell as the leader, then passed the baton to Prebble and became party president. Later he became the patron, until, unhappy that the party was seeking to become too populist and not paying enough attention to the economic goals that he continued to advocate, he resigned in 2004.

While Douglas was a divisive figure in New Zealand, he was in great demand overseas. He became a regular speaker at financial conferences around the world and a consultant to the World Bank. Douglas held senior positions in a number of prominent companies and became the managing director of Roger Douglas Associates. He was knighted in 1991.

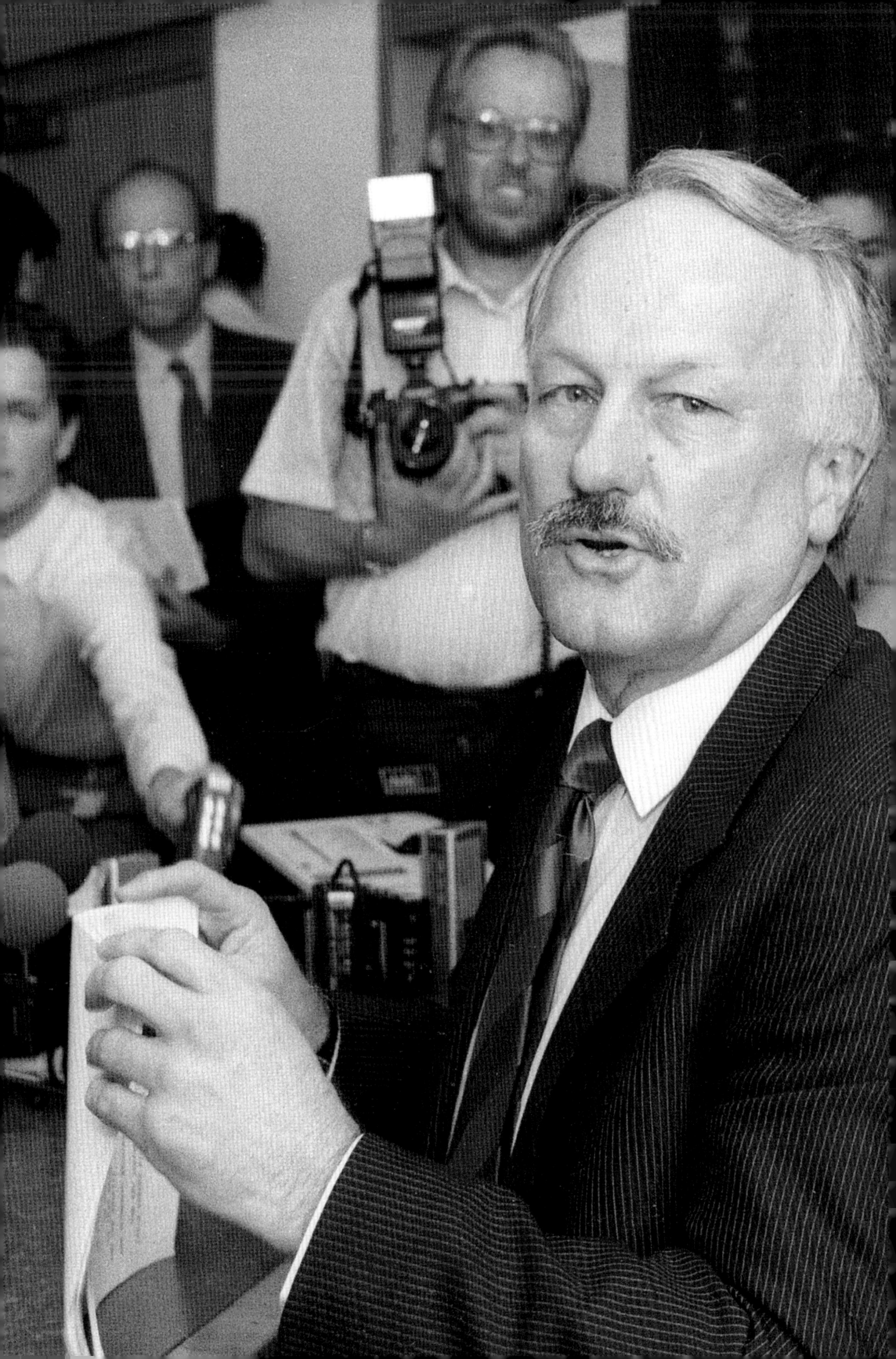

Matt During

The neuroscientist who is making a difference

BORN: NOVEMBER 30, 1956, WELLINGTON.

One of Matt During's teachers at Hamilton East School wrote in his report: "Gives the impression that one of these days he will awaken to the possibilities of hard work." During's work as a neuroscientist over the past two decades indicates that he has more than fulfilled that teacher's forecast.

During's early years were spent at Day's Bay, near Wellington. His father, an agricultural scientist who worked for the Department of Agriculture, and his mother, a doctor, were busy raising five children. Matt fitted in but didn't impress as a genius in the making.

The family moved to Hamilton in 1964. He attended Hamilton East School and Southwell Boys Preparatory School, where, despite apparently drifting through his classes, he was dux.

At Auckland Medical School he grew bored with the study. He was kicked off the course and it required some pleading from During and his mother before he was reinstated. Despite a spotty attendance record, he passed his exams and graduated in 1981. Always a lateral thinker, he funded his way through university by driving a taxi through the night, which unfortunately meant he tended to sleep during the day.

He left New Zealand in 1985, drawn to the United States by the work of Professor Richard Wurtman at the Massachusetts Institute of Technology. Wurtman was researching chemical transmission and hormone signalling in the brain and During was taken on as a junior research fellow. It was the beginning of 20 years of groundbreaking work by During. He had spells at Harvard and Yale universities, then returned to New Zealand from 1996-98 to work at Auckland University.

On returning to the United States he spent several years at Jefferson Medical College, Philadelphia, and founded the Neurologix Inc biotechnology company, now trading publicly and with headquarters in New York. He is based now at New York's Cornell Medical School, where he directs a molecular neuroscience laboratory in the department of neurological surgery. He maintains close ties with Auckland University's Medical School. He and protégée Deborah Young are the Auckland University Medical and Health Sciences Department's principal researchers in gene therapy.

During does not fit the accepted picture of a scientist. He is outspoken, colourful and talkative. However, the quality of his research work has been outstanding. His research teams at Auckland University and Jefferson University did ground-breaking work to discover a vaccine to counter stroke and epilepsy, a paradigm-shifting approach that his Auckland laboratory is developing for clinical translation.

He felt that many acquired diseases were in part caused by defective genes, and worked on manipulation of human genes, aimed at correcting the defect and combating such diseases. During has focused on the most common genetic disease, cystic fibrosis, but he has turned his attention to many others as well, including Alzheimer's, Huntington's, haemophilia, intestinal cancer and diabetes. Because his work is cutting edge, he has faced the ethical dilemma of generic engineering – does it lead to human enhancement, and should that be encouraged?

In 1996 he created headlines when his team at Auckland Hospital conducted a significant world first, implanting synthetic genes directly into the brains of two American girls, aged 19 months and two years, who were suffering from Canavan disease, a rare and fatal brain disorder. Some hailed his work, while others accused him of being a cowboy. The girls, who were expected to die within a couple of years, are alive and are leading reasonable lives. It was another eight years before similar operations were undertaken elsewhere.

In 1998 During obtained headlines again when he published in *Nature Medicine* the development of a gene pill. In collaboration with Carlo Croce at Jefferson, During showed that such a gene pill approach could be used to prevent gastrointestinal cancer.

There was another world first in 2002, when he won approval from the Food and Drug Administration to introduce gene therapy on 12 humans suffering from severe Parkinson's disease. The results have been so heartening that During is guardedly optimistic that he will find a cure for the illness.

While most scientists tend to be cautious, During pushes ahead. "I admit I upset some people, but I push hard, right to the edge. You don't just want to come up with a concept; you want to be able to put it into practice and improve people's lives. That's what it's about."

During's sister, Miriam, once told him that it was not enough just to do research, but that it had to make a difference. He has lived his professional life by that creed.

Te Kooti

Tribal leader and prophet

BORN: NEAR GISBORNE, c1832. DIED: TE KARAKA, APRIL 7, 1893.

Te Kooti was the ultimate Maori warrior – fierce, brave and inspiring. For several years he attacked his Maori and Pakeha enemies in the central North Island with his lethal guerrilla campaign. Basing himself in the Urewera mountains, he was remarkably successful at launching lightning attacks and retreating when things went awry. Though Te Kooti established the Ringatu religion, his warrior reputation earned him most fame. Yet in later life he was dedicated to peace, law and the gospel. He rejected the Christian practice of communion, which, he said, was symbolic of cannibalism.

He was a member of the Rongowhakaata tribe from Poverty Bay. As a child he attended the Whakato Anglican Mission School. In 1852 he was baptised Te Kooti, the name by which he is referred, though he mainly used his ancestral name, Te Turuki. He was strong-willed and unpredictable, and often fell out with his own chiefs and his Pakeha business partners.

The arrival of the Pai Marire (Hauhau) religion in Poverty Bay in 1865 brought civil war to the area and was a defining moment for Te Kooti. Many Maori converted to the new faith. Te Kooti did not and fought alongside Government soldiers and pro-Government Maori kupapa in the siege of Te Waeranga-a-Hika against the Hauhau. He was accused of supplying ammunition to the enemy, but maintained that he had been falsely accused. Nevertheless, he was arrested and deported to the Chatham Islands, along with men he had been fighting.

While in the Chathams Te Kooti suffered bouts of fever and experienced the visions that gave birth to the Ringatu movement. Ringatu stood for "The Upraised Hand", a reference to Te Kooti and his followers' practice of standing and raising their right hands before prayer. His religion grew from a mixture of Old Testament beliefs – Ringatu followers identified with the Israelites returning to their promised land.

On July 4, 1868, Te Kooti masterminded an audacious escape, leading 300 prisoners aboard the The Rifleman and back to the east coast of the North Island. Most escapers converted to Ringatu. Te Kooti planned to form an alliance with the Maori King movement or challenge King Tawhiao for leadership of the Maori people.

The army called on Te Kooti to surrender, but he declined, though he vowed not to fight unless attacked. A group of 120 Europeans and pro-Government Maori then hunted Te Kooti, who had settled at Turanga (Gisborne). Te Kooti's men won several ensuing battles, including a bloody massacre inflicted on Pakeha at Matawhero. There ensued years of ferocious fighting, some to gain revenge for his earlier betrayal, some to secure land. Te Kooti was an expert guerrilla fighter, but less effective when fighting from a fixed position. Colonial and Maori forces chased him and he had many narrow escapes.

In 1869 Te Kooti formed an alliance with Tuhoe, who gave him protection in the Ureweras. He then travelled to Te Kuiti to negotiate with the King movement. Tawhiao and his close ally, Rewi Maniapoto, rejected Te Kooti's suggestion that they combine their movements. At Te Porere (near National Park), Te Kooti and his followers constructed a British-style redoubt, but errors in design and location led to defeat at the hands of his kupapa and Pakeha pursuers. Once again Te Kooti escaped. His power base was shattered only when the Tuhoe were conquered by his enemies.

He moved to Te Kuiti in 1873, having been offered protection by Tawhiao in return for embracing pacifism. He remained for 10 years, while he built his religion. He developed various holy days, and composed texts and prayers, drawing always from scriptures. His teachings spread, and with them belief in his powers as a healer and prophet. People travelled great distances to listen and be healed.

Though Te Kooti was pardoned by the Government in 1883, authorities with long memories arrested him and imprisoned him at Mt Eden jail, citing an anticipatory breach of the peace. He was eventually released and there followed some complicated legal wrangling. Court of Appeal judges labelled Te Kooti "a Maori prophet, and a drunken one to boot". Yet his teachings show a commitment to the law. One of his directives was: "The canoe for you to paddle after me is the Law. Only the Law can be set against the Law."

In 1891 the Government allocated Te Kooti and his followers 600 acres at Wainui, on the Ohiwa Harbour. In February 1893, while travelling to the new settlement, he was injured. He died on the shore of the harbour soon after. A marae for the Ringatu church was established there after his death.

Te Kooti or Turuki addressing Rotorua natives at Tarawera in 1887

Hongi Hika

The Nga Puhi leader who encouraged European settlement

BORN: NEAR KAIKOHE, c1772. DIED: WHANGAROA, MARCH 6, 1828.

Hongi Hika, the all-conquering Maori warrior of the early 19th century, used muskets he obtained from Pakeha to cut a swathe of destruction from Northland through Waikato and as far east as Bay of Plenty. Many rival Maori were killed or fled, which paved the way for European settlement of the region.

He is usually portrayed as ruthless and cruel, but, while he fought ferociously, there was a softer side to him. One of his two wives, Turikatuku, was blind, and he protected her for nearly 30 years. He was generous to missionaries, negotiated sagely with Europeans and was a visionary leader who improved his people's agricultural and fishing output.

Hika was the son of Te Hotete, chief of Te Tahuna, and therefore was a member of the senior chiefly line of his tribe and related to the Nga Puhi chiefs of his day.

In 1806 the Nga Puhi were ambushed by Murupaenga, of Ngati Whatua, in the battle of Moremonui. Nga Puhi chief Pokaia was killed, as were several of Hika's relatives and many tribesmen. Hika, who barely escaped, succeeded Pokaia as the Nga Puhi war leader and sought revenge.

He was not an especially gifted fighting tactician, but discovered as early as 1808 the value of using muskets against the hand-to-hand combat methods of the Maori tribes he was encountering. Hika wrought havoc on the east coast region with a huge war party in 1818, returning with 2000 prisoners and a huge collection of dried heads. There were many other similarly successful campaigns.

Hika eagerly sought contact with European visitors. He even travelled to Sydney with his nephew, Ruatara, in 1814 to encourage Samuel Marsden to proceed with plans to establish a Church Missionary Society in the Bay of Islands. When the mission was duly established, Hika offered it full protection. He later sheltered other missions in Northland. Hika encouraged European settlers, realising the benefits they could bring his people, and severely punished any Maori who committed offences against them. He was also at pains to protect visiting sealers and whalers, with whom he traded food for muskets.

While continuing to prove virtually unbeatable in battle because of the advantage of his guns, Hika was farsighted enough to understand the importance of the iron tools offered by missionaries, who would not barter in muskets. He used the tools to bring about an agricultural revolution among his people in terms of crops and productivity.

In 1820 Hika and young chief Waikato visited England in the company of missionary Thomas Kendall. At Cambridge he assisted Professor Samuel Lee to compile a Maori grammar book for the Church Missionary Society. He became the first Maori to have an audience with the English sovereign – King George IV gave him a suit of armour. Hika used his time out of New Zealand to acquire a supply of muskets, the primary reason for his journey. Stopping at Sydney on the way home, he traded many of the gifts he had received in England for more guns, so that when he arrived back in New Zealand he was ready for war.

Over the next five years Hika was to terrorise enemy tribes in the central North Island, scoring a succession of overwhelming victories for Nga Puhi. He was brutal, often staying days after a successful battle to feast on the bodies of those he had killed. He also took many captives, using them to increase agricultural production, in order to have more produce to trade for muskets.

Away from battle, Hika, a shortish man of solid build, was said to be mild, gentle and courteous. He was regarded as shrewd and perceptive, especially of Pakeha criticism of Maori cannibal practices. He often worked alongside his people farming and fishing. But he was ceaseless in his desire to conquer, and eventually set his sights on the Ngati Uru and Ngati Pou of the Whangaroa region. During a battle in 1827 he was struck in the chest by a musket ball. He lingered for a year in declining health, but died from the injury.

One of Hika's daughters, Harata, married another famous Maori leader, Hone Heke.

A section of Highway 30, from Hinehopu on the shore of Lake Rotoiti to Te Pohue Bay on the shore of Lake Rotoehu, is known as Hongi's Track. It was along this section of land that his Nga Puhi warriors carried their canoes overland, in order to attack the Arawa people in 1823.

Chief Waikato　　　Hongi Hika　　　Thomas Kendell (missionary)

David Low 75

The free-spirited cartoonist who would not be cowered

BORN: DUNEDIN, APRIL 7, 1891. DIED: LONDON, SEPTEMBER 19, 1963.

David Low was detested by Hitler and placed on a Gestapo arrest list. Stalin and Mussolini might well have contemplated similar action. He treated Prime Ministers, notably Australia's Billy Hughes and Britain's David Lloyd-George, mercilessly and established a world reputation for unwavering integrity, not allowing himself to be swayed by the pleas of proprietors or editors of the newspapers employing him.

Low became one of the most influential journalists of his era, primarily through his cartoons, but also, especially during World War II, because of his radio broadcasts and writing.

He was raised in Dunedin, then Christchurch, by free-spirited parents who encouraged him to be independent. He was even withdrawn from Christchurch Boys' High School and more or less allowed to wander free in his early teens. Even then, Low was a gifted thinker, a passionate reader and a keen black and white artist who took to copying comic books and was especially influenced by Punch's Phil May.

As a cartoonist, Low was a child prodigy. Aged 11, he had one of his comic strips published in British publication *Big Budget*, and regularly won drawing competitions run by Australian magazine *New Idea*. Then he began to be published regularly in the *Spectator*, a Christchurch political weekly. Soon his drawings were appearing in the Salvation Army's *War Cry* and *New Zealand Truth*.

He tended to be left-leaning, and his drawings gelled with the *Weekly Herald* and *Canterbury Times*. He was the *Times*' staff political cartoonist until he refused to draw cartoons advocating compulsory military training. Low was not without a job long. In 1911, aged 20, he based himself in Melbourne and became an internationally-acclaimed cartoonist through his work for *The Bulletin*. The paper employed him to travel around Australia, drawing caricature portraits of leading figures. These provided the material for a book of 400 drawings.

In 1915 he became *The Bulletin's* political cartoonist in Melbourne, where Australia's Parliament was housed. For five years Low devoted much attention to Prime Minister Billy Hughes, whose small build, large nose and bullying personality were ideal features for distortion and ridicule. His *Billy Book* was so popular that it led to work for him in England. Low sent the book and examples of his cartoons to the *Manchester Guardian*, which reproduced some of his work.

Encouraged, he moved to London in 1919 and was soon working for the *Star*. He particularly relished drawing David Lloyd-George. Low also contributed to *Punch* and published several books in England, the first being *Lloyd-George and Co*. In 1920 Low married Madeline Kenning, of Auckland, whom he had met before leaving for London. They were to have two daughters.

In 1927 Low began a 23-year stint with the *Evening Standard*. He accepted the job on the condition that he had "complete freedom in the selection and treatment of subject matter". This was important – for example, he opposed appeasement, while the paper praised the policy that was so strongly advocated by the Chamberlain Government as producing "peace in our time".

Convinced of Hitler's hostile intentions, Low turned his sights on the Nazis. In 1933, newspapers carrying his cartoons were banned in Germany, and two years later Italy adopted the same policy. Low was asked to soften his attacks, which were evidently hampering British diplomatic efforts, but he was never one to compromise.

He introduced into his cartoons several symbols, such as Joan Bull, and, most famously, Colonel Blimp, who first appeared in 1934. Blimp was a vehicle for Low's blistering criticism of the confused thinking and stupidity of the establishment in pre-war Britain. Blimp's corpulent figure, flowing moustache and self-satisfied utterances were the vehicles for Low's intense criticism.

Low was incredibly versatile. During World War II he broadcast regularly for the BBC Overseas Service and commanded the same respect on air as did Winston Churchill. He also made television appearances and wrote for the Sunday edition of the *New York Times*. He was a good writer, but it was his ability to draw simple, clear cartoons that set him above others. In 1953 he became a world-syndicated cartoonist, with first publication in the *Manchester Guardian*.

Low had more than 30 collections of his drawings published and wrote seven books, including his autobiography in 1956. He received honorary degrees from the New Brunswick and Leicester universities and was knighted in 1962. His legacy was immense. He influenced the British cartoonists of his era, and also some of New Zealand's best, including Gordon Minhinnick, Neville Colvin and Tom Scott.

Kate Edger

Pioneer of women's education

BORN: ABINGDON, ENGLAND, JANUARY 6, 1857. DIED: DUNEDIN, MAY 6, 1935.

Kate Edger was the first woman in New Zealand to gain a university degree. She established beyond any argument the intellectual capacity of women and in her quiet, reserved way, became one of the pioneers of New Zealand education.

She was born in Abingdon, Berkshire, the daughter of a university-educated Baptist minister. When she was five the family emigrated to Albertland, north of Auckland, where her father, Samuel, continued his ministerial duties. In Northland, and later when the family moved to Auckland, Kate was home-schooled, along with her equally capable younger sister Lilian. They were industrious and hard-working and seemed able to master any subject.

In the 1870s there was no secondary schooling for girls, so Kate was permitted to attend Auckland College and Grammar School, where she studied with the top class of boys and prospered academically. They were different times – as the only girl in the class she was required to enter with her eyes down, and seldom spoke to her classmates, though, she said later, they treated her courteously. Despite the difficult circumstances she demonstrated the determination and stamina required to achieve her academic goals.

She gained a university scholarship in 1874, another in natural philosophy and chemistry in 1875, and was senior scholar in Latin and mathematics in 1876, when she qualified to study for a bachelor of arts degree. Getting accepted for university was not easy. The school was affiliated to the University of New Zealand, and when she applied she gave her age and qualifications, but not her gender. She wrote to the chancellor of the university: "I am a candidate for one of the Mathematical Scholarships of the University of New Zealand to be awarded at the Examination in May. My age is within the specified limits, and I have received instruction privately and also in Latin and Mathematics at the Auckland College evening classes."

Gaining admission to university proved more challenging than the study she was required to undertake, because she was always an excellent student. On July 11, 1877, aged 20, she achieved a BA, becoming the first woman in the British Empire to earn such a degree. More than 1000 turned out for her historic graduation. The Bishop of Auckland, William Cowie, presented her with a white camellia, which he said represented "unpretending excellence".

Shortly afterwards, Edger took a position as first assistant at the recently-opened Christchurch Girls' High School. At the same time she studied for an MA at Canterbury College and in 1882 she and Lilian were capped at the same time.

Nelson College for Girls opened in 1883 and the slightly-built Edger, only 26, was appointed the founding headmistress. She was extraordinarily busy, not only running the school administration and preparing senior girls for scholarship examinations, but also teaching English grammar, comprehension and literature, physical science, Latin, mathematics, singing and geography. She coped well with the many teething problems a new school encounters and was respected by the students.

She often paid for school equipment if there was not other funding available, and she sponsored a scholarship to enable one extra girl a year to board at the college.

In 1890 Edger married a Welsh congregational minister, the Rev William A Evans. They started a family soon afterwards – they eventually raised three boys – and moved to Wellington. While her husband preached and did voluntary work, Edger gave private tuition at her home in Mount Victoria, delivered lectures and was often to be found working among the city's poor. She assisted her husband occasionally by preaching.

By now her academic prowess was widely acknowledged. She was employed as a University Entrance examiner for nearly 40 years, until resigning in 1929, and served two years on the staff of the Department of Education.

Edger once called home-making "the noblest sphere of women's work" and was never a strident feminist, but she became involved in the suffrage movement in the 1890s. She was a key figure in the Wellington branch of the New Zealand Society for the Protection of Women and Children for more than 30 years and was also active in the Women's Temperance Union.

Her husband died in 1921, but she remained in Wellington until 1932, when she moved to Dunedin to live with her son Elwyn. In 1935, just months before her death, she was awarded the King's Silver Jubilee Medal.

In 2003 the University of Auckland named its huge Information Commons after her.

Marie Clay

The Michael Jordan of reading

BORN: WELLINGTON, JANUARY 3, 1926.

Marie Clay's Reading Recovery programme revolutionised remedial teaching practice throughout much of the world. Within a decade of the programme's introduction in New Zealand more than 200,000 six-year-olds with reading problems had been assisted to an extent where they were able to read and write well. When Clay received the David H Russell Award from the National Council of Teachers of English in 1979, she was described as "the quiet voice of reason in a field frequently jarred by the conflicting cries of the marketplace".

On leaving Wellington East Girls' College, Clay wanted to be an occupational therapist but was too young, so she went to Wellington Teachers' Training College. She gained her teacher's certificate in 1945 and specialised in teaching primary school children with intellectual disabilities. They were busy times, because she was also studying for a BA at Victoria University. She graduated in 1946 and gained an MA in 1948. Her masters thesis was "The Teaching of Reading to Special Class Children". The seeds of the Reading Recovery programme had been planted.

Clay worked for the Department of Education as a psychologist, then, in 1950-51, attended the University of Minnesota on a Fulbright Scholarship.

After a spell teaching children with special needs in Wanganui, Clay moved to Auckland. She had two children in the 1950s and became involved in the early days of the Playcentre movement. She also began teaching remedial reading at home. The sudden improvement in the reading ability of two of her pupils within a few months led her to design research to monitor early progress.

She joined Auckland University's Education Department and taught child development, normal and clinical, to educational psychologists for 30 years. In 1975 she became the first woman appointed by the university as a full professor and as a head of department.

Working towards a PhD in Education, she undertook a unique study in 1966, monitoring the weekly progress of 100 children during their first year of school. This gave her a deeper understanding of why some children have reading difficulties and exemplified one of Clay's strengths – her desire to maintain a high level of contact with children, parents and teachers.

Clay made many contributions to education, ranging from lecturing to writing books and papers. But she is most closely linked with the Reading Recovery programme, which singles out children with below-average reading and writing skills after a year in school. Child and teacher then work together in individual programmes, reading, writing and finding new ways of understanding messages. It is expensive and labour-intensive, but it is short-term, and works stunningly well, with a 90 per cent success rate.

Reading Recovery trials began in Auckland in 1978. By 1983 it had become a national education programme. It has been adopted throughout the Commonwealth and the United States, and been redeveloped for use in Spanish and French. The Americans dubbed Clay "the Michael Jordan of reading".

Many of Clay's books have become vital reading in education circles. For example, *Reading Recovery: Guidelines for Teachers in Training* has sold a million copies worldwide. A revised guidebook aims to make accelerated progress possible for children with a wider range of problems.

She is the only non-North American to be elected president of the International Reading Association, and during her term – 1992-93 – revived the association's emphasis on international activities. In 1995 she received the William S Gray Citation of Merit, being acknowledged as a "world-class scholar, researcher and visionary educator". She was inducted into the Reading Hall of Fame in 1982 and in 1993 received the Charles A Dana Award for Pioneering Achievements in Education. Five overseas universities have awarded her honorary degrees.

Despite her innate modesty and unassuming manner, Clay has received many tributes in New Zealand. She has been elected a fellow of the New Zealand Educational Institute, the New Zealand Psychological Society and the Royal Society of New Zealand, and was created a Dame in 1987. When she was made the inaugural New Zealander of the Year, in 1994, the judges described her as "a person who had a dream of improving the lives of others, although never seeking personal reward or recognition".

Clay once said that New Zealand education had the technology to "turn the elephant over". After a career in education, she summed up: "It looks as though the co-operative efforts of many people have done just that. The weighty problems of reading and writing difficulties now don't seem so frightening."

Rewi Alley

New Zealand's gift to China

BORN: SPRINGFIELD, CANTERBURY, DECEMBER 2, 1897. DIED: BEIJING, DECEMBER 27, 1987.

Rewi Alley's reputation among his countrymen fluctuated according to how New Zealand viewed China. But there is no doubt that he made a tremendous impact in the world's most populous country. American journalist Edgar Snow wrote: "Rewi Alley is unique because he has achieved greatness in a country where few foreigners manage to achieve an authentic ripple."

As the People's Republic of China became a more accepted part of the world community, there was a revision of thinking on Alley. Finally, New Zealanders openly saluted his work. In 1984 he was awarded the Queen's Service Medal and three years later Prime Minister David Lange narrated a documentary on Alley. In 1997 Prime Minister Jim Bolger announced a $100,000 grant for the Rewi Alley agricultural extension unit at Gansu University.

Alley attended Christchurch Boys' High School, where he was a keen rower and rugby player. His was a distinguished family – one of his brothers became an All Black and New Zealand's first national librarian, while his other brother and two sisters were prominent in education and/or nursing.

In 1916 Alley enlisted in the New Zealand Expeditionary Force and, fighting in France, won the Military Medal for bravery. After the war he spent six years farming a rugged piece of Taranaki terrain, before returning to Christchurch. Having read about the "Red Peril" in the Auckland Weekly News, he decided to have a closer look at the Chinese revolution. He worked as a radio operator on a boat from Sydney to China and arrived in Shanghai in 1927, when the communist rebellion was gathering force.

Alley worked for the Shanghai Municipal Council as a fireman, rising to chief fire inspector, and as a factory inspector. During the catastrophic famine of 1929, when six million people died, and the great flood in 1931, he toiled hard doing relief work.

Gradually, Alley became part of Chinese society. He represented the League of Nations in overseeing dyke repairs at Wuhan, and began translating Chinese poems and literature into English, work he continued for more than 50 years. He was an important figure in interpreting China to the world.

Alley was appalled to see the slave labour and ritual executions that were part of Chinese life. Dismayed at the way the Chinese regime was intent on exterminating communists, he became involved in an underground movement that is said to have saved thousands of lives. He also wrote for the radical journal Voice of China.

When the Japanese invaded in 1937, Alley conceived the idea of encouraging the population to move inland, and developed the creed of "Gung Ho", or working together. This expression has become popular English usage. He persuaded the Chinese Government to form Chinese industrial co-operatives, and travelled extensively to set up the factories. His plan succeeded so well that soon the factories were producing everything from cotton to grenades.

Alley was always optimistic and determined. In 1942 he began establishing technical schools in remote areas and creating co-operatives alongside them, thereby combining education and production. His most spectacular success was the Shandan School in the Gobi Desert.

After the communists gained ascendancy in 1949, Alley moved to Beijing and his international reputation grew. He attended many international peace conferences and always pushed the Chinese line. On his visits to New Zealand he was met with suspicion. He criticised American interventionist policies in Vietnam, and with New Zealand allied to the United States, this did not go down well.

Alley wrote 66 books, the first of which, *Yo Banfa!* (We Have a Way), was published in 1952. His *Shandan – an Adventure in Creative Education*, published in 1958, sold around the world. He travelled extensively and ceaselessly through the Chinese interior. In 1958 he founded the New Zealand China Friendship Society.

Alley was befriended by many world leaders, including Fidel Castro and Che Guevara, and was generally on good terms with the Chinese hierarchy, including Premier Zhou En Lai and Chairman Mao Tse-tung. In 1977 Premier Deng Xiaoping hosted a banquet for him on his 80th birthday. In 1982 he was granted honorary Chinese citizenship.

During his last visit to New Zealand, in 1972, he was given an honorary doctorate in literature by Victoria University. Waikato University has named a prize for Chinese studies in his honour. Alley lived to 90 and became a revered figure in his second homeland. He never married but adopted two boys, whom he named Alan and Mike. His portrait hangs in Beijing's national gallery. In New Zealand he is commemorated by a memorial at Springfield.

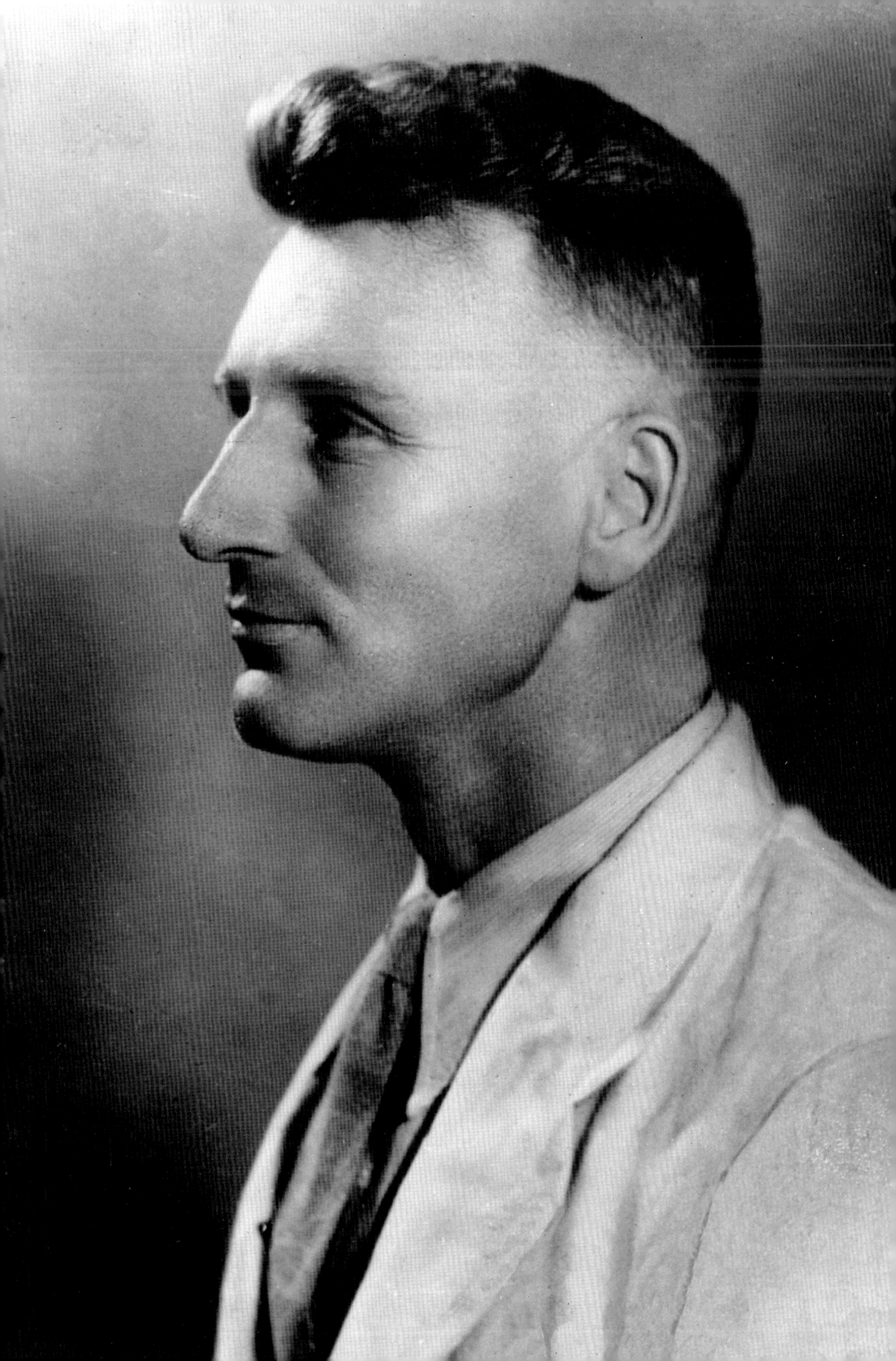

Tom Ellison

Rugby legend and astute Maori leader

BORN: OTAKOU, OTAGO, NOVEMBER 11, 1867. DIED: WELLINGTON, OCTOBER 2, 1904.

Thomas Rangiwahia Ellison (Tamati Erihana) was only 36 when he died, but during his short life he contributed much to rugby and to Maori affairs.

He was a great early thinker on rugby. After growing up in Otago – his father Raniera was a gold prospector – he gained a Makarini scholarship to Te Aute College in Hawke's Bay, where his rugby skills improved quickly. In his last two years at college the Te Aute First XV won the Hawke's Bay senior championship. On leaving school he moved to Wellington and played for the Poneke club. He represented Wellington 24 times from 1885-92, a large number in an era when representative fixtures were scarce.

Ellison was one of the best players in the famous 1888-89 Natives team that toured New Zealand, Australia and Britain. It was a gruelling tour, spanning 14 months and encompassing 107 matches. Ellison played 86 matches and scored 113 points, including 43 tries, the second-highest tally.

At the inaugural New Zealand Rugby Football Union annual meeting, in 1893, it was Ellison who successfully proposed that the New Zealand rugby team's playing strip comprise a black jersey with silver fern, white knickerbocker shorts and black stockings. The white shorts were changed to black in 1901, but the All Black jersey has remained basically unchanged for more than a century. Appropriately, Ellison captained the first fully representative New Zealand team to wear the silver fern, to Australia in 1893. He played seven matches on tour and finished his New Zealand career with the rare distinction of captaining his country every time he represented it.

Ellison, always tactically astute, pioneered the wing forward position to counter marauding halfbacks. He was regarded as a magnificently robust forward, strong and fast. In addition, he was one of the best goal-kickers of his day. Later in his career he played in the backs, helping to formulate the distinctly New Zealand five-eighths system. Ellison finished his career having played 117 matches (68 first-class), in which he scored 51 tries.

In 1898, in a move that was decades ahead of its time, he proposed that New Zealand representative players be reimbursed while on tour. "These [strict amateur] laws were never intended to apply to extended tours abroad. Such tours were never contemplated at the time the rules were framed," he argued. His proposal gained no traction at that time, but these days he'd be hailed as a visionary.

Ellison was involved in all facets of rugby. He was a Wellington union committee member from 1892-98, a selector from 1892-1902 and a referee. In 1902 he wrote the authoritative coaching manual *The Art of Rugby Football*, which offers an insight into the development of rugby from a recreation to New Zealand's national sport and into the development of tactics in rugby's early years. Ellison was a mentor of the young Billy Wallace, who became a legendary All Black figure. Such was Ellison's contribution to rugby that in 1999 he was inducted into the New Zealand Sports Hall of Fame.

His standing in rugby can be understood when reading the words on his gravestone at the Kaik on the Otago Heads: "In loving memory of Thomas R Ellison. Born Nov 11th 1867. Died Oct 2nd 1904. One of the greatest rugby footballers New Zealand ever possessed. Erected by a few friends."

However, rugby was just one string to his bow. Like his father, Ellison, of the Ngati-Awa tribe of Taranaki, was deeply concerned with Maori grievances. He took a keen interest in Ngai Tahu land claims and was appointed an interpreter in the Native Land Court in 1886. His political aspirations were thwarted when he was unsuccessful three times in standing for the Southern Maori seat in Parliament.

From 1891 he worked as a solicitor. In 1902, as a barrister in the Wellington law firm Brandon, Hislop and Johnston, he was admitted to the Bar, one of the first, if not the first, Maori to attain that distinction.

Already a well-known identity in Wellington because of his rugby prowess, Ellison became even more familiar when he bought one of the first motor cars seen in the capital. He would commute to work from Eastbourne, quite a journey in those days. In 1899 Ellison married Ethel Howell in Wellington. They had three children, two of whom died in infancy. While the family house at Muritai Hill was being built Ellison was hospitalised at Porirua Lunatic Asylum, where he died.

Rua Kenana

The Maori prophet who established his own community

BORN: MAUNGAPOHATU, 1869. DIED: MATAHI, BAY OF PLENTY, FEBRUARY 20, 1937.

Rua Kenana was such a persuasive Maori prophet and religious leader that the Government, fearful of his growing influence, was moved to push the law to its limit – and beyond – to curb him. His 1916 trial, the longest in New Zealand to that time, revealed the deep-seated suspicion in which Maori leaders were held.

Rua was born in Urewera country, the posthumous son of Kenana Tumoana, who was killed fighting for Te Kooti. He was of the Tamakaimoana hapu of the Tuhoe tribe.

After many years working on sheep stations and in shearing gangs around the Bay of Plenty and East Coast regions, Rua emerged from among the Ringatu, the followers of Te Kooti. He spoke of a supernatural experience involving the Archangel Gabriel and said he was "The One" whom Te Kooti had prophesised would follow him and complete his work by regaining his people's land.

Rua's presence split the Ringatu Church, and among his most vehement Maori opponents was the formidable Tuhoe chief, Kereru. Soon, however, many people vested their lands to Rua and he established a rapidly-expanding settlement at the foot of Maungapohatu, the sacred Tuhoe mountain.

Rua and his followers grew their hair and beards long. He had his own interpretation of the Bible, which allowed him to have seven wives. He maintained this number, so that if one wife died or departed, she was immediately replaced. Rua eventually married 12 times and fathered more than 70 children.

By 1907 Rua's community was being administered by its own parliament, centred around a circular temple, had a mining company and prosperous farm lands. Rua's vision of Maori autonomy was being fulfilled. There was financial commonsense and purpose underpinning Rua's activities. Despite protective legislation passed in 1896, the Urewera land was being earmarked for mining and settlement by Europeans and he was eager to ensure that his people staked their claim to it before it was gone.

However, not all his ventures were successful – lacking Government co-operation, he was never able to obtain road and rail connections linking his community with the main centres nearby. By 1913 his village, which at its peak boasted 600 people, had been reduced to about 30 families.

In 1914 Rua made a second attempt to establish a sizeable settlement at Maungapohatu, but this time was stymied by the Government, which was concerned that he was too disruptive. His claims to be a spiritual healer and his hostility towards the native schools that taught English caused the Government to watch him suspiciously. For years, the Government had stood over Rua. He was arrested on charges of illicitly selling alcohol in 1910 and jailed for a similar offence in 1915. Many others who broke this law escaped official attention.

Rua, a pacifist, made himself more unpopular when he opposed conscription. Rumours abounded that he was actively working for a German victory in World War I. On April 2, 1916, after he had failed to answer a summons, a large armed police party arrived at Maungapohatu to arrest him. Though there are conflicting reports of events that day, it appears incontrovertible that excessive force was used. One of Rua's sons and a bodyguard were killed and other Maori were injured.

The subsequent trial at the Supreme Court in Whakatane lasted 47 days and was to remain New Zealand's longest until 1977. Though the charges of using seditious language were thrown out, the jury found him guilty of "morally" resisting arrest. It became evident during the trial that there was perjury on both sides and some historians claim the police manipulated and even fabricated the evidence.

Rua was sentenced to a year of hard labour, followed by 18 months' imprisonment. Judge Chapman commented that Maori were a race "still in tutelage" and needed to learn that the law "reached every corner". The sentence was manifestly unfair – eight of the jurors protested its severity, and a petition was presented to Parliament – but it stood.

When Rua finally returned to Maungapohatu in 1918, he found his settlement in disarray. The destruction of Rua's Parliament marked the end of the last concerted Maori attempt for several decades to assert a separate sovereignty. However, he retained his mana and set about re-establishing his community. He had only limited success, and even this was undermined by a typhoid outbreak in 1925. After Maungapohatu had failed economically, Rua led his remaining followers down the Waimana River to a small settlement at Matahi.

After Rua's death, his Te Wairua Tapu religion waned and the number of his followers dwindled.

Rua's story has proved compelling and has been retold by film-makers, playwrights, painters, poets and authors.

Tahupotiki Wiremu Ratana

The faith-healer who spawned religious and political movements

BORN: TE KAWAU, JANUARY 25, 1873. DIED: RATANA PA, NEAR WANGANUI, SEPTEMBER 18, 1939.

Bill Ratana, as he was known, was a faith-healer who in the 1920s used his fame to start a religion. From that sprang a political movement that endures today.

Ratana, who grew up near Wanganui, had links to several tribes, principally Ngati Apa. His father was a farmer and a noted church and political figure. Ratana worked on the family property, involved himself in sport and drank heavily. In about 1900 he married Ngauta Baker and they had seven children.

He did little out of the ordinary until November 8, 1918, when he began having visions, which he and his family interpreted as the Holy Spirit visiting him and imparting messages. For a time Ratana spoke in strange voices and his family thought he was insane. When the great influenza epidemic struck, Ratana correctly prophesised the deaths of some family members and guided others to safety.

Soon he was showing an ability to heal by prayer. His first such healing was Omeka, who became ill after a needle lodged behind his knee. When it seemed Omeka would die, Ratana took him in hand and, after a week of intensive prayer, the needle emerged from Omeka's thigh. Shortly after, chief Te Kahupukoro brought his bedridden daughter to see Ratana and she recovered miraculously.

There was an ever-increasing stream of visitors to Ratana's farm and he became a national figure, "the Maori Miracle Man". A makeshift village developed at what became known as Ratana Pa, 20km south-east of Wanganui. Outside could be seen signs of his successes – discarded crutches and wheelchairs.

Ratana was anything but extraordinary in appearance, save for piercing eyes that gave him a slightly mystic air. He was tall, a habitual pipe-smoker, quietly-spoken, not given to extravagant gestures, and gentle. He shunned publicity.

Using his national celebrity, Ratana led a religious revival, mainly among Maori. He travelled widely, speaking in front of huge crowds. He uttered prophetic words, continued curing and gradually his religion took shape. It was basically Christian, but evolved its own credo and rituals. Through the 1920s the Ratana movement became more formalised. In 1923 the first Ratana federation, the United Maori Welfare League of the Northern, Southern and Chatham Islands, was set up and Ratana began to focus more on politics. The Ratana newspaper, *Te Whetu Marama o Te Kotahitanga*, was established in 1924.

Ratana spent most of 1924 in Britain, leading a large group of family and supporters in an effort to spread his religion and to petition government officials about Maori land grievances. The following year he visited North America.

On May 31, 1925, the Ratana Church was formally established, with Ratana the intermediary between God and man. Despite his growing legion of followers, Ratana was condemned in many quarters. The Anglican Church, the denomination with the most Maori followers, threatened to excommunicate those who joined the Ratana Church, though this did not weaken his influence among Maori. Ratana gave new hope to Maori in the 1920s and became an increasingly commanding figure.

Sceptics claimed his "miracles" were the results of deception, that cures were made by powers of auto-suggestion and that second-hand accounts embellished his healing ability.

But the tide was running for Ratana, and soon a political party followed. In 1932 Eruera Tirikatene became the first Ratana MP. Four years later Ratana and Prime Minister Michael Joseph Savage had a historic meeting with far-reaching consequences. Ratana placed four objects on the table: a potato, a gold watch, a greenstone tiki and a huia feather. He explained that the potato was the Maori needing his land because "a potato cannot grow without soil". The watch was broken, representing the broken machinery of Maori land law. The tiki symbolised Maori mana and the feather was a sign of chieftainship. Labour and Ratana formed an alliance and by 1943 Ratana held all four Maori seats.

Ratana showed human frailties. He took a second wife, Iriaka Te Rio, in 1925 and there were a number of other liaisons that caused consternation among his supporters. There were also problems with the Ratana federation's banking procedures. In 1927 Ratana was convicted on a charge of drunken driving. As he had predicted, Ratana gradually lost his powers of healing, but his movement continued to flourish long after his death.

Some consider Ratana was a charlatan, but what is undeniable is that through his charismatic leadership, he melded Maori religious and political movements in an unprecedented and lasting manner.

Maud Basham (Aunt Daisy)

The diminutive giant of radio broadcasting

BORN: LONDON, AUGUST 30, 1879. DIED: WELLINGTON, JULY 14, 1963.

Maud Basham, known throughout New Zealand as Aunt Daisy, began every broadcast with a hearty: "Good morning, everybody!" Those words, invariably rapped out with cheerful optimism, were a source of comfort to generations of New Zealanders. Her devoted listeners were known as the Daisy Chain.

Though she was just 1.5m (4ft 11in) tall, Aunt Daisy was a giant of radio broadcasting, a pioneer who thrived because her half-hour programme, which began at 9am every weekday, combined homespun commonsense, humour, lively comment, housekeeping tips and interesting snippets.

Maud Ruby Taylor was born in London, and was called Daisy from when she was a toddler. Her father, Robert, a carpenter, died when she was three, and a few years later her mother, Eliza, packed up her children and headed for New Zealand, settling in New Plymouth in 1889.

Already Maud was an extroverted child, who loved singing, acting on stage and even public debating. She attended New Plymouth High School, then, in 1897, qualified to be a teacher. She spent several years teaching at small coastal Taranaki schools until, in 1904, she married Frederick Basham, an English-born civil engineer. The couple, who were to have three children, moved frequently, living in Hawera, Eltham, Waipukurau and on the Hauraki Plains. Maud gave singing tuition wherever they lived.

Her radio career had its beginnings in 1923, when she took part in an experimental broadcast in Wellington. "I put my head almost inside a big horn, like the HMV dog, and sang *Il Bacio*," she recalled.

There was further radio experience in Auckland a few years later, when she wrote and sang in a series on great composers for IYA. But it was in 1930, when she filled in for a fortnight while the children's programme presenter was on holiday, that she made her radio breakthrough. On the children's programme she called herself Aunt Daisy, and the tag stuck.

From the children's programmes she branched out, filling in as a presenter wherever she was required. She was the first woman in New Zealand considered authoritative enough on air to be a regular presenter. Her natural good humour was easily transmitted through the airwaves and she was immediately popular. Though she spoke at a rapid clip – up to 175 words a minute when she had on a full head of steam – her diction was clear and precise.

She moved about during the Depression years, trying to cement a fulltime job while her husband struggled for work. There were stints on 2YA and 2ZW in Wellington and 1ZR and 1ZB (when she worked under the direction of another famous radio personality, Colin Scrimgeour) in Auckland.

By 1935 she was so popular that both major political parties asked her to stand for them in the election. She declined – radio was her life. In 1936, working for the ZB network, her programme took a commercial line. She was permitted to name and endorse products on air, which made her a powerful figure in the worlds of media and marketing.

The following year her programme, broadcast out of Wellington, went national. The signature tune of *Daisy, Daisy* that began her programme was to be heard for the next 25 years.

Basham made several trips overseas and the Americans in particular warmed to her. *The New York Post* called her "the Dynamo from Down Under". She even made a semi-official goodwill visit to the United States during World War II, when she broadcast extensively throughout the country.

In the pre-television days the impact of Aunt Daisy's radio show was immense. It was not uncommon for products she endorsed in the morning to be sold out by mid-afternoon. Her programme offered a mix of cooking recipes, handy hints, strongly-opinionated reviews, and even a bit of preaching – she was a woman of strong Christian principles. She maintained that she would not endorse a product unless she was personally satisfied that it was of good quality.

In many ways she was an ageless personality. Listeners heard a bubbly, talented woman and had little idea of her age – she was more than 50 before she broke into radio properly and was still broadcasting when she was nearly 84.

Besides her radio career she found time to write more than a dozen books, mostly cookbooks and collections of handy hints, and contributed to the *Auckland Weekly News* and the *Radio Record* (later the *Listener*). Basham was made an MBE in 1954 and in later years was commonly and correctly known as the First Lady of Radio.

Charles Upham

The ultimate soldier

BORN: CHRISTCHURCH, SEPTEMBER 21, 1908. DIED: CHRISTCHURCH, NOVEMBER 22, 1994.

It would be simplistic to state that by virtue of earning two VCs, Charles Upham was the outstanding New Zealand soldier of World War II – countless acts of bravery went, if not unnoticed, then unrewarded during the war. Nevertheless, Upham was a courageous soldier with a desperate hatred of Nazi Germany and its allies. It was said he fought with "nerveless competence". He is the only combat soldier to win the VC and Bar, although two medical officers did so during World War I. In New Zealand "Upham" became a turn of phrase, denoting fearlessness.

Upham was born into a wealthy Christchurch family and attended Christ's College from 1923-27. He pursued a farming career, gaining a Diploma of Agriculture at Canterbury Agricultural College in 1930. After several years working on high-country sheep farms, he decided to become a valuer. He gained a Diploma in Valuation and worked for the Valuation Department in Timaru.

Though nearly 31 when war broke out, Upham was eager to serve. He enlisted in the Second New Zealand Expeditionary Force and was posted to the 20th Canterbury-Otago Battalion. Upham was an impressive soldier and a natural leader. He was wiry and strong, displayed outstanding tactical sense, and soon mastered the technical skills of a soldier's craft. Promotion came quickly.

He served with the New Zealand Division in Greece in March 1941, and was evacuated to Crete soon after. In May, Lieutenant Upham earned his first VC for outstanding gallantry and leadership. For nine days he led attacks on the Germans, risked death to rescue his soldiers, and destroyed machine-gun posts by using his favourite attacking weapon, the hand grenade. He was wounded twice but, as the battle turned, continued to defend vigorously against the advancing Germans. In the most stressful situation, he was resourceful and quick-thinking.

Such was Upham's ferocious desire to get into battle that Lieutenant Colonel Kippenberger initially left him out of the Libyan campaign, fearing he would be killed quickly because of his audacity.

Upham – Pug to fellow soldiers – earned his second VC for his efforts in the Western Desert in 1942. Operating under heavy fire at Minqar Qaim, Egypt, he fought alongside and encouraged his men, eventually leading a famous breakout and over-running enemy posts. Again using hand grenades, Upham took a heavy toll of German soldiers, despite being wounded in both arms.

His actions during the New Zealand Division's attack on Ruweisat Ridge on July 14–15 were typical. He was ordered to send an officer forward to gather information from the battalions leading the assault and, typically, went himself. Later he was leading a bayonet charge when his left arm was shattered by a bullet and his leg was wounded by shrapnel. Unable to walk, he was captured when the Germans counter-attacked.

When further recognition for Upham was being considered, King George VI asked Kippenberger whether Upham deserved a Bar to the Cross. "In my respectful opinion, sir," Kippenberger replied, "Upham has won the VC several times over."

Upham was a nightmare prisoner. He was held first in an Italian camp, but, after repeated escape attempts, was transferred to Germany. His attempts grew more daring until, in 1944, he became the only New Zealand combat officer to be sent to the Colditz camp for habitual escapers.

He continued his escape endeavours and showed contempt for the Germans. When Colditz was liberated Upham was sent to Britain, where he married Molly McTamney, to whom he had become engaged eight years earlier.

Upham was immensely popular. His men recognised not only his bravery, but his modesty. He said of his second VC: "Naturally I feel some pride in this distinction, but hundreds of others have done more than I did. They could have given it to any one of them."

Back home he was lionised. Christchurch citizens raised £10,000 to buy a farm for him, but he declined the money, which was used instead to establish a scholarship fund for servicemen's sons.

Upham farmed successfully in North Canterbury for many years, largely overcoming the lingering effects of his war wounds, especially the injury to his left arm. He served on the board of Christ's College for nearly 20 years. He and Molly remained on the farm, where they raised three daughters, until just months before his death. More than 5000 people lined the streets of central Christchurch and filled the city's cathedral for his funeral, which was conducted with full military honours.

Ralph Hotere

The "black" artist

BORN: MITIMITI, NORTHLAND, AUGUST 11, 1931.

Though Hone Papita Raukura Hotere has a tribal affiliation to Aupouri, his paintings do not specifically draw on his Maori heritage. There is certainly a spiritual aspect to his work, but his subject matter is extremely varied, ranging from collaborations with poets to his views on Middle East politics and experiences of personal grief.

Hotere, one of 11 children, was educated at St Peter's College (Hato Petera) Northcote, then at Auckland Teachers' College. In 1952, when he decided he wanted to specialise in art, he moved to Dunedin to study at King Edward Technical College under Gordon Tovey. Hotere's first art exhibition was in 1952 – a one-man exhibition at the Dunedin Public Art Gallery.

After working as an arts adviser for the education department for seven years, much of that time in the Bay of Islands, Hotere was awarded a New Zealand Art Societies fellowship in 1961. This enabled him to study at the Central School of Art in London. The opportunity to travel changed his life.

Not only did he become part of the rapidly-changing art world of the early 1960s, but he received the Karolyi International Fellowship, which enabled him to study in Vence, France. He travelled extensively around Europe and made a pilgrimage to the Sangro Rive war cemetery in Italy, where his brother and other Maori Battalion servicemen from World War II were buried. This event, and the politics of Europe at the time, had a profound effect on his work, seen most obviously in the *Sangro*, *Polaris* (relating to the nuclear warhead Polaris) and *Algerie* (relating to Algerian troubles in France) series of paintings. He also rather surprisingly experimented with figurative work that has only recently come to light.

Hotere returned to Otago in 1965, settling in Port Chalmers. He began producing increasingly thought-provoking work and developed a national following that is still growing. There were important solo exhibitions in Auckland: *Sangro Paintings and Human Rights* (1965) and *Black Paintings* (1968). In 1969 he became the Otago University Frances Hodgkins Fellow. In 1973 there was a nationwide Hotere exhibition.

One of Hotere's strengths has been his ability to collaborate. He worked successfully with artist Bill Culbert in the impressive *Black Light* series. He has worked also with leading poets Bill Manhire, Hone Tuwhare and Cilla McQueen, whom he married in 1973, incorporating hand-written text into many of his works. He did four drawings for *Landfall 78* and designed the cover of *Landfall 84*.

Hotere has been well-known for his use of black since his *Black* paintings of the 1960s. He will often use black almost exclusively, but employs a variety of methods to give the work depth and sheen. Sometimes he places strips of colour against stark black backgrounds. His *Black* works have been described as "minimalist abstraction", but they are strikingly moving, because black is often associated with spirituality, death, race, silence, nothingness and infinity. Hotere leaves the interpretation to the spectator. "No object, and certainly no painting, is seen in the same way by everybody," he says. "Yet most people want an unmistakable meaning, which is accessible to all, in a work of art. It is the spectator who provokes the change and the meaning in these works."

Hotere has always been an extremely relevant artist, not afraid to comment on current affairs. When Aramoana, a wetland near his home, was being mooted as the site for an aluminium smelter, he strongly opposed the project and produced the *Aramoana* series. He protested against the 1981 Springbok rugby team's tour of New Zealand with *Black Union Jack* and against the 1985 sinking of the Greenpeace ship Rainbow Warrior with *Black Warrior*. His works relating to Middle East politics have included *Jerusalem, Jerusalem* and *This Might be a Double Cross Jack*.

There have been two extremely popular Hotere exhibitions in Wellington in recent years. In 1997 the City Gallery displayed his *Out the Black Window* and in 2000 Te Papa featured the *Black Light* series. His work has also been displayed extensively overseas, including in Britain, France, the United States, Brazil, Japan, Australia and the former Yugoslavia.

Hotere was awarded an Arts Council grant in 1970 and in 1978 was able to return to France with McQueen after being granted an Arts Council fellowship. In 1994 he received an honorary doctorate from Otago University. In 2003 he was one of 10 New Zealanders to be named in the inaugural set of Living Icons of New Zealand Arts.

Hotere's paintings are sought-after by art collectors and their prices have risen dramatically. Increasingly his art is purchased as an investment.

Richard Hadlee

New Zealand cricket's one-man destruction unit

BORN: CHRISTCHURCH, JULY 3, 1951.

In cricket, where statistics are often the measuring stick, no New Zealand player has dominated like Richard Hadlee.

His 1490 first-class wickets pushed Clarrie Grimmett (1424) into second place in the New Zealand lists. To reach his world record 431 test scalps, he passed his idol, Dennis Lillee (355), and Ian Botham (376 at the time). Before Hadlee's debut in 1973, New Zealand had won seven tests. When he retired 17 years later, that number had swelled to 29. Hadlee had played a vital role in nearly all of them.

He was primarily a pace bowler, but was such a good attacking left-handed hitter that he could have represented New Zealand as a batsman. He scored two test centuries and 14 in first-class cricket.

His career was dotted with *Boy's Own* heroics. Playing just his third first-class match, for Canterbury against Central Districts in 1972, he took a hat-trick. In 1984, he became the first player since 1967 to complete the double of 1000 runs and 100 wickets in an English season. In Brisbane in 1985 his test figures of 9–52 were among the best ever. He took 6–71 in the second innings, and in the three-match series snared 33 wickets – a one-man destruction unit.

Mike Gatting famously described playing New Zealand as like facing the World XI at one end and the Ilford Second XI at the other. It was a cruel jibe at some good New Zealand players, but indicated how Hadlee towered over his team-mates.

Cricket was in his blood. His father, Walter, was a test batsman and captain, and his older brothers, Barry and Dayle, represented their country.

Early on Richard was a tearaway fast bowler, but he was often inaccurate, not a patch on the bowler he became as he defied the ageing process through his 30s. His breakthrough came in 1976, when, fortunate not to be made 12th man, he ran through India in their second innings of the Basin Reserve test, finishing with 7–23 and match figures of 11–58 to lead New Zealand to a stunning innings victory. In 1977 he became New Zealand cricket's first cult figure, with his crashing hitting and express bowling against Australia at Eden Park inciting the crowd to frenzied chanting.

He turned professional in 1978 and for a decade spent the New Zealand winters representing Nottinghamshire. "That decision reshaped my life," he said. "I discovered the true meaning of the word professional and applied that lesson to my life outside cricket, as well as to how I approached the game."

In England he was saluted as the bowling genius he was. In New Zealand he was awarded the Winsor Cup 13 times in 14 years as the outstanding first-class bowler.

He reduced his run-up in 1982 and was heavily criticised. But he lost little pace, gained greater accuracy and extended his career by nearly 10 years. Paddles, as he was known, still began his run-up with that peculiar leg-crossing shuffle, likened by commentator John Arlott to Groucho Marx stalking a waitress. But economy became the key. Not a movement was wasted.

He bowled from nearer the umpire than anyone. His action, classically correct, became so grooved that he could bowl over after over just on or outside the off-stump, forcing the batsmen to play his bag of awkward leg-cutters and late-swinging deliveries.

Sometimes there were murmurs about the emphasis he placed on statistics, and about his lack of enthusiasm for the one-day game. Both criticisms were easily refuted by pointing to New Zealand's test successes in his era and to his one-day figures – 158 wickets and 1751 runs in 115 matches.

Team-mates occasionally complained when he went his own way. There was a row over a car, which he won for Player of the Season in Australia one year and kept for himself. Another time he criticised the New Zealand side in his newspaper column for a sloppy attitude. But Hadlee played 342 first class matches in 18 years and it's hardly surprising that he upset the odd person along the way.

He was prolific in other ways. He did radio and television commentaries, wrote newspaper columns and half a dozen books, and was a popular public speaker. He suffered stress problems in the early 1980s, and there were further serious health concerns in 1991, when he had a heart turn while commentating. He eventually had a heart operation.

Hadlee was knighted while touring England in 1990 – the first bowler to be knighted since Francis Drake, he joked. He remains close to cricket as a national selector.

Billy T James

The irreverent entertainer who was loved by a nation

BORN: CAMBRIDGE, 1949. DIED: AUCKLAND, AUGUST 7, 1991.

As with many comedians, Billy T James' public image as an endlessly comical, carefree imp did not reflect his private personality. Away from the spotlight, he was still extremely popular, but seemed rather tortured, always at pains to do a professional job. He cherished his privacy, even while conceding that his high public profile came with the career he had chosen.

William James Taitoko was a Waikato boy until his family moved to Whangarei when he was 11. He always liked music and at school become known for his guitar-playing. After leaving college he drove trucks, took a commercial art apprenticeship, then joined the army.

The physical demands of army life were too much for his rotund figure and he applied to be a traffic officer. (Years later, one of his best-known characters was a jodpur-wearing cop.) He never did become a traffic officer because show biz intervened.

He became part of a band called the Maori Volcanics, who left New Zealand in 1973 to play the club circuit in the north of England, and also appeared in the United States and Australia. Not long after, while doing cabaret work in Australia, Taitoko changed his name to Billy T James. He said he was tired of having his name's pronunciation mangled, so came up with "something the Aussies could pronounce".

James' musical and comedic talents were nurtured by Elaine Hegan, who became his agent. By the late 1970s he was one of the hottest acts around and had been nominated as the 1978 New Zealand Entertainer of the Year. The man who spotted James as a television talent was Tom Parkinson, who gave him his first major vehicle, *Radio Times*, a light entertainment show that screened on TV2. His big breakthrough followed with *The Billy T James Show*. Thereafter James was immensely popular. He earned the 1981 Entertainer of the Year award and in 1984 he was named Entertainer of the Decade.

Often dressed in a black singlet and with a yellow towel around his neck, James was an irreverent entertainer, making cheeky, often racially-based jokes that he got away with because he was Maori. Some criticised his humour as racist and claimed he was demeaning Maori, but most people thought he was uproariously funny and loved his trademark chuckle.

He starred in Ian Mune's film *Came a Hot Friday* as the Tainuia Kid, a Maori who believed he was a Mexican bandit. He parodied the American show *Entertainment This Week* with *Entertainment That's Weak* and launched a succession of other spoofs, including *Turangi Vice* (with the "Vice Squad" clamping down on illegal trout fishing), *Chocky IV* and his version of American cop show *CHiPS*. One of his most popular roles was Fast Eddie in *Last Tango in Te Kuiti*. Importantly, James was equally popular with Maori and Pakeha viewers.

He was willing to try a range of projects and in 1987 revealed his skill as a raconteur in *Billy T James' America's Cup*.

He dubbed voices in the feature cartoon *Footrot Flats: The Dog's Tale* in 1987 and two volumes of the *Billy T James' Real Hard-Case Book* were published. A sitcom, *The Billy T James Show*, on the fledgling TV3 channel, received a muted reception in 1989-90.

Amid the public highs were some private lows. In 1986 he and his wife Lynne received death threats, then had a rock thrown through a window of their Auckland home. In 1988 James suffered a heart attack and underwent a quadruple heart bypass. A year later he became New Zealand's 14th heart transplant recipient.

He continued to make public appearances, including *Billy T James: Alive and Giggling* with Howard Morrison, *The Billy T James Christmas Special* (when he sang, played the saxophone and did some stand-up comedy) and *The Comeback* concert in Aotea Centre. He revealed a different side of himself in a fine documentary, *The James Gang Rides Again*, in which, to remove the fear of heart surgery and transplants, he traced his life back to the operating table.

About a year after his transplant, his health broke down. Because of his premature death at the age of 42, he did not leave a huge body of work, but nearly everything he did displayed his rare gift of comic timing and endearing ability to be self-mocking. He seldom received a bad review and was arguably the most popular New Zealand public figure of his time.

The Billy T James Award for comedy is awarded annually at the New Zealand International Comedy Festival.

Keith Sinclair

The historian's historian

BORN: AUCKLAND, DECEMBER 5, 1922. DIED: TORONTO, CANADA, JUNE 20, 1993.

Keith Sinclair was not the first New Zealand historian, but he was perhaps the most significant. Michael King, James Belich, Judith Binney and Claudia Orange followed in his footsteps. The appeal of Sinclair's work was that he viewed history as a New Zealander, without the British slant that had often marked previous historians.

Sinclair was an accomplished writer, whose output was prodigious. He was a schoolboy when he had his first writing published – in the *New Zealand Woman's Weekly* under the pseudonym of "S.K.K.S." He wrote volumes of poetry, children's stories, academic papers and numerous magazine articles. However, his best-selling histories set him apart.

His magnus opus was *A History of New Zealand*, published in 1959 and reprinted and revised many times. Sales of this book have topped 100,000. Among Sinclair's other important books were his 1957 *Origins of the Maori Wars* and his 1965 biography of turn-of-the-century politician and business leader William Pember Reeves.

Sinclair was the oldest of 10 children in a working-class Point Chevalier family. His father was a clerk until the Depression struck, and then became a wharfie. Sinclair attended Ellerslie and Pt Chevalier primary schools and Mt Albert Grammar, where he impressed not only as a scholar but as a boxer. He had a spell at Auckland Teachers' College, then did war service in the army and the navy. After the war he attended the University of London. On his return to New Zealand he gained an MA at Auckland University.

He became a lecturer at Auckland University in 1947, received a PhD in 1954, and was a university professor of history until 1987. He taught many students who were to make a mark in New Zealand, including future Governor-General Cath Tizard and future Prime Minister David Lange, whom he recalled as "very clever but not a hard worker".

Sinclair wrote poetry throughout his career, from *Songs for a Summer* in 1952 to *Moontalk*, which was released shortly before his death. But historical writing was his bread and butter. *A Destiny Apart: New Zealand's Search for a National Identity* (1986) and *Kinds of Peace: Maori People after the Wars 1870-85* (1991) revealed a rare depth of observation and analysis.

Sinclair was opinionated and not afraid to be controversial. During the 1960s he campaigned against the Government's support of the Vietnam War and in 1981 he joined the big anti-Springbok tour marches. His biography of Walter Nash, published in 1976, led to a run-in with the Secret Service. The SIS demanded retractions for two passages in the book, one relating to Nash's failure to denounce the Rugby Union at the time of the 1959 "No Maoris, No Tour" protests, the other a section on Dr Bill Sutch. Sinclair enjoyed the publicity and the SIS eventually dropped the matter.

In 1969 Sinclair ran for Parliament, standing for Labour in Eden – he'd been a member of the Labour Party since 1949. He won the seat with a tiny majority of 35. Three weeks later, after special votes had been counted, this turned into a 67-vote deficit and National MP John Rae, the Minister of Housing, took the seat.

Sinclair was heavily involved in literary circles. In the 1950s he was in close touch with *Landfall* editor Charles Brasch and writers such as Ron Mason, Frank Sargeson, Rex Fairburn, Maurice Duggan and Kendrick Smithyman. He had special admiration for short-story writer Duggan and always classed James K Baxter as a genius.

In his autobiography, *Halfway Round the Harbour*, published just before his death, Sinclair wrote: "It is nonsense to say that only Maoris may write Maori history… but anyone writing about another culture and people must learn their language and study their culture." Sinclair did that. In the 1960s, long after he had become a professor, he learned the Maori language, and he was proud to have a Maori heritage.

Sinclair was sharp, well-researched and had a dry humour. Asked to sum himself up, he remarked that his interests were "defined by my early twenties: writing, literature, New Zealand, nationalism, history, Labour politics, boats and girls". He was married twice. His first marriage, to Mary Land, in 1947, produced four sons. When that marriage ended in 1976, he married historian Raewyn Dalziel. He died in Toronto while visiting his eldest son, Mark.

Sinclair, the founding president of the New Zealand Book Council, was knighted in 1985 for his services to history and literature. An annual scholarship at Auckland University was named in his memory.

Charles Goldie

The man who turned portrait painting into an art form

BORN: AUCKLAND, OCTOBER 20, 1870. DIED: AUCKLAND, JULY 11, 1947

The art word gets a bit sniffy about Charles Goldie. Critics claim his paintings are limited artistically – more like photographs than paintings, has been a common complaint. But their appeal is beyond argument, and his work is indisputably of historical significance.

Goldie was the son of wealthy Aucklanders. His father, David, was a timber merchant who became Auckland mayor. Goldie showed ability in art at Auckland Grammar, and won Auckland Society of Arts and New Zealand Art Students' Association prizes.

After leaving school he worked in his father's business while studying art part-time under Louis Steele, who encouraged him to pursue an art career in Paris. Sir George Grey, impressed by Goldie's two still-life paintings exhibited with the Auckland Academy of Art, backed the plan. The academy's December 1892 exhibition included Goldie's first-known Maori portrait.

In 1893 Goldie enrolled at the Académie Julian in Paris. He studied there for five years, and won prizes in the studio competitions. He copied the old masters' paintings in the Louvre and the Luxembourg galleries, and travelled extensively.

Back in Auckland in 1898, Goldie and Steele collaborated on a large historical painting, *The Arrival of the Maoris in New Zealand*. It was exhibited with the Auckland Society of Arts in 1899 and bought for the Auckland Art Gallery for £200.

But Goldie's real fame, and the high prices for his work, are associated with his range of portraits – Pakeha and Maori – some of which he presented at the Auckland Society of Arts in 1900. From there his career took off. He was soon regarded as Auckland's leading painter and art teacher. He was appointed to the Auckland Art Gallery advisory board, and served on the Auckland Society of Arts committee.

Goldie concentrated on depicting elderly Maori with moko, the "noble relics of a noble race". Like many of his time, he believed the Maori was a dying race and that he was recording the last survivors. His paintings were precise and meticulous, but some have accused him of colonial racism – at his request, elderly Maori posing for him assumed dejected poses. Many Maori believe the spirit of their ancestors resides in his portraits, but others blame him for the high rate of smoking among Maori because he painted in pipes that they claim they didn't smoke.

In the early 1900s Goldie met Ngati Mahuta chief Patara Te Tuhi, Ina Te Papatahi of Nga Puhi, and Te Aho-o-te-rangi Wharepu of Ngati Mahuta, all of whom posed for him many times. Goldie's models usually sat in his Auckland studio, draped in a cloak or other articles of clothing he kept in his studio. His studio was on the top floor of the Hobson Building, next to the *Auckland Star* newspaper in Shortland Street.

In 1903 Lady Ranfurly, wife of the departing governor, chose two large Goldie paintings as her farewell present from Auckland. *Darby and Joan* and *The Widow*, valued at £100 each, were purchased by popular subscription.

Asked in 1908 to name the best six New Zealand artists, readers of the *Weekly Graphic* put Goldie first. But critics tired of his meticulously-realistic portraits, claiming they lacked variety. In 1911 one critic described Goldie's style as "photo-realist", saying "his artistic ideal seems to be the coloured photograph".

Ignoring the critics, Goldie, a shy, reserved man, exhibited new works every year until 1919. During World War I he stopped producing large pictures, which were selling for more than £100, concentrating instead on small-scale paintings on wooden panels.

In 1920 Goldie travelled to Sydney, where, aged 50, he married Olive Cooper, an Australian. After two years in Sydney, Goldie was back in Auckland, but his behaviour became very erratic and he produced few paintings for several years. Some suggested he was an alcoholic, and he appeared to have a nervous breakdown. Most likely he suffered from lead poisoning, the result of inhalation from sanding the white undercoats on his paintings.

Goldie resumed painting in 1930, and sent work to London for exhibition with the Royal Academy of Arts and to Paris for the Salon of the Société des Artistes Français. He was awarded King George V's Silver Jubilee Medal and an OBE.

He maintained a good income by selling his oil paintings, which fetched up to 350 guineas each, but in 1941 he ceased painting because of declining health.

Although hundreds of Goldie's works are preserved in private collections, many of his important paintings are owned by New Zealand museums. He is probably New Zealand's best-known artist. His paintings fetch record-shattering prices, and are always hot items on the art market.

John Minto

The activist with an acute social conscience

BORN: DUNEDIN, MAY 16, 1953.

During 1981 the surname of the most reviled man in New Zealand began with M. Supporters of the Springbok tour of New Zealand detested John Minto, the face of the Halt All Racist Tours (Hart) movement. Those opposing the tour felt the same about Prime Minister Rob Muldoon, who would not withhold visas for the South African players.

Minto is recalled for his activism during that torrid winter, but has always battled against issues that have offended his conscience. He has been a member of Greenpeace, Corso, Campaign for Nuclear Disarmament and Citizens Association for Racial Equality. He now fronts the Quality Public Education Coalition and has targeted such things as State funding of private schools at the expense of State schools and the need for better resources for children needing Special Education. He is a spokesman for Global Peace and Justice Auckland.

Minto was taught by the Sisters of Mercy at Dunedin Catholic primary schools St Patrick's and St Edmund's, and was an altar boy. When the family shifted to Napier, he attended Napier Intermediate and Napier Boys' High School, and played rugby, swam and played squash. In 1975 he attended a Hart meeting run by Trevor Richards and knew it was a cause he believed in.

He gained a BSc in physics at Massey University, then headed to Auckland Teachers' College. He was passionate about the Hart cause, and was soon playing a leading role in the organisation.

The 1981 tour was a tumultuous time. It was an election year and the police Red Squad, protesters, barbed wire and rugby dominated the winter. The angular Minto, wielding a loud hailer and often wearing a motorcycle helmet for protection, seemed to be on the TV news every evening. He received death threats, and was arrested, tailed by the SIS, smashed over the head with bottles and rammed into a post by police, convicted, fined, required to do periodic detention and jailed. His cause divided New Zealand, though the weight of public opinion subsequently swung against maintaining sports links with South Africa while apartheid remained.

"We set out to stop the tour," said Minto, "and did not manage that. But we stopped two matches [in Hamilton and Timaru] and forced people to confront the issue here and overseas. The Springboks were not welcomed to another IRB country till apartheid was abolished." He has described his greatest sports moment as the 1981 South Africa-Waikato match, which protesters prevented from taking place. His favourite chant was, "Remember Soweto, remember Parihaka". The local angle appealed to him.

Minto was Hart's fulltime national chairman for five years. In 1983 he married fellow protester Angi Zanderigo. There was a bomb hoax before their wedding, which was held on a Sunday so that Minto could fulfil his periodic detention requirements on Saturdays.

The South Africa issue remained in the headlines. For example, Minto protested when the annual Auckland tennis tournament included players who had appeared recently in South Africa, and was arrested several times for his troubles. He was gratified when the apartheid system was dismantled in 1992, and was honoured when Nelson Mandela toured New Zealand and said Hart's 1981 protests, which were televised in South Africa, gave him hope while he was in prison.

Minto had considerable stature overseas. He addressed the United Nations Special Committee Against Apartheid in New York in 1983 and claimed that Muldoon's objection to apartheid in no way matched his hatred of Hart. In 1990 he went to Sweden to attend a United Nations conference on apartheid and sport and was appointed to chair one of the sessions.

He has continued to protest, turning up at Waitangi celebrations, and objecting when the Fiji team attended the rugby sevens tournament in Wellington immediately after a coup at home. He has been disappointed by developments in post-apartheid South Africa. "Black South Africans have gained political rights, but their social and economic position is appalling. Most are worse off under the ANC's free-market economic policies than they were under the old white regime," he said.

Minto has been a science teacher at Massey High School, Hillary College, Western Springs College and Tangaroa College. He is as intractable and dogged a campaigner on education issues as he was over apartheid. He displays calm logic in his many letters to the editor.

His advocacy of difficult causes has been pursued at considerable personal cost, certainly in financial and material terms, and probably within his professional career.

He has not attended a rugby match since 1981, but has coached his two boys' soccer teams.

Rudall Hayward

Early master of the silver screen

BORN: WOLVERHAMPTON, JULY 4, 1900. DIED: DUNEDIN, MAY 29, 1974.

Rudall Hayward was the Peter Jackson of his era. While not gaining the world fame of Jackson, Hayward was an influential and imaginative film-maker who dominated the industry in New Zealand for half a century. He was responsible for one of the earliest New Zealand films with sound, *On the Friendly Road*, in 1936, and shot New Zealand's first colour film, *To Love a Maori*, in 1972. His *Rewi's Last Stand* (1925) was nominated in 2005 by Progressive Silent Film List as one of the best 100 silent movies ever made, which put Hayward on the same footing as famous directors Alfred Hitchcock, Frank Capra, John Ford, Cecil B DeMille and Charlie Chaplin.

Hayward was born into an English show business family. His father, Rudall, and mother, Adelina, were members of West's Pictures and The Brescians, a touring entertainment company. In 1905 the Haywards moved to New Zealand with the troupe, bringing with them projectors and cameras to demonstrate the marvel of the moving film.

West's toured New Zealand for three years before disbanding. Rudall's father and his uncle, Henry, then formed Hayward's Picture Enterprises and opened a theatre in Auckland. Soon after, the family moved to Waihi and established a circuit of cinemas around the Coromandel Peninsula.

Hayward did most things in the film industry, from projectionist to actor. He branched away from films briefly, attending Wanganui Collegiate in 1916-17 and studying electricity at the Waihi School of Mines for two years. After that his life became movies. In 1920 he made his first film, a two-reel comedy called *The Bloke From Freeman's Bay*. It was screened at the Hayward cinemas and drew good crowds, but Henry Hayward was so unimpressed that he offered Rudall £50 to destroy the film.

Hayward had a spell in Australia working on film sets, then returned to Auckland and in 1922 made the first of his four silent movie feature films, *My Lady of the Cave*. The following year, when Hayward married Hilda Moren, he listed his occupation as picture-theatre manager.

His second feature, *Rewi's Last Stand*, was a drama-romance set during the Waikato wars. He used James Cowan's book *The New Zealand Wars* as a resource and made more use of Cowan when directing *The Te Kooti Trail* in 1927. His fourth big movie, *The Bush Cinderella*, attracted additional publicity because the reigning Miss New Zealand, Dale Austen, starred.

Hayward then introduced Community Comedies to New Zealand, travelling from town to town making quick-fire two-reel films with local casts and locations. He made 23 such comedies, including *Suzie of Stratford*, *Tilly of Te Aroha* and *Patsy of Palmerston*.

On the Friendly Road, which brought sound to the screen in New Zealand, was a story about life during the Depression years and featured well-known radio broadcaster Colin Scrimgeour. Hayward also shot another version of *Rewi's Last Stand*, with a soundtrack, and this proved popular when released in England. The film endured so well that it was bought by the New Zealand Broadcasting Corporation and televised in 1970.

Hayward was divorced in 1943 and within a week married Patricia Te Miha, an accomplished photographer and actress. She starred in *Rewi's Last Stand*, where she was credited as Ramai Te Miha.

During the war Hayward worked for the National Film Unit. Afterwards he spent several years in London and was making encouraging inroads into the British film industry when he decided it was time to move to Australia. He was back in Auckland by the 1950s, often working as a newsreel cameraman while making documentries and educational and travel films with his wife. One of these, *The Amazing Dolphin of Opononi*, made Opo the dolphin a national star and was shown in 26 countries.

Hayward always had left-leaning views and these dove-tailed nicely with a visit to China in 1957, when he met Rewi Alley and Mao Tse-tung and made a thought-provoking documentary, *Inside Red China*. He later spent two months filming in Albania.

His last feature movie was *To Love a Maori*, a love story about racial discrimination. He died while touring the country promoting the film.

To mark the centenary of his birth, the New Zealand Film archive undertook the massive task of restoring *My Lady of the Cave*. Ramai Hayward, who for many years directed the Hayward Historical Film Trust, was presented with a Lifetime Achievement Award at the 2005 Wairoa Maori Film Festival as the first Maori film-maker.

Witi Ihimaera

Maori storyteller, New Zealand novelist

BORN: GISBORNE, FEBRUARY 7, 1944.

During a lifetime of accomplishment and variety, Witi Ihimaera has recorded a number of notable firsts, some of far-reaching significance. His career milestones have included:
- Becoming the first Maori to have a collection of short stories published (*Pounamu, Pounamu*, 1972) and to have a novel published (*Tangi*, 1973).
- Being seconded, at the behest of Prime Minister Norman Kirk, to the Ministry of Foreign Affairs in 1972. During an 18-year career as a diplomat, he was based in Canberra (1977-80), New York (1986-88) and Washington DC (1988-89).

Underpinning Ihimaera's achievements have been his extraordinary skill as a writer, and his fearlessness in broaching subjects others had shied away from. He has described himself as a combination of Maori storyteller and New Zealand novelist.

His early years were spent on the family farm on the East Coast. He was of Te Aitanga-a-Mahaki descent, with close affiliations to a range of other tribes. When he was 10 his family moved to Gisborne. He attended Te Karaka District High School, had one year at the Mormon Church College in Hamilton, then finished his schooling at Gisborne Boys' High School. In 1963 he began studying for a BA at Auckland University, but he made little progress in four years and eventually returned to Gisborne, where he worked as a cadet on the local newspaper.

A move to Wellington in 1967 proved life-changing, even if his job with the Post Office was undemanding. He had his first writing published, a short story called *The Liar*, run by the *Listener*, and he completed his BA by studying part-time at Victoria University. In 1970 he married Jane Cleghorn and, at her urging, they travelled to England.

It was while in England that Ihimaera's writing flourished. Within a short time he had produced an impressive body of work, mainly short stories and novels. His success has proved enduring. Three of his novels, *Tangi*, *The Matriarch* (1986) and *Bulibasha: King of the Gypsies* (1994), won Watties/Montana Book of the Year awards.

Ihimaera received the Robert Burns Fellowship in creative writing at Otago University in 1975, gained a writers' fellowship to Victoria University in 1982, and was the Katherine Mansfield Fellow at Menton, France, in 1993. He developed a special affinity with Mansfield and in 1989, to mark 100 years since her birth, produced *Dear Miss Mansfield*.

The range of Ihimaera's work has been amazing. Besides his novels and short stories, he has written plays, a children's book, numerous anthologies and orchestral works – he has always been passionate about opera.

Though he and Cleghorn had two daughters, he declared himself gay in the early 1980s. He and Cleghorn separated in 1983, but have never divorced and remain friends. Some of his work since, drawing on personal experience, has dealt with the issues of sexuality, notably *Nights in the Gardens of Spain* and *The Uncle's Story*. His most outstanding commercial success was *Whale Rider*, which was made into a successful film. On the back of that publicity, the book's sales have topped 250,000 worldwide.

Belying his roguish sense of humour, Ihimaera has never been afraid to support controversial projects. He was a prominent anti-Springbok tour protester in 1981, despite his Ministry of Foreign Affairs role. More recently he was the founding chairman and public face of Te Waka Awhina Tane, a support group for gay and bisexual Maori men. He has helped to establish organisations that aim to encourage Maori writers. He has become a Books in Prison trustee, and is a director of the education publishing group Learning Media.

His writing – in all forms, from novels to anthologies – has focused strongly on Maori and he has been tenacious and dedicated to the Maori cause. During his time as a diplomat he was at pains to represent Maori perspectives in foreign policy. He was awarded an honorary doctorate from Victoria University in 2004 for "powerful documentation of 20th century experiences of rural and urban Maori". In 1987 he was awarded the QSM for his services to the Maori community and in 2004 he was made a member of the Distinguished New Zealand Order of Merit, the equivalent of a knighthood.

Since 1990 Ihimaera has worked for the Auckland University English department.

John Rangihau

Bridging the Maori-Pakeha divide

BORN: KUHA, NEAR WAIKAREMOANA, SEPTEMBER 5, 1919. DIED: ROTORUA, OCTOBER 14, 1987.

John Rangihau once said: "Mana is when you know something has to change, and you are able to change it." By such a yardstick, Rangihau epitomised mana. The quietly-spoken Rangihau was an extremely intelligent person, a visionary, and a great orator. He contributed significantly to the 20th century renaissance of Maori.

His full name was John Te Rangianiwaniwa Rangihau, and some close to him knew him as Te Nika. He was a member of the Tuhoe tribe and lived his early years in Urewera country. Rangihau attended Kokako Native School from 1926-33 and then spent three years at Wesley College, Auckland. For the next decade he undertook a variety of outdoor jobs in the Bay of Plenty, including timber-milling and working on the Waikaremoana hydroelectric power scheme.

In 1944 he enlisted in the Air Force, serving in the Delta unit. However, he then requested a transfer to the army and served overseas with the 28th Maori Battalion for a year.

On his return he worked for the Government, first at a health centre north of Wairoa, and then as a Maori welfare officer. He became a recognised leader of Tuhoe, attending conferences throughout New Zealand. He was a thoughtful person and pondered the problems of Maori, seeking solutions that would be acceptable to Maori and Pakeha.

He married Wenarata Tait in 1949. They had nine children. Though he was busy with his family life, he decided he needed more academic qualifications, and after three years' study, gained a diploma in social science at Victoria University, Wellington, in 1959.

Rangihau enhanced his stature further when he set up a branch of the Department of Maori Affairs at Taupo, then moved to Rotorua as district Maori welfare officer. There were awkward discussions during this period, including contentious issues over Lake Waikaremoana and various roading projects, but he handled negotiations skilfully. Gradually his horizons expanded. He began running classes in Maori culture and history for Tuhoe students, and he was deeply involved with the Ringatu church.

The span of his work was immense – he travelled to South Africa to debate that country's apartheid laws, helped Polynesian immigrants to New Zealand, and lectured at some of the world's foremost universities, including Oxford in England.

In 1973 Rangihau began working for the University of Waikato's Centre for Maori Studies and Research. This enabled him to research thoroughly the history of Te Kooti, who had founded the Ringatu religion, and to revise the Ringatu Church prayer book. He strove constantly for ways to preserve and revive the Maori language and in 1974 established the first Maori-language preschool groups, which were based on kindergartens.

Out of these spun the kohanga reo programme of the 1980s – Rangihau had a vision of Maori babies being nurtured in their native language from birth to age five. It was largely through his intervention that the decline in the number of Maori-speaking people in New Zealand was halted.

In the 1980s Rangihau returned to the Maori Affairs Department, as a senior consultant. He turned his attention to the problem of Maori youth in prison and encouraged Maori elders to seek out their children and grandchildren in prison and persuade them to return home upon release. In 1985 Rangihau became a member of the Parole Board. He also worked for the Department of Social Welfare, trying to improve the department's image among Maori, and in 1986 released a landmark report, *Puao-te-ata-tu* (Daybreak), which argued convincingly that there was racism in the department, and throughout most other New Zealand's institutions. This led to significant reforms and a Maori perspective in the delivery of child, youth and family services in New Zealand, including the introduction of family group conferences.

At the 1986 National Party conference Rangihau explained movingly that he was not seeking compensation or feelings of guilt, but a fair share of resources. He received a standing ovation.

Though he spoke commandingly and was an impressive performer of the haka, Rangihau was understated. He had about him an amazing aura and an obvious integrity. He was an ideal person to promote understanding between Maori and Pakeha and to try to incorporate Maori values into modern life.

His work touched health, education, history, religion and culture. In 1975 he received the British Empire Medal for services to Maori. In 1981 Michael King wrote Rangihau's biography, *Being Maori*. Two years after Rangihau's death, a teaching and research position at Victoria University was established in his name.

Dave Dobbyn

The beloved entertainer

BORN: AUCKLAND, JANUARY 3, 1957.

Dave Dobbyn was given a Lifetime Achievement Award at the New Zealand Music Awards in 2001. The same year, his *Loyal* was chosen as New Zealand's No 3 song of all time and eight of his songs made the top 50. It was confirmation of Dobbyn's enduring contribution to the New Zealand music industry as a song-writer, record-producer and musician.

Dobbyn, short, rotund and with trademark curly hair, was aptly described by the *New Zealand Herald*'s Russell Bailey as "The Beloved Entertainer".

He was a shy schoolboy who "always had a song in my head", whether it was The Beatles, David Bowie or Motown. One of five children in a working-class Glen Innes Catholic family, Dobbyn attended Sacred Heart College and Lavella College in south Auckland. While working as a bank teller, he was persuaded by two of his Sacred Heart school friends, Peter Urlich and Ian Morris, to join their band, Th'Dudes, as the lead guitarist.

The band became so popular that the following year Dobbyn abandoned a primary school teacher training course to become a professional musician. Its *Be Mine Tonight* was Single of the Year in 1979 and *Bliss* was almost as big. Th'Dudes had success touring New Zealand and Australia, but broke up in 1980 after drug and alcohol problems.

Dobbyn formed a band called Dave Dobbyn's Divers, soon renamed DD Smash. The band had a sensational beginning when its debut album, *Cool Bananas*, rocketed to No 1 in its first week of release. He wrote hit singles like *Devil You Know*, *Outlook for Thursday* and *Whaling*. In 1982 Dobbyn was named top male vocalist and his band was the top group and produced the top album. In 1983 he was again top vocalist and was named most popular artist. DD Smash was the top group, and won awards for single and album of the year.

Dobbyn was involved in a much-publicised incident in December 1984, when DD Smash was performing for 10,000 people in Auckland's Aotea Square. During a break in the music caused by a power failure, some of the crowd became restless and began causing a disturbance. Police made several arrests and the riot squad was called. Dobbyn criticised the police from the stage, which alerted the crowd to the fracas going on behind them. The concert was halted by police and a riot began, with departing concert-goers smashing shop windows along Queen Street. Prime Minister David Lange set up a commission of inquiry into what became known as the Queen Street Riot and Dobbyn was charged with "behaving in a manner likely to cause violence against person or property". He was acquitted.

The popular animated film *Footrot Flats* brought Dobbyn massive success in 1986. He wrote the theme song, *Slice of Heaven*, which spent eight weeks heading the New Zealand charts and four as the No 1 in Australia. *You Oughta Be in Love*, also from the movie, was almost as popular.

In 1986 Dobbyn formed Dave Dobbyn and the Stone People. He spent much of the next decade living in Australia, though he returned to New Zealand to tour the beach resorts during the summer.

Dobbyn has released solo albums regularly ever since. *Loyal* was used by Team New Zealand supporters during the 2002-03 America's Cup contest. He has also teamed with other leading musicians. In 1994 he recorded *Twist*, produced by Neil Finn, and worked with Eddie Rayner on Enzso, a rearrangement of classic Split Enz songs for the New Zealand Symphony Orchestra. In 1998 there was a well-received North American tour with Neil Finn. Dobbyn has also produced albums for Grant McLennan and contributed to albums by Jenny Morris and Bic Runga. He played to packed houses during a national tour with Runga and Tim Finn in 2000. *Together in Concert* was released shortly after. The trio performed at Brixton, London, on Waitangi Day, 2002.

Dobbyn's increasing maturity was reflected in his 1998 album *The Islander*, which explored New Zealand's national identity. A 1999 retrospective album of Dobbyn's career, *Overnight Success*, sold especially well. The title was ironic, considering he had been a hard-working music artist for more than 20 years.

For many years Dobbyn battled alcoholism, but he changed his life in 1997 when he quit drinking. He has become a born-again Christian. Dobbyn and his wife Annaliesje, whom he married in 1983, have two children. He was made an Officer of the New Zealand Order of Merit in 2003. Dobbyn's *Welcome Home* won him the Songwriter of the Year at the 2005 New Zealand Music Awards.

Russell Coutts

The yachtie who made the America's Cup his cup

BORN: WELLINGTON, MARCH 1, 1962.

Russell Coutts is one of those rare sportsmen for whom winning an Olympic gold medal is not their career highlight. It's not that Coutts didn't cherish winning the Finn class gold medal at the 1984 Los Angeles Olympics. But in a yachting career crammed with victories and cups, even that was just one peak in a mountain range of triumphs.

Coutts is best recalled for his America's Cup feats. He skippered Black Magic to victory in 1995, landing one of world sport's truly significant trophies. Five years later he led Team New Zealand to a historic defence of the Cup. He was accorded the sort of hero status generally reserved for the greatest All Blacks.

Then Coutts fell out so badly with the Team New Zealand hierarchy that he departed, taking master tactician Brad Butterworth with him. They joined Swiss-based Alinghi, and returned to Auckland in 2003 to deliver an emphatic message, smashing Team New Zealand 5–0 in the final. Coutts was reviled by many who had saluted him a short time earlier. There were even death threats. He was branded a traitor. Misguided "Loyal" campaign leaders attacked Coutts relentlessly.

Ironically, Coutts had a disagreement with the Alinghi boss Ernesto Bertarelli in 2004 and left the Swiss team. Therefore, under new America's Cup rules, the most successful sailor in the Cup's history – he won a record 14 finals races – was consigned to a spectating role for the next Cup regatta, at Valencia.

All this and not a mention yet of Coutts' phenomenal match-racing deeds. He claimed world titles in 1992, 1993 and 1996 and had other yachties in awe of him. There have been other winning forays too, such as in the Admiral's Cup and One Ton Cup, and he has earned world titles in the 12m and Farr 40 classes.

Coutts grew up in Wellington. When he was 11 the family moved to Dunedin, where he attended Otago Boys' High School. He was always a good sailor, but honed his craft when he moved to Auckland. In 1981 he won the world youth single-handed title in Portugal.

Coutts has the knack of extracting the maximum from any boat he steps in, and at the 1984 Olympics he was brilliant, even when he developed painful boils on his backside and had to compete in agony. There was drama at Los Angeles, though, not so much on the points table, where he won well, but in the committee room. His gear, when weighed after the final race, was too heavy, and it required a long, nervous wait while it dried – and consequently got lighter – before he was declared the gold medallist.

Coutts completed his Bachelor of Engineering degree at Auckland University in 1986. Whatever yachting project he is involved in, he offers as much in technical expertise as in tactical nous.

Small wonder that he was lured by Peter Blake to skipper NZL 32, dubbed Black Magic, in the 1995 America's Cup challenge. While Blake did the organising and built the team, Coutts concentrated on making the boat go fast. Black Magic swept to the Louis Vuitton Cup, then hammered Dennis Conner's Young America 5–0 in the final. There were joyous scenes when the America's Cup champions were accorded huge parades through New Zealand's main cities. Coutts was awarded a CBE, was named World Sailor of the Year and won the Halberg Award with Team New Zealand.

The good times continued in 2000, when Coutts and Butterworth proved an unbeatable combination and Team New Zealand walloped Prada 5–0 to retain the America's Cup. Coutts was made a Distinguished Companion of the New Zealand Order of Merit. Who'd have guessed then, looking at Coutts with that cherubic smile, that he would soon be so detested by so many of his countrymen?

The story behind Coutts' split from Team New Zealand emerged only slowly. Finally it became clear that there had been poor management and broken promises. Coutts, a proud New Zealand representative for so long, felt that he had no choice but to head off-shore. With his record he was sure to receive many lucrative offers. That he subsequently returned to Auckland in Alinghi colours and proved his class merely confirmed what a fantastic sailor he was. It should never be overlooked how ruthlessly competitive he is on the water.

Perhaps when the heat and fury have died down, there'll be a revision in thinking about Coutts. Few New Zealand sportsmen ever won as much or made their countrymen feel as good as Coutts did.

Jonah Lomu

The softly-spoken giant who took the rugby world by storm

BORN: AUCKLAND, MAY 12, 1975.

Jonah Lomu, the most recognisable player in rugby history, could not have made a more dramatic entrance on to the world stage.

The drums had been beating about Lomu for some time. He was an outstanding player for Wesley College and by 1991 was locking for the New Zealand under-17 side. He made his rep debut, on the wing, for Counties-Manukau in May 1994, but even before that the country was buzzing after his breathtaking play for the New Zealand sevens team in Hong Kong.

Lomu's second first-class game was an All Black trial, when he had legend John Kirwan at full stretch marking him. He played for New Zealand against France two weeks later. At 19 years, 45 days, he was the youngest test All Black.

It was too soon, and he lasted just two matches. Some questioned his rugby acumen, slow reactions and lackadaisical attitude to training. However, Laurie Mains included him in his All Black team for the 1995 World Cup in South Africa and that's where Lomu turned the rugby world on its head.

Lomu cut a swathe through Ireland, Wales, Scotland and England at the World Cup. There were two storming tries against Ireland, but it was England that really felt his full power. He scored four magnificent tries in the All Blacks' 45–29 semi-final victory. One, when he ran over England fullback Mike Catt while stumbling for balance, defied belief. Because he had played so well against the Home Nations, he received the full brunt of British media coverage and that turned Lomu into a world sports celebrity.

At 1.95m (6ft 5in) and 118kg, Lomu was different from previous wings. He wasn't just big, he was agile, fast (he could cover 100m in 11s) and quick off the mark, which made him a nightmare to tackle. There have been few who could engender the expectancy that arose in crowds whenever he received the ball. Colin Meads, asked if he had seen a player like Lomu, replied: "Yes, plenty of them. But they were locks and I found them in the middle of the lineout."

After that World Cup, Lomu was always big news. He remained quiet and humble, despite the adulation and publicity. He was courted by major companies like Nike and there was huge media coverage of his marriages, to Tanya Rutter and Fiona Taylor, and his other relationships, as well as his off-field pursuits, ranging from driving cars to his taste in music.

He played for Counties-Manukau, Wellington, the Blues, Chiefs and Hurricanes. While he didn't always hit his best form, there were enough rampaging runs and breathtaking tries to keep the Lomu legend alive.

Lomu excelled against Australia in 1995 and at the 1999 World Cup, and helped New Zealand win a sevens gold medal at the 1998 Commonwealth Games. But he began to be ever more affected by a kidney ailment – nephritic syndrome – that finally reduced him to a shuffle. He needed regular dialysis treatment and departed rugby in 2003, having scored 37 tries in 63 tests.

He received a kidney transplant in 2004, courtesy of radio announcer Grant Kereama, and vowed he would return to top rugby, which drew much scepticism. Amazingly, he did so, leading a team at Twickenham in Martin Johnson's benefit match in June 2005. Lomu scored a try but injured his shoulder, which put him out of rugby for the rest of the New Zealand season. He was contracted to play for North Harbour in the NPC, but was reduced to an assistant-coach role. He signed to play for Cardiff at the end of 2005.

With his enormous income, Lomu could have become the target of jealousy, but he remained so committed to the All Black cause that this never happened. Team-mates joked about his fame. Long-serving All Black captain Sean Fitzpatrick told how in South Africa he was asked by an elderly woman to sign a rugby ball. "I was halfway through signing," Fitzpatrick related, "when Jonah walked nearby. The woman screamed 'Jonah', grabbed the ball and pen and rushed towards him. Somewhere in South Africa an elderly woman has a white rugby ball which has two signatures – Jonah Lomu and Sean Fi."

Lomu was a great advertisement for rugby. Of Tongan upbringing, he told of how the game had helped him overcome a troubled childhood in south Auckland and had pulled him away from crime.

He became an increasingly confident speaker and was widely recognised, not just in traditional rugby strongholds, but in Europe and Asia. Lomu was awarded an International Rugby Players Association Special Merit Award in 2003.

Peter Mahon

The judge whose Erebus crash report made him a household name

BORN: CHRISTCHURCH, NOVEMBER 1, 1923. DIED: AUCKLAND, AUGUST 11, 1986.

Peter Mahon's phrase, "an orchestrated litany of lies", to describe the behaviour of Air New Zealand executives he felt were covering up the truth over the Mount Erebus disaster, has become one of the most famous in New Zealand history.

Mahon, a High Court judge, was appointed by Robert Muldoon's Government to form a one-man Royal Commission of Inquiry into the Air New Zealand DC-10 crash in the Antarctic on November 28, 1979. There were 257 people killed in the crash, including 200 New Zealanders. It was New Zealand's second-worst disaster, after the 1931 Napier earthquake.

Ron Chippindale, the Chief Inspector of Air Accidents, presented his report on June 12, 1980. He said pilot error was the principal cause of the tragedy and blamed Captain Jim Collins for flying too low. The report was met with scepticism and, bowing to public demand, the Government launched a Royal Commission of Inquiry.

Mahon's thorough research and comprehensive and fearless report (he reviewed 3083 pages of evidence, 284 exhibits and 368 pages of closing submissions) into the flight TE901 crash largely exonerated the crew, blaming the provision of faulty navigational information and the existence of a phenomenon called "white-out", or, as he termed it, "a malevolent trick of the polar light". During his inquiry Mahon visited North America, Europe and the Antarctic.

He said the single, dominant cause was the changing of the aircraft's navigation computer co-ordinates to a route where the aircraft was aimed directly at Mt Erebus, without the crew being advised. Because of the white-out conditions, the crew were unable to see the mountain. He also found that the radio communications centre at McMurdo Station had authorised Captain Collins to descend to 450 metres. Most sensationally, Mahon accused Air New Zealand of irregularities and deceit, "a pre-meditated plan of deception", and ordered Air New Zealand to pay $150,000 towards the cost of the commission. The Government did not expect the sort of report Mahon provided, and Prime Minister Muldoon joined Air New Zealand in angrily rejecting its findings.

The case turned Mahon into a household name – not the sort of profile he was seeking. The Appeal Court later ruled that Mahon had exceeded his jurisdiction and breached natural justice in his findings on the conduct of Air New Zealand. Mahon, feeling his integrity had been questioned, resigned from the High Court bench. His appeal to the Privy Council against the Appeal Court decision was dismissed. However, Mahon's findings and verdict on the crash stood and he emerged from the affair as a somewhat controversial public hero.

Mahon's conclusions were significant. They forced a rethink internationally on the responsibilities of airlines and crew. In 1985 he received the International Federation of Air Line Pilots' Associations Award for his work during the inquiry. He was the first non-pilot to be so honoured. His written report had the pace of a best-selling thriller. An award-winning book by Mahon called *Verdict on Erebus*, which drew on the same information, was published in 1984 and sold well.

After his retirement, Mahon headed an inquiry into a Queen Street riot and was a temporary Chief Justice for Western Samoa. He had a number of appointments as arbitrator on behalf of several statutory bodies and private litigations and at the time of his death had been appointed a senior lecturer at Auckland University. But, in large part because of the stress of the Erebus inquiry, his health declined quickly and he died in 1986.

Mahon grew up in Christchurch, where he attended St Bede's College. He served with the Second New Zealand Expeditionary Force during World War II. He was commissioned in Italy in 1943 – he became fluent in Italian – and served for a time in Japan with the British Commonwealth Occupation Forces.

After completing his law degree at Canterbury University after the war, he joined the firm of Raymond, Stringer, Hamilton and Donnelly. He was admitted to the bar in 1947. He was a Christchurch Crown solicitor from 1957-62, when he went into private practice as a barrister. He conducted three appeals before the Privy Council's judiciary committee before he was made a Queen's Counsel in 1971. Mahon and his wife, Margarita, shifted to Auckland and the following year he was sworn in as a Supreme Court judge.

Mahon always appeared a dignified and cultured person, with a generous heart. His 1985 book *Dear Sam*, a collection of letters to his three children and to friends, revealed his humour and kindness.

Georgina Beyer

From drag queen to Member of Parliament

BORN: WELLINGTON, NOVEMBER 7, 1957.

Georgina Beyer made an unforgettable maiden speech to Parliament in 1999. After mentioning that she was the world's first trans-sexual Member of Parliament, she nearly brought down the house when she said: "I was quoted once as saying that, 'This was the stallion that became a gelding and now she's a mayor'. I suppose I do have to say that now I have found myself to be a member! So I have come the full circle, so to speak."

It would be difficult to imagine a stranger path to Parliament than that walked by Beyer. She was born George Bertrand, a part-Maori who spent his first four years on his grandparents' farm in Taranaki. His mother subsequently married Colin Beyer, a prominent lawyer, and George moved to Wellington, where he attended Wellesley College, then Onslow College. In 1970 the family moved to Auckland and George attended Papatoetoe High School.

By the time George was 17 he was becoming heavily involved in the gay scene, and he came to understand that he was trans-gender. "I realised I was a woman trapped inside a male body," was how Beyer later described her situation.

There followed years of chaos and uncertainty. She adopted the name Georgina, and became a stripper and a prostitute. Beyer eventually made her way to Kings Cross, Sydney's notorious red light area. It was a dangerous life – she related later how on one occasion she got into a car with four men, who brutally raped her.

Beyer returned to New Zealand, continuing to work as a stripper and a drag queen, but gradually she sorted out her life. She underwent a sex-change operation in 1984 and began to pursue an acting career, with notable success. She appeared in *Jewel's Darl* (earning a nomination in 1987 as best actress in the Guild of Film and Television Arts Awards), *Close to Home*, *Inside Straight*, *Shark in the Park* and *Shortland Street*. She also acted in theatre and appeared in cabaret.

A move to Carterton set Beyer on a path to Parliament. She enrolled in an Access Scheme, but was soon teaching on the course and then became course administrator, employed by the Carterton Community Centre.

In 1992 she had a stint broadcasting for *TodayFM*. Increasingly she found herself drawn to politics. She dipped her toe in the water by winning an election to a local school board. She missed a place on the Carterton District Council by just 14 votes in 1992, but won a by-election comfortably the following year. Beyer quickly developed a strong following. People recognised her intelligence and wit and she made no secret of the problems she had encountered during her life. In 1995 she became the world's first trans-sexual mayor, when Carterton citizens voted her in with a 48 per cent majority. She proved so popular that in the next election, in 1998, she was re-elected with a stunning 90 per cent majority.

By now Beyer had her eye on national politics. In 1999 she caused a shock by winning the seat of Wairarapa for Labour. National's Deputy Prime Minister, Wyatt Creech, had won the seat with a 7867 majority in 1996, but Beyer claimed the seat for Labour with a 3033 majority – a swing of 32 per cent to Labour – when most had expected National's Paul Henry to win it.

Beyer retained the seat in 2002, increasing her majority to 6372. During the next parliamentary term she chaired the Social Services committee and was a member of the Law and Order committee. She served on a variety of Labour's caucus committees, but seemed to become disenchanted with politics. Labour's foreshore and seabed policy caused her problems and she began to find the political scene unnecessarily spiteful.

After announcing she intended retiring from Parliament at the 2005 election, she changed her mind. She did not stand for Wairarapa but was returned to Parliament as a Labour list member.

Beyer has become a distinguished New Zealander and an inspiration to many. She is an internationally-known advocate for gay and lesbian rights, but her work has extended into many other areas. She became a JP in 1997 and was for some years a trustee of the New Zealand Aids Foundation. She had *Change for the Better* published in 1999 and in 2002 was the subject of a moving television documentary, *Georgie Girl*.

New Zealanders often boast of their we-can-do-anything spirit, in the face of the country's isolation and lack of population. No-one exemplifies the ability to triumph over adversity better than Beyer.

A J Hackett

The man who took bungy-jumping to the world

BORN: AUCKLAND, MAY 26, 1958.

Incredibly, Alan John Hackett once sold encyclopaedias door-to-door. These days the man who began the bungy-jumping craze is one of the world's most famous thrill merchants. No-one calls him Alan John any more. He's simply A J.

Hackett grew up on Auckland's North Shore. After leaving school at 16 he became a carpenter, but spent much time snowboarding and skiing. It was the pursuit of ever faster and steeper slopes that eventually led to the bungy. He was always looking for that extra adrenalin rush.

He began experimenting with bungy-jumping in the mid-1980s. It wasn't new – there is a centuries-old Pacific Islands coming-of-age ritual, where men tie vines to their feet, then fling themselves off towers. Picking up on that, a group of Oxford University students formed the Dangerous Sports Club and one of their pastimes was throwing themselves off bridges, with rope tied to their ankles.

But Hackett and an Auckland mate, Chris Sigglekow, brought what we now call bungy-jumping to New Zealand. Hackett, always on the lookout for excitement, would regularly jump into the water off 20m-high cliffs. Hackett and Sigglekow had their first recorded jumps off Auckland's Greenhithe Bridge in 1986. Sigglekow, a video editor, was responsible for filming it. The pair progressed to a 30m bridge near Hamilton, then the Auckland Harbour Bridge, 40m at its highest.

Expanding his horizons, Hackett decided to jump off Paris's Eiffel Tower. That jump, done in June 1987, without the permission of the French authorities, was quite an exercise in planning and received tremendous media exposure. It was really when bungy-jumping as we know it was born.

Within a short time, Hackett had gone into business with downhill mountain biking champion Henry van Asch, of Christchurch. The word bungy was derived from New Zealand slang for elastic strap. Bungy cords were made from latex rubber.

In 1988 Hackett and van Asch opened the first bungy site, at Ohakune, but the sport's spiritual home was to be Queenstown's Kawarau Bridge. On November 12, 1988, the day bungy-jumping was first offered there, 28 people paid $75 each to leap off the 43m bridge. The bridge now attracts 27,000 jumpers annually and seven per cent of tourists to Queenstown take the jump. Among those who have jumped there have been the Queen's grand-daughter, Zara Phillips, singer Kenny Rogers, actor Billy Boyd, Slash from Guns n' Roses and various All Blacks and America's Cup yachties.

The long-haired Hackett, with his bubbly personality and boundless energy, became a national identity. He was also a savvy businessman, with an eye for publicity and marketing opportunities. For 10 years he and van Asch built their business, not just around New Zealand but overseas, too. There was A J Hackett (the name became the brand) bungy-jumping in such exotic locations as Bali, Las Vegas, Normandie, Cairns and Macau. The company has an annual turnover of $14 million and caters for 70,000 jumpers a year. The oldest man to bungy jump was 91, the oldest woman 84. Bungy-jumping has become so popular that the company has had many rivals, but none have prospered like the originals.

Hackett settled with his three children in the French Alps and in 1997 there was a split with van Asch. Hackett now runs the company's overseas operation and van Asch is the New Zealand boss. However, Hackett returns to New Zealand frequently. He made a much-celebrated jump from the Auckland Sky City Casino Tower in 1998 and regularly speaks at seminars. There have been other commercial spin-offs, including a television series, *Can U Hackett*, and a string of television commercials. In addition, there is an AJ Gear brand of outdoor clothing.

The explosion in bungy-jumping has been incredible. More than two million people have jumped at one of the company's sites. It's a curious phenomenon, which Hackett explains is not thrill-seeking, but overcoming fear: "People aren't paying us to jump off a bridge tied to a rubber band. We are selling them the opportunity to face their greatest fear."

People often talk about how the All Blacks have spread New Zealand's reputation through the world. Hackett has done the same thing in recent years, and not just in rugby-playing nations. Bungy-jumping takes place in all sorts of places, from Acapulco, Mexico, to Victoria Falls, Zimbabwe.

Through the Hackett bungy-jumping connection, New Zealand has marketed itself as one of the world's adventure capitals. Not surprisingly, Hackett has received several top New Zealand Tourism awards.

Denny Hulme

The quiet achiever who snared the greatest prize in motor sport

BORN: NELSON, JUNE 18, 1936. DIED: BATHURST, OCTOBER 4, 1992.

Denny Hulme was known throughout the motor racing world as "The Bear". A brilliant driver, but tough and taciturn, frugal with words. Gruff, grumpy even.

Friends claimed Hulme was misunderstood, that he was a fine person and a loyal team member. This was confirmed at the New Zealand Sports Hall of Fame's inaugural induction ceremony, in 1990. Hulme, the 1967 world Formula One champion, was not among the inductees. This was absurd. The Formula One title draws acclaim from all around the world. It transcends sport.

Hulme's friends were appalled. But Hulme's reaction was superb. "It doesn't matter," he said quietly. "Bruce [McLaren] is there and that's more important. There's plenty of time for me." At the ceremony, Hulme was clearly moved when he read the citation to his long-time friend McLaren, who'd died 20 years earlier. His reaction spoke volumes for Hulme as a person and was an insight into the camaraderie that existed between McLaren and Hulme – and Chris Amon, the third flying Kiwi – during the 1960s, when they were among motor racing's superstars.

Sadly, Hulme was wrong about there being plenty of time for him. He died when he suffered a heart attack while racing at Bathurst in 1992 and was inducted into the Hall of Fame posthumously in 1993.

The first vehicles Hulme drove were tractors and trucks. His father Clive, a Victoria Cross winner, owned a small trucking business in Pongakawa, and young Denny would get a buzz out of driving the trucks. From his late teens he raced throughout New Zealand. Then he was sent overseas on the Driver to Europe scheme in 1960. Australian Jack Brabham recognised his ability and included him in his Formula One team.

Hulme was 11th in the 1965 world drivers' championship and thereafter was repeatedly among the leading drivers – fourth in 1966, champion in 1967, then third, sixth and fourth. When Hulme retired in 1974 he'd raced in 112 Grands Prix and been placed 61 times. He won eight races, including two – Monaco and Germany – in 1967, his golden year.

The New Zealander was locked in a battle with his boss Brabham as the 1967 championship reached its climax. He'd begun the season well, fourth in South Africa, then a sensational winner at Monaco. After that, consistently good results meant that with two Formula One championship races remaining, Hulme had 43 points, Brabham 40. At Watkins Glen, Hulme ran out of fuel on the last lap and puttered to the finish on a dead engine for third. Brabham was fifth. Before the final race, at Mexico City, Hulme led by five points. He drove conservatively, knowing fourth would earn him the title. Jim Clark won the race by a huge margin, Brabham was second and Hulme third. His championship victory was built on consistency – he scored in nine of the 11 races. Hulme was a runaway winner of the Sportsman of the Year award that year.

There were other great motor racing moments for Hulme. He won two Can Am championships, was Rookie of the Year at the 1967 Indianapolis 500 (when he finished fourth), and was second at Le Mans in 1966. After his Formula One days, Hulme turned to saloon cars, trucks and the classic car racing series in Europe and the United States. Even into his mid-50s he was competitive and loved the thrill of racing.

He was always extremely courageous. He had several bad smashes, including one at Atlanta in 1972, when his car was destroyed in a 290km/h (180mph) back flip that put Hulme in hospital. His stickiest moment was in 1970, when his car caught fire during Indianapolis. He was badly burnt and by the time he jumped from his blazing car – which was still doing more than 110 km/h (70mph) – his body was engulfed in flames. He nearly had to have some of the fingers of his left hand amputated and had both hands placed in splints. But he still raced a fortnight later, determined to succeed for the McLaren team in the Can Am series, in memory of McLaren, who had just been killed in a crash while test driving.

Adriano Cimarosti summed up Hulme in *The Complete History of Grand Prix Motor Racing*: "As cool and collected in the cockpit of the car as he was outside it, the quiet, unassuming Hulme was a man who never sought publicity or press attention in the way many of his predecessors had. He was tough and strong, anything but a showman."

Russell Crowe

Rough diamond, brilliant actor

BORN: WELLINGTON, APRIL 7, 1964.

Russell Crowe is New Zealand's most celebrated Hollywood actor. He fulfils the popular concept of what it means to be a movie star, from his award-winning acting to being a gossip magazine favourite because of his romantic liaisons and tempestuous behaviour.

Crowe had an Australasian upbringing. His family moved from Wellington to Australia when he was four, but he spent his teenage years in Auckland. He attended Auckland Grammar, where he followed his cousins, Jeff and Martin Crowe, both New Zealand cricket captains. Russell never showed much aptitude for sport, but was interested in music and acting.

He was the son of movie set caterers and was drawn to the film-making craft. At seven he made his screen debut in the Australian television programme *Spyforce*. In 1978 he had a role in *The Young Doctors*, a popular Australian soap.

Back in New Zealand, he changed his professional name to Rus Le Roq and formed the band Roman Antix. His first single was called *I Want to Be Like Marlon Brando*. Crowe was an enthusiastic though ordinary musician. As Rus Le Roq he became known in the Auckland rock scene as a disc jockey.

He showed far more ability as an actor. In 1983 he was in an Australian stage production of *Grease*. From 1986-88 he toured Australia and New Zealand with *The Rocky Horror Show*. There were several appearances in 1987 as Kenny Larkin on the much-watched Australian soap *Neighbours*.

His breakthrough movie role was playing a neo-Nazi in *Romper Stomper* in 1992. This was followed by *The Sum of Us*. Crowe was on his way. A-list actress Sharon Stone was so impressed by Crowe in *Romper Stomper* that she wanted him in her Western, *The Quick and the Dead*, and delayed filming until he was available.

Other good roles followed. In 1995 he was a serial killer of sorts in *Virtuosity*, which starred Denzel Washington, and he really cracked it as tough cop Bud White in the much-acclaimed *L.A. Confidential*.

Crowe sought variety in his acting. *Mystery, Alaska*, *The Insider*, *Proof of Life*, *Gladiator*, *A Beautiful Mind*, *Master and Commander: The Far Side of the World* and *Cinderella Man* offered diverse challenges. He directed two films in 2002, including *Texas*, which he also produced.

Crowe earned his first best actor Oscar nomination playing tobacco industry whistle-blower Jeffrey Wigand in *The Insider*. The following year, as Maximus in *Gladiator*, he went one better and won the best actor Oscar. In 2002 he was nominated for the third straight year in the best actor category, for his portrayal of John Nash, a mathematician who was schizophrenic but recovered to win a Nobel Prize, in *A Beautiful Mind*.

Crowe appeared regularly with talkshow high-fliers like Jay Leno, David Letterman, Oprah Winfrey, Rosie O'Donnell and Michael Parkinson.

He made even more headlines off screen than on. After *Proof of Life*, he began a relationship with co-star Meg Ryan that had Hollywood buzzing. However, on April 7, 2003 (his 39th birthday), he married long-time girlfriend Danielle Spencer, whom he'd met in 1989 when they co-starred in *The Crossing*.

Though New Zealanders claim him, his Australian links are strong – he is a passionate supporter of rugby league club South Sydney and owns a 560-acre farm in New South Wales. Crowe has contemplated taking out Australian citizenship, while retaining his New Zealand citizenship. Not surprisingly, given his family links, Crowe follows cricket closely and even has a full-sized cricket field, with appropriate spectator facilities, at his New South Wales property.

His hot temper has landed him in trouble. He has been involved in headline-making brawls in Sydney and London, and when his acceptance speech for the best actor award during a British Film Awards ceremony was edited, he shoved the producer of the show, Malcolm Gerrie, against a wall. Perhaps his lowest moment was in June 2005, when he was arrested and charged with secondary assault after an incident with a staff member of the Mercer Hotel in New York.

Crowe is a complex character who can be erudite and thoughtful – he proudly displayed his grandfather's MBE while making his Oscar-winning speech in 2001.

He marches to the beat of his own drum. After *The Gladiator*, he and some friends made a 6500km motorcycle trip around Australia. His rock group is now called 30 Odd Foot of Grunts. It played its first United States concert in Austin in 2000. Ticket prices hit $US500 on the black market.

Index

Abrahams, Harold 90
Allen, James 122
Alley, Rewi 174-175, 198
Amon, Chris 216
Anderton, Jim 72
Annaliesje (wife of Dave Dobbyn) 204
Arlott, John 188
Armstrong, Neil 44
Aubert, Suzanne 152-153
Azcona, Marie 132

Bader, Douglas 82
Bailey, Russell 204
Baillie, Bill 98, 124
Baker, Ida (Lesley Moore) 56
Baker, Ngauta 180
Ballance, John 64
Bannister, Roger 98
Barnard, Christian 40
Barratt-Boyes, Brian 40-41
Bartram, Fred 134
Basham, Frederick 182
Basham, Maud (Aunt Daisy) 182-183
Bassett, Michael 144, 160
Batchelor, Denzil 148
Batten, Ellen 37-38
Batten, Jean 37-39
Baxter, Archie 94
Baxter, Jacquie (Sturm) 94
Baxter, James K 94-95, 192
Bayi, Filbert 130
Beath, Mary 13
Beauchamp, Leslie 56
Beaverbrook, Lord (William Aitken) 82
Beccali, Luigi 90
Bedbrook, John 9, 92-93
Beeby, Beatrice (Newnham) 88
Beeby, Clarence 88-89
Begg, Heather 80
Belich, James 192
Benedict XV, Pope 152
Benson-Pope, David 72
Bertarelli, Ernesto 206
Beston, John 48
Beyer, Colin 212
Beyer, Georgina (George Bertrand) 212-213
Binney, Judith 192
Blackett, Patrick 10
Blake, Peter 86-87, 206
Blake, Pippa 86
Blatchford, Robert 118
Blond, Elaine 114
Blond, Neville 114

Bohr, Niels 10
Bolger, Jim 104, 174
Bonaparte, Napoleon 19
Bonthron, Bill 90
Botham, Ian 188
Bowden, George 56
Bowie, David 204
Boyd, Billy 214
Brabham, Jack 216
Brasch, Charles 94, 192
Brown, Alan 100
Brownlee, Joe 78
Brunner, Thomas 154
Brydone, Thomas 9, 58-59
Buck, Margaret (Wilson) 66
Buck, Peter 26, 66-67
Buck, William 66
Buckman, Rosina 9
Bunbury, Thomas 50
Bunkle, Phillida 72
Busby, James 34
Butterworth, Brad 206

Campion, Jane 48
Capra, Frank 198
Carco, Francis 56
Carr, Harold 136
Carrington, Dora 56
Carroll, James 26, 54
Carter, Jimmy 106
Castro, Fidel 174
Catchpole, Ken 52
Catt, Carrie Chapman 14
Catt, Mike 208
Caygill, David 160
Chadwick, James 10
Chamberlain, Neville 168
Chaplin, Charlie 198
Chapman, Frederick 178
Charles, Bob 9
Charles, Prince 80
Chekhov, Anton 56
Chippindale, Ron 210
Chunn, Geoff 100
Chunn, Mike 132
Churchill, Winston 76, 82, 168
Cimarosti, Adriano 216
Clark, Helen 72-73, 86
Clark, Jim 216
Clark, Russell 110
Clarke, Don 148
Clarke, George 36
Clarke, Helen 120

Clarke, John (Fred Dagg) 120-121
Clay, Marie 172-173
Cleghorn, Jane 200
Coates, Gordon 128
Cockroft, John 10
Collins, Jim 210
Colvin, Neville 168
Conner, Dennis 86, 206
Connon, Helen 9
Cook, Captain James 9, 50
Cooper, Whina 54-55, 144
Cooper, William 54
Cornes, Jerry 90
Coutts, Russell 86, 206-207
Cowan, James 198
Cowie, Bishop William 170
Cram, Steve 130
Creech, Wyatt 212
Crick, Francis 70
Croce, Carlo 162
Crombie, Noel 132
Crowe, Jeff 218
Crowe, Martin 218
Crowe, Russell 218-219
Crump, Barry 9
Culbert, Bill 186
Cullen, Christian 148
Cunningham, Glenn 90
Curnow, Allen 68

Dalziel, Leanne 72
Dalziel, Raewyn 192
Daniels, Stacey 9
Dauga, Benoit 52
Davidson, Caroline (Thierens) 58
Davidson, Jane 58
Davidson, William 9, 58-59
Davies, John 124
Davis, Peter 72
De Cleene, Trevor 160
DeMille, Cecil B 198
Deng, Xiaoping 174
Devlin, Johnny 74
Devoy, Susan 9
Dickens, Charles 134, 156
Dixon, Rod 130
Dobbyn, Dave 100, 132, 204-205
Dorée, Victor 37
Douglas, Norman 160
Douglas, Roger 72, 104, 160-161
Dowding, Hugh 82
Doyle, Harry 158
Drake, Francis 188

220

Duff, Oliver 158
Duggan, Maurice 158, 192
Du Preez, Frik 52
Durham, Lord (John Lambton) 102
Dunne, Peter 104
During, Matt 9, 162-163
During, Miriam 162
Dyson, Ruth 72

Eden, George (Lord Auckland) 34
Edger, Kate 170-171
Edger, Lilian 170
Edger, Samuel 170
Edmonds, Jane (Irvine) 108
Edmonds, Thomas 108-109
Einstein, Albert 10
Elachi, Charles 44
Eliot, T S (Thomas) 56
Elizabeth II, Queen 80
Elliott, Herb 42
Elliott, Peter 130
Ellis, Charles 10
Ellis, John 92
Ellison, Ethel (Howell) 176
Ellison, Tom 176-177
Evans, Elwyn 170
Evans, Rev William 170
Exel, David 120

Fairburn, Rex 158, 192
Falwell, Jerry 104
Favaloro, Rene 40
Fay, Michael 86
Field, Robert 110
Field, Taito Phillip 72
Finn, Elroy 100
Finn, Liam 100
Finn, Mary 132
Finn, Neil 100-101, 132, 204
Finn, Tim 100, 132-33, 204
Finn, Sharon 100
FitzGerald, James 102
Fitzpatrick, Sean 208
FitzRoy, Charles 19, 28, 50
Flavell, Dick 92
Fletcher, Andrew 150
Fletcher, Hugh 150
Fletcher, James 150-151
Fletcher, Jim 150
Fletcher, John 150
Fletcher, John jnr 150
Fletcher, Lottie (Cameron) 150
Fletcher, William 150
Foley, Mina 80
Forbes, Gordon, 26
Ford, Gerald 44
Ford, John 198
Fox, Michael J 46
Fox, William 68
Frame, Janet 48-49, 144, 158
Franklin, Rosalind 70
Fraser, Janet (Munro) 118
Fraser, Peter 22, 24, 76, 88, 118-119, 128, 134, 144, 150
French, Alf 22

French, Elizabeth 22
Freyberg, Barbara (Jekyll) 76
Freyberg, Bernard 76-77, 118

Gallagher, Bill 142-143
Gallagher, Bill jnr 142
Gallagher, Henry 142
Gallagher, John 142
Gallagher, Millie (Murray) 142
Gallagher, Viv 142
Gandhi, Mahatma 62
Garbo, Greta 37
Gatting, Mike 188
Gaugin, Paul 110
Geiger, Hans 10
George IV, King 166
George VI, King 22, 82, 184
Gerrie, Malcolm 218
Gifford, Charles 44
Gilbert, Richard 54
Gillies, Harold 78-79, 114
Gillies, Kathleen (Jackson) 78
Gillies, Marjorie (Clayton) 78
Gillies, Robert (father of Harold) 78
Gillies, Robert (musician) 132
Glasgow, David 13
Glover, Denis 158
Goldie, Charles 194-195
Goldie, David 194
Goldie, Olive (Cooper) 194
Gray, Ken 52
Gregory, Herbert 66
Grey, Eliza 20
Grey, George 19-21, 28, 50, 62, 102, 154, 194
Grey, George snr 19
Grimmett, Clarrie 188
Grodotzki, Hans 98
Guevara, Che 174

Hackett, A J 214-215
Hadlee, Barry 188
Hadlee, Dayle 188
Hadlee, Richard 188-189
Hadlee, Walter 188
Hadlow, Mark 114
Halberg, Murray 42, 98-99, 124
Hall, John 13, 62
Hamilton, Peggy 138
Hamilton, William 138-139
Harata 166
Hardie, Keir 118, 160
Haskell, Ernie 124
Hayward, Adelina 198
Hayward, Henry 198
Hayward, Hilda (Moren) 198
Hayward, Ramai (Patricia Te Miha) 198
Hayward, Rudall 9, 198-199
Hayward, Rudall snr 198
Heaphy, Catherine (Churton) 154
Heaphy, Charles 9, 154-155
Heaphy, Thomas 154
Heeger, Alan 84
Hegan, Elaine 190
Heke, Hone 9, 19, 28-30, 34, 166
Henry, Paul 212

Henry, Ros 144
Hester, Paul 100
Hika, Hongi 9, 28, 116, 166-167
Hillary, Edmund 16-18, 86
Hillary, Richard 114
Hine-i-te-aparangi 126
Hitchcock, Alfred 198
Hitler, Adolf 82, 90, 168
Hoar, Stuart 114
Hobbs, Marian 72
Hobson, Eliza (Elliott) 34
Hobson, William 19, 28, 34-36, 102
Hodgkins, Frances 146-147
Hodgkins, William 146
Holland, Harry 22
Hollows, Fred 96-97
Hollows, Gabi (O'Sullivan) 96
Hollows, Mary (Skiller) 96
Holmes, Paul 120
Holyoake, Keith 9, 106
Hooper, Craig 100
Hornibrook, Fred 122
Hotere, Ralph 186-187
Howard, Harriett 74
Howard, Mabel 74-75
Howard, Ted 74
Hough, Mark 100
Hughes, Billy 168
Hulme, Clive 216
Hulme, Denny 216-217
Hunt, John 16
Hutter, Frank 78
Huxley, Aldous 56
Hyde, Robin 158

Ihimaera, Witi 200-201

Jackson, Peter 46-47, 198
James, Billy T 190-191
Jarden, Ron 84
Jelley, Arch 130
Joel, Grace 146
Johnson, Amy 37
Johnson, Martin 208
Johnson, Samuel 156
Jordan, Michael 172
Judd, Phil 100, 132
Julian, Jeff 124
Jungowska, Maria 144

Kakahi, Hone 62
Kakahi, Tohu 62
Kan, Raybon 9
Katipa, Rewi Tumoko 128
Kawatihi, Kare Pauro 54
Kawiti, Te Ruki 28
Kenana, Rua 178-179
Kendall, Thomas 166, 167
Kereama, Grant 208
Kereru, Numia 178
King (Millar), Bella 32
King, Lawrie 124
King, Lew 144
King, Michael 144-145, 192, 202
King, Nellie 144

King, Thomas 31
King, Truby 31-33
Kingsford-Smith, Charles 37
Kipling, Rudyard 37
Kippenberger, Howard 184
Kirk, Norman 140-141, 160, 200
Kirk, Ruth 140
Kirklin, John 40
Kirwan, John 208
Knox-Johnston, Robin 86
Kohere, Reweti 25
Korokoro 116
Koteliansky, Samuel 56
Kreymborg, Fr Charles 54
Kupe 9, 126-127

Ladoumegue, Jules 90
Land, Mary 192
Landy, John 98
Lange, David 72, 104-05, 106, 160, 174, 192, 204
Lange, Naomi (Crampton) 104
Langwell, Robyn 9
Lawrence, D H (David) 56
Lawrence, Frieda 56
Lawrence, Keith 52
Lee, John A 24, 74, 118, 134-135
Lee, Molly (Guy) 134
Lee, Samuel 166
Leno, Jay 218
Leo, Sister Mary 80
Letterman, David 218
Lillee, Dennis 188
Lloyd-George, David 168
Lloyd-Jenkins, Douglas 9
Lochore, Brian 52
Lomu, Jonah 148, 208-209
Lousich, Colin 124
Lovell-Smith, William 14
Lovelock, Jack 90-91, 130
Low, David 168-169
Low, Madeline (Kenning) 168
Lowe, George 16, 18
Luxton, Jack 72
Lydiard, Arthur 42, 98, 124-125

MacDonald, Ginette 120
MacDonald, Ramsay 160
Macquarie, Lachlan 116
Magee, Barry 98, 124
Mahon, Margarita 210
Mahon, Peter 210-211
Mahuta 128
Mains, Laurie 208
Major, Malvina 80
Makaro (Kupe's daughter) 126
Malam, Liz 132
Manchester, William 78
Mandela, Nelson 62, 196
Mander, Jane 158
Manhire, Bill 186
Maniapoto, Rewi 164
Mansfield, Katherine 56-57, 158, 200
Mao Tse-tung 174, 198
Marore (wife of Te Rauparaha) 50

Marsden, Elizabeth (Fristan) 116
Marsden, Martha 116
Marsden, Samuel 50, 116-117, 156, 166
Marshall, Jack 106
Marx, Groucho 188
Mason, Ron 192
Massey, William 122
Matiu (Kupe's daughter) 126
May, Phil 168
McBride, Willie John 52
McCahon, Annie (Hamblett) 110
McCahon, Colin 110-111,146
McCombs, Elizabeth 13, 74
McCormick, Fergie 52
McDiarmid, Alan 84-85
McDiarmid, Marian (Mathieu) 84
McIndoe, Adonia (Aitken) 114
McIndoe, Archie 78, 114-115
McIndoe, Constance (Belcham) 114
McIndoe, John 114
McIndoe, Mabel 114
McLaren, Bruce 216
McLay, Jim 106
McLennan, Grant 204
McQueen, Cilla 186
Meads, Colin 52-53, 148, 208
Meads, Rhonda 52
Meads, Stan 52
Minhinnick, Gordon 168
Minto, John 196-197
Moens, Roger 42
Moore, Mike 72, 104, 160
Monester, Sara 40
Morestin, Hippolyte 78
Morris, Albert 150
Morris, Ian 204
Morris, Jenny 204
Morrison, Howard, 190
Morton, James 58
Moser, Elder 148
Mowlem, Rainsford 78
Moyes, Warren 72
Mozart, Wolfgang 80
Muldoon, Robert 104, 106-107, 160, 196, 210
Mune, Ian 190
Murdoch, Colin 9, 112-113
Murry, John Middleton 56
Murupaenga 166
Mussolini, Benito 168
Muturangi 126

Naki, Katerina 25
Nash, John 218
Nash, Walter 24, 74, 134, 150, 192
Nathan, Waka 52
Neill, Sam 46, 120
Nene, Tamati Waka 28, 34
Nepia, George 148-149
Nepia, George jnr 148
Nepia, Huinga 148
Nerli, Girolamo 146
Newton, Isaac 10
Ngake (Ngahue) 126
Ngarongo-ki-tua 66
Ngata, Apirana 25-27, 66, 128, 144

Ngata, Paratene 25
Nolan, Melanie 9
Nordmeyer, Arnold 140
Norgay, Tenzing 16, 18

O'Donnell, Rosie 218
Omana, Tiaki 26
O'Maonlai, Liam 132
Omeka 180
Ono, (wife of Hone Heke) 28
Oppenheimer, Robert 10
Orange, Claudia 192

Palmer, Geoffrey 72, 160
Parata, Ned 148
Parekowhatu 50
Park, Desmond 80
Park, Dol (Parish) 82
Park, Keith 82-83
Parker, Honorah 46
Parker, Lyn 52
Parkinson, Michael 218
Parkinson, Tom 190
Patuone, Eruera Maihi 29, 34
Pearse, Richard 60-61
Pere, Wi 26
Peters, Winston 104
Phillips, Linda 80
Phillips, Zara 214
Pickering, Inez (Chapman) 44
Pickering, William 44-45
Plunket, Victoria 32
Plunket, William Lee (Governor) 32
Pokaia 166
Pomare II 28
Pomare, Maui 9, 26, 66
Pompellier, Bishop Jean Baptiste 152
Pope, Margaret 104
Porritt, Arthur 9, 90
Prebble, Richard 104, 160
Puckett, Ray 124

Quax, Dick 130
Quigley, Derek 160

Rae, John 192
Randall, John 70
Ranfurly, Lady 194
Ranfurly, Lord (Uchter Knox) 194
Rangihau, John 144, 202-203
Rangi-kawau 62
Ratana, Tahupotiki Wiremu 180-181
Rayner, Eddie 100, 132, 204
Redwood, Archbishop Francis 152
Reed, Alfred 156-157
Reed, Clif 156
Reed, Isabel (Fisher) 156
Reed, James 156
Reed, Marian 156
Reeves, William Pember 64, 192
Reid, John 84
Reti 126
Richards, Trevor 196
Richmond, Dorothy Kate 146
Richmond, Henry 31

Riemenschneider, Johannes 62
Rina (Peter Buck's mother) 66
Robb, Douglas 40
Rodger, Bill 124
Rogers, Kenny 214
Rolleston, William 62
Romanos, Joseph 9
Rongo, Hariata 28, 30
Ross, Hilda 74
Rout, Ettie 122-123
Rowling, Bill 54, 104, 106, 120, 160
Ruatara 116, 166
Runga, Bic 100, 132, 204
Russell, Bertrand 56
Rutherford, Ernest 10-12, 44, 70
Rutherford, James 10
Rutherford, Martha 10
Rutherford, May (Newton) 10
Rutter, Tanya 208
Ryan, Meg 218
Ryun, Jim 130

Samuels, Dover 72
San Romani, Archie 90
Sargeson, Frank (Norris Davey) 48, 144, 158-159, 192
Sargeson, Oakley 158
Sassoon, Siegfried 56
Savage, Joseph 22
Savage, Michael Joseph 22-24, 118, 134, 180
Scott, Bob 148
Scott, Tom 168
Scrimgeour, Colin 182, 198
Sebold, Alice 46
Seddon, Louisa (Spotswood) 64
Seddon, Richard John 13, 64-65
Selwyn, Bishop George Augustus 154
Seymour, Nick 100
Shelley, James 88
Sheppard, Douglas 13
Sheppard, Kate 13-15
Sheppard, Walter 13
Shipley, Jenny 72
Shirakawa, Hideki 84
Sigglekow, Chris 214
Sinclair, Keith 144, 192-193
Sinclair, Mark 192
Slash (Saul Hudson) 214
Smith, Lockwood 104
Smithyman, Kendrick 192
Snell, Miki 42
Snell, Peter 42-43, 98, 124, 130
Snow, Edgar 174
Spencer, Danielle 218
Spencer, Diana 80
Spielberg, Steven 46
Stafford, Edward 68
Stalin, Joseph 168
Steele, Louis 194
Stephens, Tainui 9
Stone, Oliver 46
Stout, Anna 122
Stout, Robert 20, 64

Strachey, Lytton 56
Strauss, Richard 80
Stoddart, Margaret 146
Stone, Sharon 218
Sullivan, Daniel 108
Sutch, Bill 192
Swainson, Mary Anne 56
Symonds, William 34

Tait, Wenarata 202
Tamati, Arihia, 25
Tamihere, John 72
Tasman, Abel 9
Tawhiao 128, 164
Tayler, Dick 124
Taylor, Eliza 182
Taylor, Fiona 208
Taylor, Robert 182
Te Akau (wife of Te Rauparaha) 50
Tedder, John 82
Te Haratua 28
Te Hotete 166
Te Kahupukoro 180
Te Kanawa, Kiri 80-81
Te Kanawa, Nell 80
Te Kanawa, Tom 80
Te Kira, Hene 26
Te Kooti 164-165, 178, 198, 202
Te Pahi 28, 116
Te Papatahi, Ina 194
Te Puea Herangi 128-129, 144
Te Rangihaeata 50, 102
Te Rauparaha 9, 19, 50-51, 116, 154
Teresa, Mother 152
Te Rio, Iriaka 180
Te Rongo (wife of Te Rangihaeata) 50
Te Tuhi, Patara 194
Te Wake, Heremia 54
Te Whiti 62-63
Thomson, Joseph 10
Tirikatene Eruera 180
Titore, 28
Tizard, Cath 192
Tovey, Gordon 186
Tremain, Kel 52
Trotter, Ron 150
Trowell, Garnet 56
Truman, Fred 37
Tuhou, Te Riringi 26
Tulloh, Bruce 42
Tumoana, Kenana 178
Turbott, Harold 128
Turikatuku 166
Turner, Ellen 102
Tuwhare, Hone 186

Upham, Charles 184-185
Upham, Molly (McTamney) 184
Urlich, Peter 204

Valadier, Auguste 78
Van Asch, Henry 214
Van Damme, Ivo 130

Vianney, Abbé 152
Victoria, Queen 30, 34, 36
Vogel, Julius 20, 68-69
Vogel, Mary 68

Wahawaha, Ropata 25
Waikato 166, 167
Wakefield, Arthur 102
Wakefield, Charles 37
Wakefield, David 102
Wakefield Edward (Felix's son) 102
Wakefield, Edward Gibbon 102-03
Wakefield, Eliza (Pattle) 102
Wakefield, Felix 102
Wakefield, Jerningham 102
Wakefield, Oliver 102
Wakefield, William 34, 50, 102
Walker, Helen 130
Walker, John 130-131
Wallace, Billy 148, 176
Walsh, Fran 46
Walter, Edward 37
Walton, Ernest 10
Washington, Denzel 218
Watkins, David 52
Watson, Jim 70
Watt, Hugh 140
Wattie, Gladys 136
Wattie, Gordon 136
Wattie, James 136-137
Wattie, Ray 136
Webster, Michael 124
Weir, John 94
Wellesley, Arthur (Duke of Wellington) 19
Wellmann, Paul-Heinz 130
Wells, H G (Herbert) 122
Wera Wera 50
Wharepu, Te Aro-o-te-rangi 194
Whineray, Wilson 52
White, Andy 132
White, Patrick 48
Wigand, Jeffrey 218
Wilby, Thomas 146
Wilkins, Henry 70
Wilkins, Maurice 9, 70-71
Wilkins, Patricia (Chidgey) 70
Williams, Henry 28, 34, 50, 116
Winfrey, Oprah 218
Wooderson, Sydney 90
Woodham, Kerrie 9
Woolf, Leonard 56
Woolf, Virginia 56
Wright, Orville 60
Wright, Wilbur 60
Wurtman, Richard 162
Wynyard, Robert 102

Yarrow, Sid 40
Young, Deborah 162
Young, Jeff 52

Zanderigo, Angi 196
Zhou En Lai 174